Deleuze and the D

Bloomsbury Studies in Continental Philosophy

Bloomsbury Studies in Continental Philosophy is a major monograph series from Bloomsbury. The series features first-class scholarly research monographs across the field of Continental philosophy. Each work makes a major contribution to the field of philosophical research.

Adorno's Concept of Life, Alastair Morgan
Badiou, Marion and St Paul, Adam Miller
Being and Number in Heidegger's Thought, Michael Roubach
Deleuze and Guattari, Fadi Abou-Rihan
Deleuze and the Genesis of Representation, Joe Hughes
Deleuze and the Unconscious, Christian Kerslake
Deleuze, Guattari and the Production of the New, edited by Simon O'Sullivan and Stephen Zepke
Derrida, Simon Morgan Wortham
Derrida and Disinterest, Sean Gaston
Derrida: Profanations, Patrick O'Connor
The Domestication of Derrida, Lorenzo Fabbri
Encountering Derrida, edited by Simon Morgan Wortham and Allison Weiner
Foucault's Heidegger, Timothy Rayner
Gadamer and the Question of the Divine, Walter Lammi
Heidegger and a Metaphysics of Feeling, Sharin N. Elkholy
Heidegger and Aristotle, Michael Bowler
Heidegger and Logic, Greg Shirley
Heidegger and Nietzsche, Louis P. Blond
Heidegger and Philosophical Atheology, Peter S. Dillard
Heidegger Beyond Deconstruction, Michael Lewis
Heidegger, Politics and Climate Change, Ruth Irwin
Heidegger's Early Philosophy, James Luchte
Idealism and Existentialism, Jon Stewart
Kant, Deleuze and Architectonics, Edward Willatt
Levinas and Camus, Tal Sessler
Merleau-Ponty's Phenomenology, Kirk M. Besmer
Nietzsche, Nihilism and the Philosophy of the Future, edited by Jeffrey Metzger
Nietzsche's Ethical Theory, Craig Dove
Nietzsche's Thus Spoke Zarathustra, edited by James Luchte
The Philosophy of Exaggeration, Alexander Garcia Düttmann
Sartre's Phenomenology, David Reisman
Time and Becoming in Nietzsche's Thought, Robin Small
Who's Afraid of Deleuze and Guattari? Gregg Lambert
Žižek and Heidegger, Thomas Brockelman
Žižek's Dialectics, Fabio Vighi

Deleuze and the Diagram

Aesthetic Threads in Visual Organization

Jakub Zdebik

Bloomsbury Studies in Continental Philosophy

BLOOMSBURY
LONDON • NEW DELHI • NEW YORK • SYDNEY

Bloomsbury Academic
An imprint of Bloomsbury Publishing Plc

50 Bedford Square	1385 Broadway
London	New York
WC1B 3DP	NY 10018
UK	USA

www.bloomsbury.com

Bloomsbury is a registered trade mark of Bloomsbury Publishing Plc

First published in 2012 by Bristol Classical Press an imprint of Bloomsbury Academic
Paperback Edition first published 2013

© Jakub Zdebik 2012

Jakub Zdebik has asserted his right under the Copyright, Designs and Patents Act, 1988, to be identified as Author of this work.

All rights reserved. No part of this publication may be reproduced or transmitted in any form or by any means, electronic or mechanical, including photocopying, recording, or any information storage or retrieval system, without prior permission in writing from the publishers.

No responsibility for loss caused to any individual or organization acting on or refraining from action as a result of the material in this publication can be accepted by Bloomsbury or the author.

British Library Cataloguing-in-Publication Data
A catalogue record for this book is available from the British Library.

ISBN: HB: 978-1-4411-1560-7
PB: 978-1-4725-2619-9

Library of Congress Cataloging-in-Publication Data
A catalog record for this book is available from the Library of Congress.
Zdebik, Jakub.
Deleuze and the diagram: aesthetic threads in visual organization/Jakub Zdebik.
pages cm. – (Continuum studies in Continental philosophy)
Includes bibliographical references and index.
ISBN 978-1-4411-1560-7 (hardcover) – ISBN 978-1-4411-7872-5 (ebook (pdf) 1. Deleuze, Gilles, 1925–1995. 2. Aesthetics. 3. Art and philosophy. I. Title.
B2430.D454Z42 2012
194–dc23
2011049275

Typeset by Newgen Imaging Systems Pvt Ltd, Chennai, India

For Barbara

Contents

Acknowledgements	viii
Introduction: What Is a Diagram?	1
1. System	24
2. Black Line, White Surface	66
3. Gilles Deleuze's Diagram (Complicated by a Comparison to Immanuel Kant's Schema)	109
4. The Extraordinary Contraction	141
5. Skin, Aesthetics, Incarnation: Deleuze's Diagram of Francis Bacon – An Epilogue	178
Conclusion	193
Notes	196
Bibliography	224
Index	231

Acknowledgements

I would like to thank Daniel Vaillancourt and Calin Mihailescu for their invaluable guidance, feedback and encouragement. Gary Genosko has been tremendously helpful with his commentaries, insights and advice. Jonathan Murphy has been especially instrumental in the making of this book: his comments were constructive, patient and helpful. I would like to thank Andrew Pendakis for reading through the manuscript. Colette Stoeber edited the manuscript with precision and efficacy and for this I thank her. I would like to thank Sarah Campbell, Colleen Coalter and Rachel Eisenhauer at Continuum for the opportunity to publish my work and for their support. Elżbieta, Zbigniew and Magda have always been there and supported me and for this I thank them. And, of course, I would like to thank most of all Barbara. Without her tireless and constant support this book would not have been possible. I am forever in your debt.

Earlier versions of some chapters or chapter sections appeared in various journals. Permission to reprint was kindly granted by *The Semiotic Review of Books*, *The Brock Review* and *ESC: English Studies in Canada*.

Introduction: What Is a Diagram?

A diagram is commonly understood as a drawing conveying information about something incorporeal. From the Greek *diagramma*, it means to mark out by lines, to draw – where *dia* is through, across, apart and *graphein* is to write. The diagram is defined as a geometrical figure used to illustrate theorems. It can also be a sketch, a drawing or a plan that explains a thing by outlining its parts and their relationships – basically, delineating its inner workings. Finally, a diagram can be defined as a chart or a graph explaining or illustrating ideas and displaying statistics.

A diagram can be seen in the form of three different types of drawings: a plan, a map and a graph (or a schema). A plan represents a building that is not yet built. A map represents terrains on which we have not yet travelled. A graph displays relations between variable quantities. No matter what form it takes as a representation, a diagram is a configuration of lines, whether they are drawn or written.

In a conceptual diagram, the lines marking out a space are abstract traits. The diagram thus does not represent, but rather maps out possibilities prior to their appearance, their representation. This new dimension lies between the visible and the articulable, and therefore traits are not exactly pictures or written language. A conceptual diagram is not like a flow chart, for example, which represents economic fluctuations in a schematic visual shorthand. The diagram does not resemble particular elements in an imitative way; rather, it displays abstract functions that make up a system. The diagram, then, is the dynamic, fluctuating process occurring between static structures. As a concept, it describes the flexible, elastic, incorporeal functions before they settle into a definitive form. The diagrammatic process could be imagined as a physical state or system being atomized into incorporeal abstract traits and then reconfigured into another state or system. The first and second system will be different, but their abstract functioning will be the same.

The concept of the diagram revamps hylemorphic theory – the push and pull between form and matter – as well as the relationship between content and expression, the connection between thought and image, and the difference between representation and non-representation. It values the unformed, the state of flux, the dynamic, the movement towards actualization. It also deals with organization, forces at work in social and cultural constructs; it is a way to travel from one system to another. The diagram allows a glimpse of the state that comes before the formation of an object, and of what goes into its formation. In a cultural object such as a painting, for example, the theory of the diagram offers something more than typical hermeneutics because it searches for essential states of abstraction within the actual figuration of an image. It also shows the far-reaching connections at play in a work of art, and the multiple parts that come to work in its assemblage. The theory of the diagram is based on a philosophical concept devised by Gilles Deleuze, who was inspired by Michel Foucault.

This chapter is divided into two major parts. First, I will look at two definitions of the diagram as they appear in Deleuze's *Foucault*. After a brief summary of these passages, I will show how architecture and cartography are fundamental to the conceptualization of the diagram. In the second part, I will pinpoint the locations of the diagram in Deleuze's corpus. This is important because Deleuze does not dedicate a single work to the diagram. His presentation of the diagram remains indefinitely unformed – from its first to last appearance in Deleuze's corpus, the diagram changes shape. First mentioned in an essay on Foucault titled 'Écrivain non: un nouveau cartographe' (1975), it then appears in *A Thousand Plateaus* (1980) and *Francis Bacon: The Logic of Sensation* (1981) and is later developed in more detail in *Foucault* (1986). Taken all together, these texts seem to form a small system revolving around the notion of the diagram. And this system has a circular form: starting and looping back onto Foucault after a process of transformation. By tracing the sources of the concept of the diagram, I will provide an introductory map of the diagram's situation in Deleuze's thought – and, by extension, this map will reveal the diagram's characteristics.

Definitions of the Diagram in Deleuze's *Foucault*

In *Foucault*, the book in which he finally explains the workings of the diagram most completely, Deleuze defines his concept twice. The first time, the diagram is a new informal dimension; the second, it is a display of relations as pure functions.

Diagram as a new informal dimension

Deleuze explains the diagram as an informal dimension by analysing the relationship between two practical formations. One is discursive and the other non-discursive. Discursive types of formations involve statements: for example, statements of eighteenth-century clinical medicine or penal law. These discursive formations are involved with non-discursive formations defined as environments: for example, institutions or prisons. Environments determine discursive formations, or statements; and statements, conversely, determine environments. But the discursive and non-discursive formations are different, heterogeneous: 'Even though they may overlap: there is no correspondence, or isomorphism, no direct causality or symbolisation.'[1] Two heterogeneous formations are not linked in any way that could be understood as representational.

Deleuze explains how, in *Discipline and Punish*, Foucault resolves the problem of incongruity between differing systems. The two systems used as an example are the prison and penal law. The prison system is a formation with a content: 'Even a "thing" like prison is seen as an environmental formation (the "prison" environment) and a form of content (where the content is the prisoner).'[2] Deleuze explains that the prison formation does not refer to a word or a signifier for which it would stand in as a signified. That is because a prison environment, much more than a simple 'thing' that can be represented succinctly, is an assemblage of various abstract functions. Yet a non-discursive formation, such as a prison, refers to another incongruous 'thing', a discursive formation, namely, penal law.

The two heterogeneous systems, an environment and a statement, are related. This relationship emerges from the shift both systems incurred at a particular point in time. In the eighteenth century, penal law shifted from revenge to what is articulable, and at the same time prison shifted from hiding away prisoners to making them visible. As Deleuze explains, penal law, the discursive formation, concentrates on what is articulable: 'Penal law [the discursive formation] concerns those aspects of criminal material that can be articulated: it is a system of language that classifies and translates offences and calculates sentences; a family of statements that is also a threshold.'[3] Prison, the non-discursive formation, focuses on visibilities: 'Prison, for its part, is concerned with whatever is visible: not only does it wish to display the crime and the criminal but in itself it constitutes a visibility.'[4] The prison environment is not defined by its materiality: stone walls and prison bars. It is defined by its function: seeing without being seen. For its part, the penal law is defined by what can be articulated in language: 'A system of light and a system of language are not the same form, and do not have the same formation.'[5]

But both systems share more than a similarity, especially when abstracted into their essential traits of the visible and the articulable. In-between these two heterogeneities, there is an intermingling. They 'seep into one another and steal bits for themselves'.[6] The abstract function is what links two incongruous systems together. And so, according to Deleuze, Foucault solves the problem of incongruence between two formations by abstracting them to the level of their function.

Two questions remain for Deleuze. First, what is the link between two systems in the social field that is not based on their outside forms? And second, how do the assemblages between two heterogeneous forms come together and remain respectively varied?

Before Deleuze proceeds to his answer – the diagram or the new dimension that these forms share – he differentiates between two meanings of 'form'. On the one hand, form means to organize matter; on the other, it means to distribute function. Prisons are formed matter and punishment, formalized function. How can there be a correspondence, a commonality, between two irreducible forms? Deleuze explains: 'The reason lies in the fact that we can conceive of pure matter and pure functions, abstracting the forms which embody them.'[7] The function and matter can be, in effect, abstracted to their essential traits and connected together on that level. The prison is abstracted to its function of seeing without being seen; it is an abstract machine that 'also passes through every articulable function'.[8] Seeing without being seen imposes '*a particular conduct on a particular human multiplicity*'.[9] The multiplicity is constrained, formed into a particular formation with a particular content, and it operates according to the same function working in another system. Between different systems there is 'unformed and unorganized matter and unformalized, unfinalized functions'.[10] This abstract level of intermingling functions is what constitutes the dimension called the diagram.

Deleuze asks and answers: 'What can we call such a new informal dimension? On one occasion, Foucault gives it its most precise name: it is a "diagram", that is to say a "functioning, abstracted from any obstacle [. . .] or friction [and which] must be detached from any specific use".'[11] It is because two systems can be linked together based on their abstract function that systems can be linked across social fields without having to be of similar form, which answers Deleuze's first question. Furthermore, because the diagram promotes independence of function within a multiplicity, each system continues to constitute its own abstract functions according to its own assemblage, which answers the second question. For example, the diagram activates the exercise of auto-discipline on the part of an individual who is subjected to the seeing-without-being-seen function. A diagram is not specific, but it is pure abstracted function – so that it can pass from one system to the next without the need to follow any similarity of form and it can intermingle with other functions, giving two incongruous systems their respective operative fields. In this way, the diagram is not merely a simple model that traces similarities between things, but is also a generative device that continues working once embodied:

> The *diagram* is no longer an auditory or visual archive but a map, a cartography that is coextensive with the whole social field. It is an abstract machine. It is defined by its informal functions and matter and in terms of form makes no distinction between content and expression, a discursive formation and a non-discursive formation. It is a machine that is almost blind and mute, even though it makes others see and speak.[12]

The diagram makes abstracted function pass from one formation or system to the next. In this way, it is a virtual map behind heterogeneous formation not only irreducible in its actual form, but also heterogeneous in its level of materiality: like prison and the penal code, an architectural structure and a set of laws.

Diagram as a display of relations as pure functions

In the second definition of the diagram, Deleuze is concerned more with the abstract content of the diagram. Within the newly discovered informal dimension, he focuses on the display of relations of pure function.

The prison example Deleuze uses is not random. In fact, it is part of the architectural point of origin of the concept of the diagram. The prison in question, which yields the function of seeing without being seen, is a particular architectural structure. The visual mechanism that inspired the conception of the diagram is Jeremy Bentham's panopticon, which Foucault describes in *Discipline and Punish*. The panopticon is a prison where inmates are placed in cells stacked around a central tower from which a single guard can observe all the prisoners without being seen by them. It is an architectural structure that operates on visual transparency: the prisoners are controlled through knowing that they can be surveilled at all times.

But the panopticon does not constitute a diagram. Rather, the function of the structure of surveillance is labelled as a diagram. Not the cells and the walls and the tower, but the relationship between the guards and the prisoners within that environment. This relationship, abstracted from the prison structure, can be transposed to other structures – such as schools, barracks and hospitals – which are built around a similar relationship involving surveillance for the purpose of control. But surveillance is just one example of a diagrammatic function. In other places, Deleuze writes of a feudal diagram,[13] a Napoleonic diagram,[14] a Greek diagram,[15] or even a pastoral diagram.[16]

Deleuze asks the question, 'What is a diagram?' and in the answer he describes the abstract function of the device. In the span of his answer, he begins with an architectural basis and ends by comparing the diagram to a map:

> It is a display of the relations between forces which constitute power in the above conditions: 'The panoptic mechanism is not simply a hinge, a point of exchange between a mechanism of power and a function; it is a way of making power relations functions [sic] in a function, and of making a function through these power relations.' We have seen that the relations between forces, or power relations, were microphysical, strategic multipunctual and diffuse, that they determined particular features and constituted pure functions. The diagram or abstract machine is the map of relations between forces, a map of destiny, or intensity, which proceeds by primary non-localizable relations and at every moment passes through every point, 'or rather in every relation from one point to another'.[17]

Right away, it is important to note the visual element in the explanation. The translator here chooses the word 'display' for the original French word *expose*. *Display* means to exhibit (this latter being a closer word to the French *exposer* than display) or show – in this case, relations between forces. The word hints at a visual aspect in the diagram's function. Display is made up of *dis* from the Latin *dia*, which is the same prefix as in diagram. It means *through, apart, between* and hints at the multidimensional aspect of display. The second syllable comes from *ply* or fold. The fold is an important concept for Deleuze and is the title of the book he wrote after *Foucault* – *The Fold: Leibniz and the Baroque*. To *display*, then, is to show by unfolding. The diagram folds together abstract relations of forces, and then unfolds them in another system.

The diagram is the abstract state of these processes as they are transferred from one system, or mechanism, to the next. Therefore, the abstract surveillance function is translated from the prison system to the school system or the barracks system. Even though they are different social environments, the prison school or barracks share the function of surveillance, or seeing without being seen. As social organizations, the prison, school and barracks are vastly heterogeneous. But the diagram of surveillance that operates in each system is the same. The seeing-without-being-seen function makes any analogy between these systems actual: they are the same on a diagrammatic level. As Deleuze argues, the panoptic mechanism does not mediate between power and function; it does, however, create a template, in this case a mechanism of surveillance, that has deeper consequences than simple observation. The diagrammatic operation has concrete consequences in each environment. On a microphysical – or abstract – level, power relations in the function of surveillance influence the relations between the subjects of each system. As Bentham says himself, surveillance provides the mind with the power over the minds of others.[18] The insidiousness comes from the fact that the function is abstract, and it is non-representational. We are being surveilled but we cannot see it.

The diagram makes us aware of abstract forces at play in the organization of systems. Insofar as it brings to light these connective traits between isomorphic systems, the diagram is a map. Deleuze states this clearly: 'A diagram is a map, or rather several superimposed maps. And from one diagram to the next, new maps are drawn.'[19] This superimposition of maps illustrates the passage from one abstract system to the next, and in-between them another one is made. But we see immediately that Deleuze does not have a typical map in mind. This is an abstract map of relations of forces, of destiny or of intensity. This map of virtuality shows all possibilities before they are actualized – which is why it is so nimble. The diagram is not precise, or representational, but charts the relation of forces that can be utilized or made manifest in various situations.

Architecture and cartography

From this description of a diagram, I would like to isolate two terms that will be instrumental in the articulation of the many aspects of the diagram: architecture and cartography. On the one hand, the diagram, following from the panopticon, gets its point of origin from an abstract architecture; and on the other, the diagram is 'a map, a cartography that is coextensive with the whole social field'.[20] It is a fluid, virtual map that is under the fabric of things – before their formation into something actual – just as much as it is an architecture, appreciated for its abstract forces and not its material walls and foundations. Because the diagram is abstract and elusive, touchstones of some sort are necessary for us to grasp what it is. Architectural and cartographic representations give a preliminary image of the diagram. These two spatial markers are important because they are an attempt to capture the fluid and unstable dimension of the diagram. This is why architectural and cartographic representations of a diagram help us understand, or see, the concept of the diagram.

The architectural diagram is important to the theory of the philosophical diagram because it raises the issue of translation of data from one medium to another. The diagram is that stage between the idea of the building and the actual building. It displays the amorphous passage from one structure to the next: from the virtual to the actual, the abstract to the specific.

Peter Eisenman, the architect often associated with deconstructive architecture, makes diagrams integral to his creative process. Eisenman differentiates between diagram on the one hand and sketch and plan on the other. The diagram, as an analytical tool, 'attempts to uncover the latent structure of organization'.[21] Through a diagrammatic visual approximation, the architect can superimpose or tease out from structures of buildings other patterns that will not make it to the final plan or structure but that nevertheless exist in the interaction of the lines on the level of the page: 'The diagram not only is an explanation, as something that comes after, but also acts as an intermediary in the process of generation of real space and time.'[22] A diagram connects between the theoretical and the real stages of the construction of a building.

Here is how Eisenman defines his idea of an architectural diagram:

> Generically, a diagram is a graphic shorthand. Though it is an ideogram, it is not necessarily an abstraction. It is a representation of something in that it is not the thing itself. In this sense, it cannot help but be embodied. It can never be free of value or meaning, even when it attempts to express relationships of formation and their processes. At the same time, a diagram is neither a structure nor an abstraction of structure. While it explains relationships in an architectural object, it is not isomorphic with it.[23]

Eisenman's description of the diagram is revelatory because of certain crucial elements he bestows on the concept from an architectural point of view. First is the notion of embodiment. This part of the architectural diagram is an approximate sketch that reveals a building's overarching yet implicit structure. Therefore, the diagram is going to be embodied because it cannot remain at that approximate level and be helpful architecturally. Eisenman then says that the diagram can never be free of value and meaning. This indicates the difference between an architectural diagram, which must be following the path of the actual plan of the building, and a conceptual diagram, which is devoid of value and meaning because it is pure abstract function. But the architectural diagram reveals the becoming of forms and how they function – their processes. The diagram is not a structure; instead, <u>it traces the flow of forces</u> that are part of a rigid organization of a particular building. It shows forces at play in a structure, but not the structure; it shows the stages before a form comes into being, but not the form; and because it is something that must be embodied, it is not isomorphic with the final product.

But an architectural diagram must be compared to the conceptual diagram. Deleuze and Guattari's diagram is not part of the history and representation of architecture and therefore their concept of the diagram remains detached from architectural practice. The Deleuzoguattarian diagram is able to discover new dimensions because it is free from the burden of representation.[24] Eisenman provides a concise definition of Deleuze's diagram:

> The diagram, then, is both form and matter, the visible and the articulable. Diagrams for Deleuze do not attempt to bridge the gap between these pairs but rather to widen it – to open the gap to other unadorned matters and functions that will become formed. Diagrams, then, form visible matter and formalize articulable functions.[25]

An example of this widening gap, or dissolution towards abstraction, can be seen in Deleuze and Guattari's own treatment of architecture. Whereas the architect needs to bridge the gap between matter and form in order to actualize a house at the end of his creative process, Deleuze and Guattari atomize the structure of the house into, what is according to them, its essential function: the frame. In a way, Deleuze and Guattari's treatment of architecture shows the discrepancy between Eisenman's architectural diagram – still rooted in practice – and their own diagram – which dissolves into abstraction. But it is this dissolution into abstraction that gives the conceptual diagram its strength to create something new instead of falling back into representation. And if the diagram does not bridge the gap between matter and form, it opens the gap and connects it to the universe.

In *What Is Philosophy?* Deleuze and Guattari consider architecture for its essential traits. Because the diagram is abstract, it can be applied – beyond a single specific state – to heterogeneous situations. Unlike specific elements that have been subtracted from the original structure, the traits of the diagram are peripatetic. Diagrammatic traits can be connected to other traits devoid of specificity and form new arrangements. Deleuze and Guattari, instead of discussing architecture in specific terms write about a generic house.[26] The essential element of the house is the frame. After all, architecture is the 'first art of the frame'.[27] We can look at the frame like the trait of a diagram. But the frame is also the essential function of the house. The frame of the house is more than simply a part of the structure of an architectural building. On a philosophical level, it makes connections possible. In this process of abstraction, the house is seen not in particular terms, as a singular house, but in terms of essential traits like an ensemble of frames, vectors and abstract lines:

> Interlocking these frames or joining up all these planes – wall section, window section, floor section – is a composite system rich in points and counterpoints . . . a vast plane of composition that carries out a kind of deframing following lines of flight that pass through the house-territory to town-cosmos, and that now dissolve the identity of the place through variation of the earth, a town having not so much a place as vectors folding the abstract line of relief.[28]

What Deleuze and Guattari try to make us understand in this passage is that architecture functions diagrammatically. Frames are the connecting element of the structure of the house. Consequently, taken abstractly, the function of architecture is the idea of a connection. The lines that make up the house are vectors abstractly negotiating the relationship of architecture to space. All these abstract elements can then connect with others, constantly challenging the stability of the house's position on the earth. As Deleuze and Guattari write, 'Not only does the open house communicate with the landscape, through a window or a mirror, but the most shut-up house opens to a universe.'[29] The diagram of a house widens its connective possibilities to a vast spatial dimension.

How do we find our bearings in such a wide, open dimension? This is where cartography comes in, the other analogue of the diagram. The cartographic element of the diagram cements the concept within the boundaries of space. The map is a metaphor, or an image, for the potentiality, the newness, the visual organization and the discovery at work in the diagram. The map also underscores the conceptual element of the spatial nature of the diagram. The diagram is not simply a map of geographical elements but also constitutes a mental geography. The map speaks to how we spatially organize our surrounding space and, by extension, how we organize our thoughts. It does this by being generative – it creates new vistas instead of simply representing what is already there. And being connective is part of its function as a conceptual tool.

The map should be perceived as lines and traits that connect the mental landscape to the outside world in an interweaving network. Deleuze explains the connection between map and diagram in *Negotiations*:

> What we call a 'map', or sometimes a 'diagram', is a set of various interacting lines (thus the lines in a hand are a map). There are of course many different kinds of lines, both in art and in a society or a person. Some lines represent something, others are abstract. Some lines have various segments, others don't. Some weave through a space, others go in a certain direction. Some lines, no matter whether or not they're abstract, trace an outline, others don't. The most beautiful ones do. We think lines are the basic components of things and events. So everything has its geography, its cartography, its diagram.[30]

The notion of diagram is put on the same plane as the map. A map is described as dynamic according to its essential trait, the line. Or rather, any lines can make a map. Accordingly, the new dimension can be wrenched from a multiplicity and made to fluctuate between heterogeneous ensembles.

In 'What Children Say?' Deleuze is showing the dynamic aspect of mapping in relation to memory-dependent psychoanalysis. Deleuze's concept of the map is an alternative to the redundant psychoanalytic approach to reconfiguring the psychic space: 'They have to put away their maps, underneath which there is no longer anything but yellowed photos of the father-mother.'[31] Children are made to rely on photographs instead of their mapping instincts. Contrasted to the photograph, which repeats reality, the map is generative of difference.

In *A Thousand Plateaus*, the map is also opposed to static tracing, which behaves like the representational photograph:

> [The tracing] is instead like a photograph or X ray that begins by selecting or isolating, by artificial means such as colorations or other restrictive procedures, what it intends to reproduce. The imitator always creates the model, and attracts it. The tracing has already translated the map into an image; it has already transformed the rhizome into roots and radicles. It has organized, stabilized, neutralized the multiplicities according to the axes of significance and subjectification belonging to it.[32]

The connections made by the map are always full of potential for new connections. Maps are superimposed, and new connections are made. This idea of the superimposable map is explicitly part of the definition of the diagram in *Foucault*:

> Maps, on the contrary, are superimposed in such a way that each map finds itself modified in the following maps, rather than finding its origin in the preceding one: from one map to the next, it is not a matter of searching for an origin, but of evaluating *displacement*.[33]

From map to map, a rhizomatic network is created. Superimposable maps stack up to a diagram.

One of the 'approximate characteristics' of the rhizome, as laid out by Deleuze and Guattari,[34] follows the principle of cartography and decalcomania (which is the artistic process of transferring pictures or designs from one medium to another[35]). There is a link between the tree-model and decalcomania since both function through 'tracing', – essentially showing us what is already there. Deleuze and Guattari go on to explain that the rhizome operates like a map rather than a tracing. And what characterizes a map is the fact that it is more dynamic than a tracing: '[I]t is entirely oriented towards an experimentation in contact with the real. The map does not reproduce an unconscious closed in upon itself. . . . It fosters connections between fields.'[36] Deleuze and Guattari fold the rhizome onto the tracing in order to avoid a duality between tracing and mapping all the while trying to avoid dualities in the rhizome model – 'It is a question of method: *the tracing should always be put back in the map.*'[37] They see two ways of approaching the diagram: in one state, the diagram still relates to movements of deterritorialization and the content and expression can still be distinguished – this would be akin to the tracing; in the other state, 'an absolute threshold of deterritorialization has been reached' – content and expression are indistinguishable in a zone of indiscernibility.[38]

A diagrammatic drawing is not wholly representational (some details are omitted so as not to overburden the design) but cannot be absolutely abstract (or the viewer would be unable to receive actual information). If the tracing functions like a photograph, as Deleuze and Guattari contend, and the map represents pure potentiality, the diagram takes a snapshot of a multiplicity in a constant state of flux. In this sense, tracing and mapping together can make a diagram visible – a reified potentiality. The map is connective, and this connection is made through its zone of indiscernibility with its virtual elasticity.

The architectural and the cartographic incarnations of the diagram are important because they help give us an approximate image of a non-representational device. Architectural and cartographic elements will appear in the overall discussion of the diagram in the chapters of this book.

Sources of the Diagram in Deleuze's Corpus

We can draw a map of the places where the diagram appears in Deleuze's corpus. In 'Écrivain non: un nouveau cartographe' (1975), Deleuze writes for the first time about the diagram, a concept he found in Foucault's *Discipline and Punish*. The diagram returns in *Mille plateaux* (1980) in the context of a theory of language. A year later, Deleuze writes about the diagram from an artistic point of view in *Francis Bacon: Logique de la sensation* (1981). Finally, Deleuze revisits his essay from 1975 and adds to it in *Foucault* (1986). Starting and ending with Foucault, Deleuze seems to close the loop on the diagram – in effect, tracing a small system of the evolving concept.

When *Deux régimes de fous* came out in 2003, two other texts that deal with the diagram became available: '*Désir et plaisir*', written in 1977 but not published until 1994, and '*Sur les principaux concepts de Michel Foucault*', written in 1984 and later incorporated in *Foucault*.

The concept of the diagram, without being named as such, also comes up in other sources. 'What is a *dispositif*?' describes the diagrammatic function using the word *dispositif* instead of the *diagram* that Foucault used in *Discipline and Punish*. In 'Bartleby, and the Formula', an essay in *Essays Critical and Clinical*, zones of indiscernibility take on the role of the unformed dimension. Of course, in *What Is Philosophy?* Deleuze and Guattari describe the plane of immanence. There, the plane fulfils a diagrammatic role: Deleuze and Guattari write about geographic landscapes of the mind and abstract architectures. The plane was, however, already announced as a possible alternative to the diagram in *Foucault*.[39] Finally, *The Fold* seems to pick up the concept of folding where *Foucault* left off.

Or perhaps the diagram was there before Foucault and *Foucault*. In *Difference and Repetition*, Deleuze already introduced us to the notion of plicature (which operates through a series of foldings) in conjunction with Geoffroy St-Hilaire. Also in *Difference and Repetition*, Deleuze discusses the Kantian schema he likens to the diagram years later. And lastly, Manuel DeLanda identified proto-diagrams in Deleuze's use of nineteenth-century thermodynamics in *Difference and Repetition*, which DeLanda developed into models of environmental systems.

For now, I will focus on the first, main sources of the diagram. The appearances of the diagram in Deleuze's corpus have been compiled into two lists: the first, by Yves Abrioux under the entry 'Diagramme' in *Le Vocabulaire de Gilles Deleuze*;[40] and the second, by Noëlle Batt in 'L'expérience diagrammatique: un nouveau régime de pensée', the introductory essay of *Penser par le diagramme: de Gilles Deleuze à Gilles Châtelet*, which she edited. I will here follow these two authors' compilations. The little system of the concept I will trace will focus on organizational facets of the diagram: first, the diagram and function; second, the diagram and language; third, the diagram and painting; and last, the diagram and thought.

Foucault as a cartographer

'Écrivain non: un nouveau cartographe', published in 1975 in *Critique*, is a book review of Foucault's *Discipline and Punish*, and the title can be translated as 'Not a writer: a new cartographer.' In one section of the essay, Deleuze refers to the chapter in Foucault's book describing the Panopticon as 'one of the most beautiful'.[41] The panoptic model – seeing without being seen – is an abstract model that can be applied to a variety of concrete spaces organized around surveillance and control. The abstract architecture of the panopticon consists of a science of control in which the visual field is converted into a field of knowledge.[42] The schema of this system is 'Power – (perception) – knowledge.'[43]

Deleuze tells us that panopticism is a machine defined by a pure function: 'It is a machine, which works, but a very special type of machine. It is defined by *pure function*, independently of sensible configurations and categorical forms where this function incarnates itself.' The function of seeing without being seen is also defined: 'It is defined by *pure matter*, independently from qualified substances into which this matter enters.'[44] Matter here is human multiplicity, a multiplicity that needs to be controlled. Panopticism is, in effect, an abstract machine. An abstract machine is pure function and pure matter. It abstracts forms that hold functions, and dissolves substances that qualify matter. This, Deleuze writes, is the diagram.[45]

The diagram is likened to a map: 'The diagram, it is the map, cartography.'[46] The diagram is a particular kind of map that is coextensive with the social field. It operates an exhaustive grid. The diagram puts into work relations within a multiplicity, a multiplicity that it organizes and activates. The diagram functions according to two dualities: anonymity–individuation and continuity–contiguity. The first duality concerns the fact that power is diffuse, non-localizable, invisible, and that it reaches individuals all the way to the smallest detail. The second, very important, duality describes the passage of abstract function from one system to the next. There is continuity between institutions (e.g. the school, the army, the factory, the prison) but each institution carries its own multiplicity – you are constantly asked to go to another office. This model is abstracted, and the diagram enacts this type of double movement of continuity and contiguity between formations of various material registers, be they concrete buildings or regimes of thought.

Deleuze finally tells us that two diagrams communicate by reciprocally exchanging elements. Not only do diagrams organize multiplicities, rendering possible the passage of abstract function from one formation to the next while leaving the multiplicity in flux in each formation; but they also involve an extra degree of complexity when they themselves are brought together. For example, a sovereign diagram connects to the panoptic diagram with the help of the Napoleonic diagram, in effect complicating function – multiplying multiplicities in what appears to be controlled chaos. The diagram does not represent an objective world but rather creates a new type of reality. Diagrammaticism, this new type of organization, defies reason and constitutes a new cartography.

A Thousand Plateaus and the linguistic diagram

Language, or linguistic expression, also stands problematically vis-à-vis the concept of the diagram. With the diagram, Deleuze complicates the primacy of linguistic expression. By showing the fluidity of language, he reveals another spatial function of the diagram: deterritorialization. *A Thousand Plateaus* offers the diagram as an alternative to the semiotic linguistic model. It is the abstract machine that works outside of the formalized regimen of language. In a way, the linguistic model is spatialized. Specifically, the diagram is subverted from Charles Sanders Peirce's semiotic theory.

Peirce explains that in order to answer a question about wishing for a thing, a human being resorts to abstract observation:

> He makes in his imagination a sort of skeleton diagram, or outline sketch, of himself, considers what modifications the hypothetical state of things would require to be made in that picture, and then examines it,

that is, *observes* what he has imagined, to see whether some ardent desire is there to be discerned.[47]

Peirce mentions the importance of the diagram in relation to desire. Here, the Sign, representamen, 'stands to somebody for something'.[48] There is a displacement of signs: 'It addresses somebody, that is, creates in the mind of that person an equivalent sign, or perhaps a more developed sign. That sign which it creates I call the *interpretant* of the first sign.'[49] In the diagram, as explained by Peirce, there is an abstracting function that makes the diagram a productive mechanism of thought instead of simply something with which to represent reality: 'The sign stands for something, its *object*.'[50] The diagram is an image of something to come rather than something that is already there.

In *A Thousand Plateaus*, Deleuze and Guattari complicate the relationship of the diagram with regard to representation: 'The diagrammatic or abstract machine does not function to represent, even something real, but rather constructs a real that is yet to come, a new type of reality.'[51] The diagram is like the prep work of a reterritorialized stratum.

> Everything escapes everything creates – never alone, but through an abstract machine that produces continuums of intensity, effects conjunctions of deterritorialization, and extracts expressions and contents. This Real-Abstract is totally different from the fictitious abstraction of a supposedly pure machine of expressions. It is an Absolute, but one that is neither undifferentiated nor transcendent. Abstract machines thus have proper names (as well as dates), which of course designate not persons or subjects but matters and functions.[52]

For Deleuze and Guattari, this is a question of pragmatics and it works diagrammatically: semiotically non-formed matter in relation to physically non-formed matter connected through the abstraction machine.[53]

> For a true abstract machine pertains to an assemblage in its entirety: it is defined as the diagram of that assemblage. It is not language based but diagrammatic and superlinear. Content is not a signified nor expression a signifier; rather, both are variables of the assemblage.[54]

The abstract machine is the diagram of the assemblage. And content and expression are variables of the assemblage. This is a way to show that language is a construction that plugs into a social field.

diagram/model — immanent utopia

Introduction 17

The example of an assemblage (stirrup–man–horse), and the consequences for society, relationships between individuals, and culture that proliferate from it, resemble the assemblage example from '*Desire and Pleasure*'.[55] It shows how language is not the primary element of a social manifestation, but is rather part of all of the other parts of the assemblage: 'The abstract machine as it relates to the diagram of the assemblage is never purely a matter of language, except for lack of sufficient abstraction.'[56] A sufficient level of abstraction would have shown all of the dimensions of various elements flattened out on a single plane and part of the same assemblage. Language is dependent on the abstract machine and not the other way around, because the assemblage operates on a broader level than the specific function of language.

Deleuze and Guattari then tell us that:

> [W]e may distinguish in the abstract machine two states of the diagram, one in which variables of content and expression are distributed according to their heterogeneous forms in reciprocal presupposition on a plane of consistency, and another in which it is no longer even possible to distinguish between variables of content and expression because the variability of that same plane has prevailed over the duality of forms, rendering them 'indiscernible'. (The first state relates to still relative movements of deterritorialization; in the second, an absolute threshold of deterritorialization has been reached.)[57]

Deleuze and Guattari see the diagram as having two successive states. In the first state, content and expression can still be distinguished. At this stage, the diagram is representational enough to be communicated. To this stage, we can compare the notion of tracing which made up part of the duality characterizing the rhizome. The tracing is representational in relation to mapping which indicates pure potentiality. The second part of this duality is here described in different terms in the second state of the diagram. In the second state, absolute deterritorialization is attained and content and expression are rendered indistinguishable. We are at a level of total abstraction. This is not to say that the elements of the previous state have disappeared; rather they have become incorporeal. What is important here is that Deleuze and Guattari are describing the representational possibility of the diagram in relation to the limitations of language, which is not abstract enough to fully contend with the degrees of variability within assemblages. If we take, for example, a graph or a chart, a diagrammatic drawing is not completely representational nor is it absolutely abstract, we see that incorporeal data must be embodied in order to be analysed. Even if the concept of the diagram captures an indiscernible zone of abstraction, this abstraction still needs to be articulated through language.

Bacon and the sensation diagram

Deleuze situates the notion of the diagram squarely within the field of art. The third source of the diagram is *Francis Bacon: The Logic of Sensation*, in which Deleuze explains what is at work in the diagram in the context of painting.[58] Bacon, who often blurs his figures, calls erased zones of distortions 'graphs'. The word graph, which he used in an interview with David Sylvester, was translated into French as *diagramme*. This is where Deleuze steps in. Despite the opportune translation,[59] Deleuze's definition of the diagram is quite complete in this book. I would like to focus on two elements of this diagram: the zone of indiscernibility and the means of passing from one form to the next (or staying within the same form).

First, the chapter titled 'The Diagram' explains the concept as preparatory work, as catastrophe or chaos, and finally as a zone of indiscernibility: 'There is thus a preparatory work that belongs to painting fully, and yet precedes the act of painting. This preparatory work can be done in sketches, though it need not be, and in any case sketches do not replace it.'[60] Deleuze describes the work of distortion that Bacon performs on his canvas: scrubbing, sweeping and wiping to create spaces or zones. These are 'more or less virtual, more or less actual' and they are on the canvas and in the painter's head. These zones are wiped, brushed, rubbed or covered over; mouths are stretched out and heads split with abstract shapes:

> This is what Bacon calls a 'graph' or a *Diagram*: it is as if a Sahara, a zone of the Sahara, were suddenly inserted into the head; it is as if a piece of rhinoceros skin, viewed under the microscope, were stretched over it; it is as if the two halves of the head were split open by an ocean; it is as if the unit of measure were changed, and micrometric, or even cosmic, units were substituted for the figurative unit.[61]

These painterly distortions are diagrams. These marks, or traits, 'are irrational, involuntary, accidental, free, random. They are nonrepresentative, nonillustrative, nonnarrative. They are no longer either significants or signifiers: they are a-signifying traits.'[62] These traits disturb the preordained, clichéd organization of the painting. The diagram is a set of non-representational lines or zones and its function is to be suggestive.[63] Deleuze says that the diagram is 'indeed a chaos, a catastrophe, but it is also a germ or order or rhythm'.[64] It is the zone between the prep work and the painting. But because it is chaotic, it must resist participating and creating more chaos. Instead, the hand of the painter needs to control it: 'Being itself a catastrophe, the diagram must not create a catastrophe. Being itself a zone of scrambling, it must not scramble the painting.'[65] The diagram is the germ of organization within chaos.

In the 'The Eye and the Hand', the final chapter of *The Logic of Sensation*, Deleuze explains how the diagram within the context of a painting is involved in the passage of one form to another – or rather, where a single form modulates, 'where we only move across a single form'.[66] The example he gives comes from Bacon's *Painting* (1946), in which a shadowy figure with a Mussolini grimace, flanked by two sides of beef, sits under an umbrella. The diagram in this context acts as a transformative agent. Deleuze contends that in this painting the diagram is located 'in the scrambled zone', towards the middle of the painting, or 'below and to the left'.[67] This is the darkest area of the painting, with aleatory brush strokes jumbled black upon black in a confused zone. Deleuze writes, 'It is from the diagram – at the center of the painting, at the point of close viewing – that the entire series emerges as a series of accidents "mounting on top of another".'[68] Bacon intended to paint a bird and ended up with a complex and morbid painting full of heterogeneous features. In this painting, Deleuze reads analogues of the bird features: 'the arms of the meat that are raised as analogues to wings, the sections of the umbrella that are falling or closing, the mouth of the man as a jagged beak.'[69] The traits that make up the intentioned figure of the bird have been put into a different series of relations, and the traits of the birds have spawned different objects: 'The diagram-accident has scrambled the intentional figurative form, the bird: it imposes nonformal color-patches and traits that function only as traits of birdness, of animality.'[70] The diagram is what is responsible for the elasticity of the bird-figure, which is topologically redistributed into other forms on the canvas:

> Thus the diagram acted by imposing a zone of objective indiscernibility or indeterminability between two forms, one of which was no longer, and the other, not yet: it destroys the figuration of the first and neutralizes that of the second. And between the two, it imposes the Figure, through its original relations. There is indeed a change of form, but the change of form is a deformation, that is a creation of original relations that are substituted for the form the meat that flows, the umbrella that seizes, the mouth that is made jagged.[71]

The diagram seems to cover over a zone and then redistributes traits from one form to another, or, as is the case with *Painting*, the same form is topologically distorted. The diagram distributes 'formless forces'.[72] The diagrammatic function is something that changes shapes from one stage to the next based on the function of contraction within a visual field. Batt explains the double movement of expansion and contraction that occurs at this stage.[73] The diagram can thus be considered a kind of synthesizer modulator: it ingests, digests and redistributes.[74] This modulation of the diagram creates new possibilities in the visual field for a form. The form can be redistributed, organized differently, depending on the heterogeneity of the assemblage of its traits.

Foucault, diagram and thought

In a final note on the diagram, Deleuze shows how it is connected outside of philosophy. Deleuze solidifies his concept of the diagram in *Foucault*. He takes the notion he started developing in 1975 and augments it with its permutations since *A Thousand Plateaus* and *The Logic of Sensation*. Batt enumerates the new additions of this most complete treatment of the concept. According to Batt, Deleuze considers the diagram from the point of view of becoming and associates it with the notions of force, *puissance* and the abstract machine. He differentiates the diagram from structure in order to make sure that it is not confused with a structuralist process, a notion that was 'omnipresent in the intellectual landscape of the time'.[75] Deleuze focuses the social field and clarifies the idea of immanence. However, notions such as dimension, the informal, multiplicity and *dispositif* are new to the overall concept of the diagram:[76] 'The concrete machines are the two-form assemblages or mechanisms, whereas the abstract machine is the informal diagram.'[77]

The diagram is spatial, and the space it occupies is indeterminate: 'The diagram is such a non-place, constantly disturbed by changes in distance or by changes in the forces in relation. It is only a place for mutation.'[78] Most importantly, Deleuze here reveals that the diagram is a non-space between the visible and the articulable. This is something that Batt also brings up:

> Between the visible and the articulable a gap or disjunction opens up, but this disjunction of forms is the place – or 'non-place' as Foucault puts it – where the informal diagram is swallowed up and becomes embodied [*incarner*] instead in two different directions that are necessarily divergent

and irreducible. The concrete assemblages are therefore opened up by a crack that determines how the abstract machine performs.[79]

Two important changes in the concept of the diagram in *Foucault* since the 1975 essay involve it becoming part of a philosophy. First, Deleuze compares the diagram to Kant's concept of the schema, and then he situates the concept as outside of thought.

In 'Écrivain non: un nouveau cartographe', Deleuze had already borrowed a term from Kant to describe the abstract nature of the panoptic architecture, likening it to Kant's architectonic – since, Deleuze tells us, this is the term Kant used to describe the conversion of vulgar knowledge into a science.[80] And Kant does in fact name his system an architectonic, a systematic arrangement of philosophical principles. The panoptic architectonic could then be understood as the abstract organization of functions that are poised to connect to other systems.

But in *Foucault*, Deleuze hones in on a particular concept within Kant's architectonic. Deleuze says that Foucault needs a third agency to bring together the two different forms of the visible and the articulable. This third thing is in fact a dimension that is heterogeneous with two forms: 'Foucault says that the visible figures and the signs of writing combine, *but in a different dimension to that of their respective forms.*'[81] What is this dimension, Deleuze asks? We already know the answer. The dimension is that of the diagram, and Deleuze compares it to the Kantian schema:

> Kant therefore had to invoke a third agency beyond the two forms that was essentially 'mysterious' and capable of taking account of their coadaptation as Truth. This was the *schema* of imagination. The word 'enigmatic' in Foucault corresponds to mystery in Kant, although it is part of a completely different whole and distributed differently.[82]

Based on this analogy of terms, Deleuze takes a step in connecting the diagram to a larger systematic philosophy.

In *The Critique of Pure Reason*, Kant writes that the schema is 'a hidden art in the depths of the human soul, whose true operations we can divine from nature and lay unveiled before our eyes only with difficulty'.[83] The schema is responsible for the conversion, through subsumption, of empirical objects of intuition into concepts of pure understanding. The device is powered by imagination. But Kant acknowledges an incommensurability between objects *in concreto* and their pure concepts. Therefore, a third term is necessary to maintain a relation of homogeneity between empirical objects, or 'phenomena', and concepts, which are part of the 'categories'. This third, mediating representation straddles the intellectual and the sensible sides.[84] From an aesthetic perspective, and in very broad strokes, it could be said that the schema bridges the empirical (objects) and the intellectual (the concept of the object). In order to do so, this third term must provide an image to the concept. But images are sensible things (they appeal to the senses), whereas concepts are part of pure understanding (therefore, not part of sensible things). So a question arises: what is this image of an object that cannot look exactly like an object? This image, what Kant calls the schema, is a bit sketchy. Kant likens the schema to a monogram. A monogram is a picture in lines only, otherwise known as an outline.

A little later in *Foucault*, Deleuze is much more explicit in his comparison between Kant's and Foucault's respective concepts:

> Foucault's diagrammaticism, that is to say the presentation of pure relations between forces or the transmission of pure particular features, is therefore the analogue of Kantian schematism: it is this that ensures the relation from which knowledge flows, between the two irreducible forms of spontaneity and receptivity.[85]

The comparison between the diagram and the schema gives the diagram an antecedent in the history of philosophy. The diagram's relationship with the schema is complex and must be analysed in conjunction with Deleuze's views on Kant and his schematism.

But the diagram, as a connection between two incongruous elements, becomes part of the mechanism of thought that comes from the outside. Because the diagram organizes unformed matter between various systems, it depends on these systems to generate thought. Deleuze writes, 'This is the outside: the line that continues to link up random events in a mixture of chance and dependency.'[86] Thought is generated from formations out of which traits are abstracted. Deleuze explains how relations of forces 'concern not only men but the elements'.[87] So there is a loss of control over what will spark thought: thought depends on formations, whose diagrams are already working in connection with other diagrams before they touch us, navigating at random in their multiplicity: 'Consequently, thinking here takes on new figures: drawing out particular features; linking events; and on each occasion inventing the series that move from the neighbourhood of one particular feature to the next.'[88] Deleuze traces a whole topology between the inside and the outside of thought – how the diagram connects

Introduction

these two dimensions and creates a new dimension between the incongruous system of the visible and the articulable. In order to articulate this topology, he comes up with another concept – that of the fold: 'To think is to fold, to double the outside with a coextensive inside.'[89] At the end of *Foucault*, Deleuze even draws a map, or a cross-section, of strata that separates the inside from the outside but connects the two different spaces. Before knowledge is stratified, it is shuffled in a diagrammatic zone. The diagram does not notice the strata; and the strata, once plumbed, lead to an interior chamber. This empty chamber connects back to the outside. Because thought is generated according to this connective topology, which feeds the void with material that is already in a diagrammatic flux, Deleuze shows us how thought comes from the outside.

Conclusion

The concept of the diagram marks a zone of abstraction in which concrete systems shed their specificity and interact on the level of pure function. I have shown how Deleuze defines this concept in two ways: first, as an informal dimension and second, as a display of relations as pure functions. Since the diagram is non-representational, it needs to be embodied in some kind of image so that it can be grasped. That is why the concept of the diagram can be initially seen in architectural and cartographic terms. These two visual strategies will guide the connections that I will be making throughout this book. The sources in the Deleuzean corpus where the diagram appears seem to trace a small yet dynamic philosophical system. First, the diagram is a device that shows us how abstract terms come together between social systems. Then, it is a negotiation between different levels of representation. In the context of visual arts, it determines the process of abstraction. And finally, it constitutes a philosophy of abstraction and a way of mapping thought as something that affects us from the outside. The sources of the diagram surveyed in the second part of the introduction reveal a drive towards an organizational function of the diagram. This is what we will explore in the first chapter.

Chapter 1

System

In this chapter, I illustrate the crucial element of diagrammatic operations and suggest an emerging possibility of considering the diagram as a methodology. The diagram displays relations of forces and translates them from one system to another. The mechanism through which it performs this task is difficult to discern since the diagram is non-representational. The diagram consists of abstract forces (e.g. surveillance) that make up a particular system (e.g. prison system) and can be applied to another system (e.g. schools or barracks).

How does the diagram travel from one system to another? The minimal elements of surveillance are abstracted from one context – the prison – and shifted to another system – the barracks. This movement, from the concrete case of the prison to the stage at which the forces that constitute the surveillance element of prison are abstracted, is made through contraction or constraint. The superfluous is taken out – walls, bodies, bars – and only the elements of surveillance are left – seeing without being seen, spatial arrangements benefiting the person in a position of authority, the prisoner's feeling of paranoia.

Each section of this chapter illustrates a facet of the passage of function from one state to another. To show the nimbleness of the abstracted function and how it passes from one heterogeneous state to another, I will present instances where the function moves from an abstract, or conceptual, state to a real, or concrete, state.

In the first section, I discuss the notion of assemblage, an integral part of the diagram and the minimal unit of systematic organization. Deleuze and Guattari provide the image of the wasp and the orchid coupling with reference to assemblage. I will locate this image in Marcel Proust's *À la recherche du temps perdu* and show how Proust uses the image of heterogeneous coupling between a bumblebee and an orchid as an analogue to the homosexual coupling between M. de Charlus and Jupien. While the function of coupling between the bumblebee and the orchid is similar to that of the two men in Proust's novel, Deleuze and Guattari use the function of heterogeneous coupling to provide an image for their concept of assemblage – or the bringing together of heterogeneous matter. I will exemplify this function by comparing Proust's novel to Diderot and d'Alembert's *Encyclopédie*, a comparison that will lead to the concept of the rhizome. The rhizome is also a manifestation of the diagrammatic passage of function from one state to another, since its functions – heterogeneity, multiplicity, connectivity – are shared by the plant structure and the concept that took the plant structure's name.

In the second section, I will excise the notion of constraint from Alain Badiou's *Deleuze: The Clamor of Being*.[1] Badiou argues that Deleuze is far from being the exuberant philosopher of multiplicities, free flows and desire that readers have pegged him to be. Rather he is the monotonous philosopher of a single idea repeated in different philosophical cases. Through his critique of Deleuze, Badiou actually illustrates my thesis of the passage of function from one state to another as it occurs in the diagram. It seems that Deleuze's system is organized according to the principle of constraint, which abstracts the idea of the One and conjugates it from one concrete case to the next.

In the third section, I first look at Gilbert Simondon's concept of analogy to consider how the idea of function changing form can be expanded into a systematic philosophy. Analogy is a comparative device through which an element of two heterogeneous objects is abstracted and compared. But in Simondon's hands, the analogy becomes the actual link between heterogeneous matter, such as crystalline formations, coral reefs and human society. What is more, Simondon articulates a theory that makes the link between two heterogeneous states possible by giving them ontological depth and moving away from a simple analogical comparison. He calls this device the *allagmatic*. The allagmatic brings into perspective the abstracted function between two states and provides a way of theorizing the abstract matter that is constrained and transported from one state to the next in a diagrammatic operation. Finally, I will use Manuel DeLanda's description of proto-diagrams to illustrate the passage of abstracted function from one state to the next: I will show how systems such as geological formations and mercantile agglomeration are not simply similar but are the same at the level of their function.

Assemblage

The assemblage is the minimal element of Deleuze's system: 'The minimum real unit is not the word, the idea, the concept or the signifier, but the *assemblage*.[2] The assemblage is connective, heterogeneous and multiple. It brings together disparate elements and organizes them. The assemblage connects, links up, creates relations between terms and objects of differing nature. Deleuze illustrates this with a description of a particular assemblage: the feudal assemblage: 'The feudal machine combines new relationships with the earth, war, the animal, but also with culture and games (tournaments), with woman (courtly love): all sorts of fluxes enter into conjunction.'[3] Actual events are linked to concepts and ideologies, as well as to persons and their roles in society. Elements abstracted from their specificity circulate in an assemblage, and heterogeneous things connect on this abstract level.

We can see why the assemblage is so essential to an all-encompassing corpus such as Deleuze's. 'What is an assemblage?' asks Deleuze. 'It is a multiplicity which is made up of many heterogeneous terms and which establishes liaisons, relations between them, across ages, sexes and reigns – different natures. Thus, the assemblage's only unity is that of co-functioning: it is a symbiosis, a "sympathy".'[4] The non-linear, non-hierarchical model of organization of assemblage brings together incommensurate objects of knowledge, and sometimes it overflows into altogether different material realities.

This is more than a simple analogy between terms or an equivocation between elements in a comparison. The assemblage is 'always collective, which brings into play within us and outside us populations, multiplicities, territories, becomings, affects, events'[5] – these disparate elements differ in their degree of abstraction. The assemblage accounts for the whole system and is able to bring together objects from different philosophical, scientific and aesthetic levels, spilling out into the actual state of affairs. In effect, it is a pluridisciplinary process. The assemblage navigates between the abstract and the concrete.

Deleuze and Guattari have succinctly summarized their principle of assemblage in an eye-catching image: the duality of the wasp and the orchid. A perfect literary example of this duality can be seen in Marcel Proust's *À la recherche du temps perdu*. What is interesting about its location in Proust's novel is that this image interacts with another duality and is already part of an assemblage. Here, the notion of assemblage is illustrated through the literary analogy between two doubly heterogeneous systems. On the one hand, we have a missed encounter between the bumblebee (an insect) and the orchid (a plant); and on the other, Proust describes the connection between M. de Charlus (an aristocrat) and Jupien (a tailor), two homosexual men of such divergent social classes that the fact they met at all was, what the narrator calls, a miracle of nature. Each coupling depends on particular functions that make the analogy viable: camouflage, lure and subterfuge on the part of the orchid and the portly M. de Charlus (the orchid resembles a bumblebee and the aristocrat, Proust tells us, a woman, and yet, because of its round shape, the bumblebee resembles M. de Charlus, effectively scrambling the analogy). With the comparison between the meeting of two men and a flower with an insect, Proust, in *Sodom and Gomorrah*, illustrates the principle of heterogeneous assemblage.

We find the fictional Marcel, the narrator, observing a hotel lobby from the top of the stairs as if on a mountaintop: '. . . the splendid vantage point, so comfortably installed at the top of the house, from where you can take in the uneven inclines by which ascent is made to the de Bréquigny *hôtel*'.[6] Marcel 'abandons' this vantage point which has offered him the perspective of the geologist: he comes down the stairs to investigate the garden outside the window in the lobby and thus adopts the perspective of the botanist.[7] There, a small area of vegetation inspires him to ruminate on the reproductive system of plants: he wonders if a bumblebee will ever arrive to pollinate a solitary flower outside the window whose shade he hides behind. Soon this vegetal thread is superimposed onto human sexuality – more specifically, homosexuality:

> I had lost sight of the bumble-bee, I did not know whether it was the insect that the orchid needed, but I no longer doubted the miraculous possibility of a very rare insect and a captive flower being conjoined, now that M. de Charlus (a simple comparison of the providential chances, whatever they might be without the least scientific pretension to drawing a parallel between certain botanical laws and what is sometimes quite wrongly called homosexuality) . . . had encountered the waistcoat-maker.[8]

Marcel sees M. de Charlus and Jupien meet and retire together to the tailor's shop. From his point of view, Marcel is able to observe the potential encounter between two heterogeneous beings and superimpose this function on the encounter between two men, whose chances of meeting, according to the narrator of the novel, were very slim.

The encounter between the insect and the flower holds a special place in Deleuze and Guattari's writings. This image of pairing is of course central to Deleuze and Guattari's famous concept/image of the orchid/wasp assemblage, except that Proust's bumblebee is traded in for a wasp.[9] A wasp is a less productive animal than the bumblebee, less social and less organized. Whereas the bumblebee is part of a social hierarchy, the wasp is independent. It seems the philosophers are sharpening the writer's image by using an animal that has no role in the reproduction of flowers; one way wasps get their honey is by killing bumblebees. The fact that the orchid is itself rhizomatic must be underlined, since a rhizomatic plant, unlike a plant with roots, is also organized in a non-hierarchical manner. And it is no accident that Proust's digressive writing style continuously spreads like overflowing vegetation.

The independent wasp is more ready than the bee to form a unit with the heterogeneous orchid: they are two lines of a multiplicity that form a block which is a zone of indiscernibility or indeterminate relation between two heterogeneous elements:

> The line or block of becoming that unites the wasp and the orchid produces a shared deterritorialization: of the wasp, in that it becomes a liberated piece of the orchid's reproductive system, but also of the orchid, in that it becomes the object of an orgasm in the wasp, also liberated from its own reproduction.[10]

The line the wasp and the orchid cross in their coupling liberates them: it is a line with depth. But what is more interesting is that the function of the insect/plant coupling, transferred by Proust onto M. de Charlus and Jupien, is transferred again onto the concept of assemblage. So a biological function passes onto a heterogeneous disciplinary and material system: a philosophy.

The wasp and the orchid are an emblem of connectivity and assemblage: two heterogeneous species coming into contact. Guattari explains that the concept of assemblage is larger in scale than the notions of structure, form and process, but that it is also larger than system. 'An assemblage', he writes, 'contains heterogeneous elements on a biological, social, machinic, gnoseological,[11] or imaginary order'.[12] As a multidisciplinary process, the assemblage can cross the lines between different types of disciplines, and it can make connections across several modes of being. Not only can processes between the biological and social domains be compared, they can also be connected. Furthermore, the imaginary and the social can be put on the same plane. Guattari compares the concept of assemblage to the block. The block is 'the crystallization of systems of intensities that traverse psychogenic strata and are susceptible or operating through perceptive cognitive or affective systems of all kinds'.[13] From this point of view, the notion of the block provides a pluridisciplinary perspective on the mechanism of assemblage.

Proust's *À la recherche du temps perdu* in its totality is also an assemblage. First, because it is qualified as encyclopedic; second, because it is expansive and non-hierarchal (qualities illustrated via vegetal metaphors); and third, because it is self-reflexive, which indicates a systematicity of heterogeneity.

First, it must be acknowledged that *À la recherche du temps perdu* has been compared to an encyclopedia. Proust's work is encyclopedic because it contains a vast amount of heterogeneous material, and also because of the procession of learning experiences and the education of Marcel – as *encyclopedia* comes from the medieval Latin meaning 'course of general education'.[14] For Deleuze, Proust's book describes the progress of an apprenticeship.[15] And this apprenticeship is manifest in a network of signs that intermingles several different domains, disappears, reappears somewhere else in the oeuvre, and is finally the revelation of art in its systematic whole. We could read this as a description of a system that aims at education. The *Recherche* is, according to Deleuze, 'the story of an apprenticeship'[16] in signs.[17] The work keeps growing, ever expanding, amassing knowledge and reflecting on it.

Secondly, it appears that Proust's work is a peculiar type of encyclopedia. Best considered from the perspective of heterogeneity and not strict ordering of knowledge, Proust's novel is described in vegetational terms to underscore the effusiveness of the work. Take, for example, Nicola Luckhurst, who, in order to illustrate the encyclopedic span of Proust's writing, quotes the Italian novelist Italo Calvino's pronouncement that the *Recherche* is an unfinished (open) system:

> Not even Marcel Proust managed to put an end to his encyclopedic novel, though not for lack of design, since the idea for the book came to him all at once, the beginning and the end and all the general outline. The reason was that the work grew denser and denser from the inside through its own organic vitality.[18]

According to Luckhurst, via Calvino, Proust's book is organic and this organic aspect can be described in vegetative terms. Vegetation itself illustrates the profusion of information but also its non-hierarchical, heterogeneous juxtapositions – seen in Proust's many asides, references and descriptive digressions. The vegetational image of such effusive systems are necessary because, as Alberto Gualandi explains in his book on Deleuze: '[t]he system of Nature is not a hierarchical system, separated into domains the importance of which is measured through their degrees of proximity and resemblance to a supreme principle that possesses Being in an immanent way.'[19] Vegetational images serve then to emblematize this view of a non-hierarchical system of nature, or of a system of philosophy that can be concrete without being stable. Ronald Bogue solidifies the systematic aspect of the vegetational metaphor by comparing its progress to another rhizomatic image – that of the crystal. He describes the growth as something that is constantly spreading: 'If there is a unity in these artworks, it comes not from a preconceived plan or an organic necessity, but from the anomalous parts, which like seed crystals induce a process of transformation and reconfiguration.'[20] We can see that Proust's novel is considered from the perspective of a heterogeneity more or less illustrated by images of profusion.

Thirdly, we can say that the description of Proust's encyclopedic and heterogeneous novel is tied to its self-reflexive nature. The self-reflexivity makes the work a system (in which the last parts must reflect the first part in a classical, circular understanding of a philosophical system) that contains encyclopedic amounts of information brought together in the form of a heterogeneous assemblage. Deleuze's description of Proust's oeuvre in a passage of *Proust and Signs* could be applied to his own corpus. He tells us that Proust's antilogocentric style continuously breaks off into detours, the various fragments of which we need to pick up at different speeds, and each fragment refers (*renvoie*) to a wholly different ensemble.[21] Deleuze also tells us that the various parts cease to function as an organic totality, instead they function like fragments that spur crystallization.[22]

Deleuze sees in *À la recherche du temps perdu* a *systématisation finale*. The *Recherche*'s final systematization is the product of its own englobing self-reference as a work of art. This final systematization refers to the final part of the *Recherche*, where the narrator reflects on the process of writing the book which has not yet come to an end. He calls it his construction, saying that it has never left his mind. But he wonders whether it will be a church where followers will meet to discover harmonies and a grand master plan, or a forgotten ruin on an island.

This final systematization as self-reflexivity is what David Bates, who discusses cartographic analysis of the encyclopedia, had in mind when the entry *ENCYCLOPÉDIE* appeared in the Encyclopedia of Diderot and d'Alembert. In the *Encyclopédie*, this opening within the system relies on the *renvois*: the references in the entry that link up to other entries and definitions. These create a malleable, dehierarchized system that has led some critics to see it as a whole other dimension within the text of the encyclopedia: 'the final dimension of the text' is 'the jeu de *renvois*'.[23] The network of cross-references makes for a dimension that is an unstable multiplicity because it defies mapping.[24] The heterogeneity of connections between entries sparks the imagination and has led some to compare the imaginary textual dimension potentially created by the network of *renvois* to a constantly shifting labyrinthine structure.[25] From a Deleuzean perspective, we could see the network as a subterranean burrow beneath the main alphabetical organization of the entries, linking up the encyclopedia in a rhizomatic arrangement. The alphabetical ordering of the encyclopedia falters because of the vast underground passages from one entry to the next; the soil is weakened by the number of tunnels underneath the illusorily stable and rigid order. Furthermore, the alphabetical method of arranging the entries contributes to a heterogeneous organization: 'More recently, the *Encyclopédie* has been called an "unintegrated juxtaposition", with only a superficial order arising from the arbitrary alphabetical series.'[26]

A comparison between Proust's novel and the encyclopedia does not make the novel rigid; rather, it is the encyclopedia that becomes a heterogeneous assemblage. That is why we must explore the images that describe the encyclopedia in its organizational function. First, I will examine the branches according to which knowledge is organized and the labyrinth that seems to be a secondary structure beneath the ordered façade of scientific architecture. Second, I will compare these two images to the root and the rhizome as differing yet ultimately complementary organizational methods described by Deleuze and Guattari.

During the Enlightenment, Diderot and d'Alembert undertook the difficult enterprise of emancipating knowledge in the form of the *Encyclopédie*. This was not only a perilous enterprise, with regard to ruling powers and the sheer fortune invested in the project,[27] but also a mammoth one, in its aim to reconfigure how knowledge was to be captured, ordered and disseminated. David S. Ferris – in his article on multidisciplinarity, the systematization of knowledge and the disciplinary boundaries of science – quotes at length d'Alembert's claims for the encyclopedia as a tool for philosophers:

> The encyclopaedic order consists in gathering together our knowledge in the smallest place possible, and, to place, so to speak, the Philosopher above this vast labyrinth at a greatly elevated point of view from where he may be able to perceive the principal arts and sciences at the same time; to see with a glance of the eye the objects of his speculations, and the operations he can perform on these objects; distinguish the general branches of human knowledge, the points that separate them and the points that unite them; and even sometimes catch a glimpse [*entrevoir*] of the secret paths that unite them. It is a kind of map of the world.[28]

Ferris's passage is an example of the use of visual cues in the discursive field of the encyclopedia – where visual metaphors come into relation with spatial ones. Initially, the encyclopedic order and its systematizing principle are considered as a place, the smallest place where knowledge is gathered. But almost simultaneously, it becomes a space or a site where knowledge is siphoned; it functions as a spatializing device reaching outside its parameters, spilling out of the boundaries configuring a site. It places the philosopher *above* knowledge, 'at a greatly elevated point of view'. Even a scale of sorts is suggested here: the encyclopedia appears to him as a map of the world. This high vantage point is crucial because it brings into relation things at first not perceived to be in proximity to each other. Depending on the scale of the map, the distance between Paris and Istanbul can roughly span twice or thrice the width of a thumb. But standing on the ground, in the streets of Paris, one can look south-east in vain without catching a glimpse of another world. And so, looking down at the encyclopedia-map, the philosopher 'may be able to perceive the principal arts and sciences at the same time'.

What the philosopher sees is branches and a labyrinth. In the last part of Ferris's passage, he presents the differences and similarities between the branches of human knowledge of the *tableau* or *phylum* in the likeness of a tree. In discussing the *Système figuré des connoissances humaines*, a visual organization of the categories of knowledge represented through a linear network of connected lines, he suggests that this image becomes the synecdoche of the 'map of the world', as the 'tree or figured system'. The tree-as-phylum duality can be compared to a map pictured as a diagram.

The metaphorical constellation of map-tree-book is taken up by Deleuze and Guattari in *A Thousand Plateaus* when they differentiate between possible models of systems and books. The representation of systems through books is crucial here, since books are argumentative systems. The model in the shape of a tree is what Deleuze and Guattari call the root-book. Through a concise analogy, they make the tree the image of the world and then equate the root with the image of the world tree. They seem to juggle the terms through an analogical operation – they who stand against a representational, analogical philosophy – in order to stay integral to the concept of the root-book they consider classical: 'This is the classical book, as noble, signifying, and subjective organic interiority (the strata of the book).'[29] Through analogy, they move from the representational to the unrepresentable concrete. 'The book imitates the world, as art imitates nature: by procedures specific to it that accomplish what nature cannot or can no longer do.'[30] Deleuze never dismisses the classical model of the root-book: it has a beautiful organic interior and it functions through imitation, mimesis (the reproduction of nature by nature) or representation (the reproduction of nature by artificial means).

Underneath the classical tree-model is a rhizomatic labyrinth. The tree is left to dry in favour of the impossible architecture of the labyrinth.[31] The labyrinth is the counterpoint to the systematic spirit of the age of Enlightenment. The entanglement of these two operating models can be seen at work during the Enlightenment, an era Deleuze believed to have been far from stable, but instead intellectually tumultuous: 'Classical thought is certainly not serene or imperious', he writes.[32] While acknowledging the post-modern view that the Enlightenment, with its grand narratives and historical teleology based on a view of ever-evolving progress, is the source of the present state of political hegemony and unbounded capitalism, Julie Candler Hayes sees in it possibilities for resisting this trend.[33] She observes that the *Siècle des Lumières*, with its drive towards ordering and systematizing, hides a 'subversive counter-discourse';[34] its 'discursive heterogeneity' makes systematic reason 'a powerful critical tool'. In fact, it gives flexibility to its structure, so that it does not crack and collapse. As thinkers of the twentieth century have noticed, a system that tries to be all encompassing is bound to contain the material of its own undoing. The heterogeneity as a function must be filtered out of systems.

In *A Thousand Plateaus*, Deleuze and Guattari present two different organizational models of thought – the tree and the rhizome. One is classical, static and hierarchical, the other is multiple, fluctuating and aleatory. There seems to be a strong divergence between these two models and it seems that one should be rejected in favour of the other. Yet, Deleuze and Guattari find that the function of connectivity brings the two together and that the tree and the rhizome complement each other. This function has assembled two heterogeneous systems, one of which is the emblem for heterogeneity, making this coupling especially self-reflexive.

The classical tree structure is teeming underneath: '[A] labyrinth is perpetually available within the most carefully conceived geometric space, within every system and every language; . . . within the general system, fiction and seduction are ineluctably bound to knowledge of self and of the world.'[35] The notions marking this discussion have the spatial and organizational characteristics of the labyrinth, the rhizome and the burrow. Together, they designate a multidimensional and non-linear path through the theory of the systematic organization of thought, and, by extension, its capture in the form of a philosophical system, a philosophy that is not very stable, but productive – in other words, flexible.

This imitative function of the root-book is developed further by Deleuze and Guattari in the coupling of the tracing and the map within the diagram. Tracing, although necessary, cannot offer anything new to thought because its function is to copy and represent what is already there. The map, on the other hand – and here the map is taken away from the classical model, but without losing the classical spirit that induced it – is an exploration device, something that does not imitate but that constantly explores the unknown.

The map, then, does not necessarily function in an imitative way like the root-book or, by extension, that other classical tree, the encyclopedia. Rather, it functions in the spirit of difference and its emblem is the rhizome. The rhizome is another model where roots spread not through bifurcations but through an undetermined disorder. It spills out of the botanical and spreads into the biological, the animal. Deleuze and Guattari write:

> A system of this kind could be called a rhizome. A rhizome as subterranean stem is absolutely different from roots and radicles. Bulbs and tubers are rhizomes. Plants with roots or radicles may be rhizomorphic in other respects altogether: the question is whether plant life in its specificity is not entirely rhizomatic. Even some animals are, in their pack form. Rats are rhizomes. Burrows are too, in all of their functions of shelter, supply, movement, evasion, and breakout.[36]

If – as Deleuze and Guattari state in *What Is Philosophy?* – 'Everything begins with Houses', the rhizome as burrow is a strange house with which to begin indeed.[37] The burrow 'begins' because it is a point of entry, as Deleuze and Guattari state on the first page of *Kafka: Towards a Minor Literature*. The burrow has only one entrance and it is designed as a decoy, a trap to exclude the enemy, which, in this case, is the signifier. An entry point, it must be underlined, is not a point of origin. In *Kafka*, Deleuze and Guattari walk into the work through random points of entry. They are not there to interpret the work; they are there to draw a map, a diagram that is made up of connecting points. The underground lair of a mole, an animal, is a strange blueprint of a system that shares a characteristic with the diagram in Deleuze's *Foucault*: the diagram and the mole are both blind, except that the diagram is a blind device making seeing possible.[38] The burrow does indeed constitute a strange architecture when taken to symbolize the structure of a system.

The encyclopedia is a link between terms of knowledge, but also, overflowing into other systems, it becomes an assemblage of incongruous matters. One could even see the encyclopedia as a multidisciplinary map linking together, liaising, between vegetal, animal and individual.[39] Relationality at work in the organization of knowledge in the encyclopedia resembles Guattari's definition of the assemblage, where the assemblage also seems to overflow particular categories and where social and biological domains can be compared and connected. Guattari valorizes the liaison, the connection between different domains. The function of relationality that is at work in the encyclopedia shifts onto other systems. This interpretation is a little different from d'Alembert, since the individual – d'Alembert's philosopher, but also the individual as represented and included in the encyclopedia – is here put side by side with the rest of the world, is included in the series, and becomes part of the system.

In the discussion of the rhizome in *A Thousand Plateaus*, Deleuze and Guattari explain how the first principle of the concept is the duality of connection and heterogeneity. These are the two elements that we particularly need to consider in describing certain elements of the assemblage and how they pertain to the concept of the diagram. What we have tried to do here is to set the stage for a description of the diagram as a methodology that will allow us to pass from one state to another through the abstraction of functions from specificities. Deleuze and Guattari explain their difficulty with linguistic models: they cannot be abstract enough to reach the abstract machine. As a result, Deleuze and Guattari develop other models to structure knowledge and connect it to the social field. In effect, the abstract machine is sometimes made synonymous with the diagram in Deleuze's corpus. Here, Deleuze and Guattari reaffirm the necessity of abstraction from specific function so that the diagram can perform its particular organizational operation. This is something that cannot be achieved through logocentric models such as linguistic models, since they cannot detach the language from meaning:

> Our criticism of these linguistic models is not that they are too abstract but, on the contrary, that they are not abstract enough, that they do not reach the *abstract machine* that connects a language to the semantic and pragmatic contents of statements, to collective assemblages of enunciation, to a whole micropolitics of the social field. A rhizome ceaselessly establishes connections between semiotic chains, organizations of power, and circumstances relative to the arts, sciences, and social struggles.[40]

Through abstraction, we can make assemblages between the social field and concepts, connecting across disciplines and heterogeneous elements of differing nature, bringing together previously unnoticed elements.

Constraint and Monotony

Constraint and monotony are two terms not often associated with the multidisciplinary and expansive philosophy of Deleuze. Yet, I focus on them here in order to draw attention to the process of creating concepts and putting together a philosophical system. In an interview during which Deleuze was discussing the possibilities of expression – specifically, the space formed by two people to foster communication and separate them from surrounding noise – he mentions the word *vacuole* (in the original French) to describe the space of the couple. I use it here to describe the need for constraint in the production of concepts, specifically in the couple that Deleuze forms with his writing partner, Guattari. By looking at other metaphors Deleuze uses to describe his concept production, I show how constraint is necessary for the production of thought. Then, I focus my attention on Alain Badiou who also sees this idea of constraint in the production of Deleuze's system. But he sees this from a rather negative viewpoint, qualifying Deleuze's philosophy as monotonous. I attempt to recuperate from Badiou's critique productive notions of constraint and monotony so as to later describe the mechanism of the diagram.

'The Couple Overfloweth' is the translation of the *Le couple déborde*, the pregnant title of a short dialogue – a brief interview conducted by Claire Parnet and Antoine Dulaure with Deleuze – that was first published in *L'Autre Journal* in 1985 and republished in *Pourparlers* in 1990, later translated into *Negotiations* in 1995. The couple referred to in the title is the generic couple Deleuze uses to exemplify the idea of expression during a time of oversaturation of background noise. The couple filters out, from the multiplicity, something meaningful. In a more intimate setting – a retreat if you will, from his clearly philosophical works – Deleuze organizes the couple spatially by articulating it through a fluid geographical image: the couple is treated as a space that overflows, as a river overflowing its banks. A minimal unit can be isolated within this dynamic in the way that Deleuze demonstrates the elements of constraint and expression within the space of the couple.

This space is organized through expression and silence. Expression and silence can be considered from this aphoristic text, not as positive and negative elements, but as organizing notions. The couple is organized around a gap, a space that makes communication possible: 'So it's not a problem of getting people to express themselves', Deleuze explains, 'but of providing little gaps of solitude and silence in which they might eventually find something to say'.[41] What Deleuze is speaking against – and what is accented by the fact that silence is not the negative of expression – are the positive and negative values inscribed in expression and silence, respectively. Silence is a necessary element of expression and is intricately linked to it. It is a productive element of expression rather than an absence of it or its negative. Deleuze's neutralizing of the negative in silence is articulated through a spatial strategy. He shifts attention from the couple's relation to language to the couple's spatial essence. In moving from language to space, Deleuze shifts the whole economy of negative and positive values articulated through language. As a result, the strategic and rhetorical purpose of language disintegrates in a space that is beyond an immediate critical scrutiny, which allows the re-evaluation of such already philosophically and socially determined objects as language and the couple.

The space in question takes the form of *gaps*, a translation of the original French *vacuoles*: 'Si bien que le problème n'est plus de faire que les gens s'expriment mais de leur ménager des vacuoles de solitude et de silence à partir desquelles ils auraient enfin quelque chose à dire.'[42] Vacuoles are indeed gaps, but gaps are not vacuoles. 'Vacuoles of solitude and silence' is a telling space. A vacuole is a tiny space within the cytoplasm of a cell containing air, fluid and food particles. It is a space within the cell that in the original Latin means empty. So it is a tiny, empty space, certainly, but a space that, articulated in Deleuze's ongoing interest in evolutionary biology, opens to all of the conceptual mechanics of folding, unfolding and refolding in his work, and also to a direct notion of writing style. The originary fold of the cell, the originary egg, is a model towards which Deleuze aims to bend his own writing as a process.

Yet, getting back to the constellation that contains the notions of expression and silence, language and its breaks, Deleuze's use of the term vacuoles, the origin of which is *vacuus*, underlines the emptiness that is at the operative core of language. The notion of style in language that Deleuze elaborates in terms of interruptions in the flow of expression, or breaks in language, is here directly incarnated: vacuous can also mean lacking in expression or unintelligent – perhaps even unintelligible: someone whom, lacking in both expression and intelligence, we cannot understand. The movement towards intelligibility, originating in this emptiness, is a structuring movement, a movement operating by constraint. It is the manifestation of the idiot, *idios* or the idiom.[43] Or the idiot as stupid, *bête*, the beast, the animality of the desiring subject speaking.[44] The vacuoles in the couple are the space of a particular idiom. These vacuoles summarize Deleuze's antipathy towards a logocentric philosophy and challenge us to find a non-discursive mode of thought.

I would like to read the notion of constraint into the space of the vacuoles because, still in 'The Couple Overfloweth', Deleuze says, 'Repressive forces don't stop people expressing themselves but rather force them to express themselves.'[45] Repression is not constraint; but a necessary force does link these two terms. This is indeed a compact formula: the forces of repression do not prevent; they encourage. This formula illustrates quite well Deleuze's cavalier attitude towards the negative and the positive as poles of a real productive opposition. Within the human landscape of the spatially organized couple, after geographical boundaries are drawn and spaces constructed, there is an undercurrent from which the mechanism of constraint emerges as an organizing and structuring device.

The link between repression and expression is translatable to the relationship between Deleuze and his writing partner, Guattari. This is because, putting the theory of constraint into practice in order to compose their book, Deleuze and Guattari did not engage in a dialogue, but rather forced thought by forcing each other to speak. Deleuze explains, '[D]uring our meetings, we didn't dialogue: one of us would speak, and the other would listen. I refused to let Félix stop, even when he had had enough, and Félix would push me in turn, even when I was exhausted.'[46] What Deleuze suggests here is that there was an element of force, of going beyond the limit of mere conversation, in his discussions with Guattari. Once the borders of conversation had been thus breached, there could be a meaningful production of concepts. Deleuze and Guattari were not exchanging 'ideas or points of view'.[47] Rather, instead of discussing things, they were creating concepts. The idea is to get passed inane chatter and get to the productive aspect of the exchange within the couple. Deleuze says that there is too much noise, and in order to get to the meaning of things, one has to filter out the point of communication: 'What we're plagued by these days isn't any blocking of communication, but pointless statements. But what we call the meaning of a statement is its point.'[48] He equates this meaning of a statement with the novelty of a statement, of inventing or creating something new, like concepts.

A gap in the Deleuze and Guattari partnership prevents their respective individual approaches to writing from coinciding. There is an incommensurability in their approach to thinking. Deleuze says that his approach is verbal, whereas Guattari's style is visual: 'Guattari's ideas are like drawing, or even diagrams. Concepts are what interest me. . . . Between Félix with his diagrams and me with my verbal concepts, we wanted to work together, but we didn't know how.'[49] This rift in style is also productive. Their divergent approaches to communication – Deleuze's verbal concepts and Guattari's visual diagrams – led to an overflowing of ideas.

System

In another interview in which Deleuze describes his writing partnership with Guattari, he refers to this idea of overflowing using a vegetal metaphor. Explaining how he saw this push and pull between Guattari and himself, Deleuze states that 'the weed overflows by virtue of being restrained. It grows in between. It is the path itself.'[50] The weed spreads like a rhizome. What is essentially a metaphor describes Deleuze and Guattari's approach to the production of concepts. From a space of constraint and incommensurability, illustrated through the space of the vegetal vacuole, Deleuze and Guattari begin the production of their ideas. These, in turn, spread like weeds and form a system based on rhizomatic connections. From the originary vacuole of unintelligibility, they form together an idiom.

The idiom – or *idios* (as in, 'one's own, private and peculiar') – in this case is that of the monotonous – from *monos* (as in, 'alone, single') and *tono* ('tone'). The monotonous, the single tone, is the bass line of Deleuze's system: or, according to Alain Badiou's *Deleuze: The Clamor of Being*, Deleuze's philosophy is 'monotonous'.[51] Badiou insists, contra what he considers to be a leftist contingent,[52] that Deleuze is a machinic thinker.[53] By this characterization, Badiou reveals that Deleuze's philosophy is organized around the function of constraint.

Badiou's book provides a very clear impression of Deleuze as a systematic writer. But the acerbic tone of Badiou's reading in fact does a great favour for readers of Deleuze. Indeed, Badiou's rough treatment of Deleuze is almost necessary to tame a corpus based on multiplicities, lines of flight and disjointed rhizomes rather than tree-models and precise dialectics. Badiou looks to the constraining instances of Deleuze's concepts to cull an effusiveness that is often the most popularly celebrated aspect of Deleuze's philosophy.

In fact, Badiou pinpoints with exactitude the process in Deleuze's philosophy. The accuracy of his interpretation lies in the very notion of constraint defining Deleuze's notion of system. According to Badiou, Deleuze is conjugating the single idea of the One by constraining it into the various theories of other philosophers. Badiou very diligently pulls this operative notion out of Deleuze's philosophy by observing the systematic mechanics of his philosophy: 'It is therefore necessary to maintain that Deleuze's philosophy is particularly systematic in that all the impulsions are taken in by it according to a line of power that is invariable precisely because it fully assumes its status of singularity.'[54] It appears as if these clarifications were designed to curb the effervescence of Deleuze's nimble thought. Badiou explains that Deleuze's system is monotonous since it constantly repeats the same idea (of the One) in different contexts. The first example

Badiou provides is the cinema-case: 'Let us understand that, under the constraint of the case of cinema, it is once again, and always (Deleuze's) philosophy that begins anew and that causes cinema to be there *where it cannot, of itself, be.*'[55] It may seem that Deleuze is an encyclopedic philosopher who wants to enumerate everything, Badiou tells us, but he is really just repeating the same thing and conjugating it through different cases (the cinema-case, the Foucault-case, the Leibniz-case). Badiou insists that Deleuze is thus constrained by his use of philosopher-cases. I would like to propose, however, that Badiou in fact suggests the reverse of his stated intention. The constraint operating in Deleuze's writings through other philosophers' texts functions as a mechanical constraint: it is the necessary mechanism of a structure. A structure that constrains an object through its mechanism, in order to classify it or represent it, is in fact filtering it.

This reversal of value can also be seen at the level of the concept. Badiou describes the nuances between a concrete concept and a concept of the concrete:

> It is therefore necessary to consider that Deleuze's philosophy is 'concrete' only insofar as, in his view, the concept is concrete. This in no way means that the concept is a concept of the concrete; rather, in the same way as with all that is, it makes the impersonal deployments of a local power that is obliged to manifest itself as thought by the concrete case through which the unique voice of Being makes itself heard in its multiple declension.[56]

In this passage, Badiou insists on the concreteness of the mechanism of the concept and, by extension, of Deleuze's philosophy. The concept's function is concrete, Badiou is saying, even though the concept is not necessarily concrete. He expands on this notion by shifting from a term or element that is concrete to a mechanism of the concrete: concreteness is manifest in that which functions, something that does something, the concrete case that conjugates a concept concretely. The concreteness of the concept, apart from the fact that its function is concrete within the larger context of working out a philosophy, should be seen as a concreteness within the context of the philosophy that makes the concepts real. The concepts are concrete because, englobed in the system of Deleuze's philosophy, they are part of a concrete reality.

The rhizome is a concept within the context of Deleuze and Guattari's system. But we must not forget that there are also rhizomes, or the wandering roots of plants such as the orchid, that exist in an empirical reality outside of the philosophical system. The rhizome in the system is not simply an image that is analogous to the root of the plant. The rhizome in the system functions like the rhizome of an orchid. In this respect, the rhizome of an orchid is already a 'concept' – a concrete concept before it is captured in an abstract philosophical system. In other words, the rhizome in the system is not a representation of the way the plant survives by pumping its nutrients from the soil: it *is* itself a rhizome. Thus understood, as Deleuze and Guattari explain, 'Concepts are concrete assemblages, like the configurations of a machine.'[57]

Now, we have seen how assemblages link between heterogeneous elements on various registers of abstraction, and do so according to the same function that passes from one system to another. Badiou inadvertently seems to be suggesting a similar process despite his critique of Deleuze's systematicity. In Deleuze's philosophy, the concept-rhizome does not represent a way of thinking, but is the function of thought in that system; the rhizome does not organize the system, but opens up an ontological dimension to the concept. It becomes emblematic of the materiality of thought cemented into the form of a system. This further concretization is what is lacking in Badiou's argument.

The singular idea of Deleuze is repeated, or conjugated, according to constraint through various philosophy-cases; for example, the cinema-case: according to Badiou, 'The entire interest of these cases lies in this generation, but *what* is generated bears no resemblance to the generating power.'[58] But of course it has no resemblance. The very effusiveness generated from the concreteness of the concept and the function of the concept takes the concrete concept on a line of flight. The difference produced by the trajectory from the generating power to what is generated is precisely how mapping functions – as opposed to tracing. The duality of tracing and mapping is introduced in *A Thousand Plateaus*. Whereas tracing repeats, mapping shows new possibilities. The tracing generates the same through an analogous repetition, but a map is not something that necessarily represents what is there; rather it marks the process of discovery. What is not there originally – as in the case of cinema – grows, overflows, must be mapped anew. This is the function of the concrete concept, which can also spill out in order to turn thought into a creative mechanism. Thought creates objects that are themselves concrete.

According to Badiou, Deleuze's philosophy is always the same stubborn philosophy filtered through 'concrete cases',[59] be they other philosophers' theories or objects such as cinema. Deleuze's production of philosophy is the result of his reliance on immanence: 'Immanence requires that you place yourself where thought has already started, as close as possible to a singular case and to the movement of thought.'[60] Badiou explains on numerous occasions Deleuze's conviction that thought does not just happen but needs to be forced out of necessity. As he puts it: 'Thinking happens "behind your back" and you are impelled and constrained by it.'[61] Thought not only binds and restrains you, but also forcefully pushes you forward. This euphemistic reference to sodomy is an urgent image of thought violently punishing a passive subject. Each of the objects raised by Deleuze in his books becomes a constraining mechanism through which his theories are filtered. The book is the little machine that constrains thought and builds structures by being part of a larger network. Deleuze's philosophy pushes thought outwards, towards unexplored countries, and it overflows.

What does thinking mean for Deleuze? Badiou explains that for Deleuze thought is not about spontaneity but, on the contrary, about being forced to think. Thought only comes out of constraint. But how does thought organize itself around constraint? Badiou believes that constraint is at the centre of Deleuze's philosophical system. Philosophical systems have been repudiated by thinkers, and the word still has a stifling connotation for some – including Badiou. But others ask instead: Is a system not an occasion to rejoice? This is Arnaud Villani's rhetorical question in response to accusations laid by Badiou against Deleuze's philosophy.[62] Badiou criticizes Deleuze's philosophy as 'abstract and systematic'.[63] Villani is stumped by the terms in this dual label since they could each be taken in two opposing ways. If a wounding tone generally chimes in people's ears when a text is described as abstract, Villani reminds us that for Deleuze abstract has a precise meaning: not one that is negative, but is '"ideal-virtual" or "transcendental"'.[64] The problem for Deleuze is not that things are too abstract; it is that they are not abstract enough. As for Badiou's pairing of the term 'systematic' with 'abstract', Villani cannot find any precise referent inside Deleuze's philosophy. While Villani can rescue 'abstract' from Badiou's charge by providing an accurate demonstration of the way Deleuze uses and celebrates abstraction, this is not the case for 'systematic'. Villani does not dip into Deleuze's philosophy to find positive mention of the concept of system. He fails to show how the notion of system, unlike that of the 'abstract', is instrumental to the smooth articulation of Deleuze's philosophy. Rather, Villani interjects subjectively well outside of Deleuzean grounds. 'On the other hand', he writes, 'that the philosophy of Deleuze be systematic, what can be more joyful? It is the signature of a great philosophy.' Alberto Gualandi[65] agrees: 'Deleuze . . . represents for contemporary philosophy something special: he is the thinker who has pushed philosophy to the extreme limit of its systematic possibilities in a time when it is declared from all sides that it is the end of all systems.'[66] It seems the polemics for and against systems that has ebbed and flowed since the first use of the term within philosophy is re-enacted on the terrain of Deleuze's corpus.

Even though Badiou wants to denounce the notion of system as limiting, he shows that constraint is part of Deleuze's system. Badiou articulates the importance of the mechanism of constraint in his attempt to reveal the monotony of Deleuze's philosophy. But Deleuze has already expressed, albeit metaphorically, the value of constraint for the production of thought. Deleuze's interpellation of vacuoles seems to be a call for sobriety in the face of excess, silence as an alternative to noise and constraint as instrumental to production. Whether we see the system in a negative or positive light, Badiou has demonstrated that the system is the field on which the relationship between the abstract and the concrete are played out through constraint. Seen in this way, the system is integral to the operation of constraint which can make the diagrammatic operation overflow and suffuse Deleuze's extended corpus.

Analogy, Allagmatic and Proto-Diagrams

In this section, we train our sight upon a philosopher who shares a strong kinship with Deleuze: Gilbert Simondon. What this section strives to determine from outside Deleuze's philosophy is the possibility of collapsing the distance between images and concrete things. First, I will look at the way the concept of analogy streamlines the notion of the system and gives us a way of understanding how connections can be made between disparate elements. Secondly, I will look at Simondon's notion of the allagmatic. Allagmatic is an ontological study of the crux of the relation between structure and operation. Allagmatic theorizes a schism, a blind spot that is productive in its articulation of thought. The theory of the allagmatic provides the opportunity to visualize an unrepresentable process that is no less actual because it is virtual, reversing a cleft into a depth. This theory proposes a visual semiotic tool of interpretation of aesthetic objects. Finally, I will show how connections based on pure functions between material elements illustrate the diagrammatic process by using examples Manuel DeLanda considers to be proto-diagrams in Deleuze's corpus.

'Sobriety, sobriety', Gilles Deleuze and Félix Guattari announce in *A Thousand Plateaus*, 'that is the common prerequisite for the deterritorialization of matters, the molecularization of material, and the cosmicization of forces'.[67] It is a rallying call without exclamation. In its quiet way, sobriety links the flower to the cosmos. And the philosopher Gilbert Simondon shows how the individual plant is opened on either end to that which is geological, as it pumps nourishment out of the soil and to the cosmos, as it imbibes the sun's rays through photosynthesis.[68] If, as Badiou suggests, Deleuze is the monotonous philosopher of the One,[69] then Simondon is parsimonious with his concepts. With Guattari, Deleuze has constructed a system populated by deterritorializations, molecularizations and cosmicizations, a kaleidoscopic multiplicity of concepts. While constructing such concepts as the Body without Organs (BwO), the Rhizome and the Diagram, Deleuze and Guattari have given a number of philosophers a new life. Simondon is not just another figure holding up the Deleuzoguattarian assemblage. He is at once subterranean and ubiquitous in their corpus,[70] but most importantly, he is sober.

Simondon's system is an 'entire philosophy',[71] as Deleuze calls it, and links the formation of crystals to the splitting of cells, the formation of coral reefs and termites' nests to the psychic make-up of individuals and their composition of a society with very few key concepts: transduction,[72] metastability, hylemorphism, structure and operation, crystallization, and modulation are all woven together through the notion of analogy.

Simondon, who was born a year before Deleuze, in 1924, and died in 1989, is mostly known for his ontological theory of technology. His work on the process of individuation is fascinating. Simondon's system materially holds everything together in the universe under the banner of this concept. His work was, until recently, divided into two volumes: the first published in 1964 and titled *L'individu et sa genèse physico-biologique: l'individuation à la lumière des notions de forme et d'information*; and the second titled, *L'individuation psychique et collective*, which was only published in 1989. These are now published as *L'Individuation à la lumière des notions de forme et d'information*, which has not yet been translated into English. If Deleuze is a systematic philosopher of one single idea, a similarly ascetic method is found in the philosophy of Simondon, Deleuze's precursor, whose system is at once tight and expansive.

Let us start with the very sober brick. And the very sober mould and earth needed to form the brick. The 'entire philosophy' begins with an evocative example involving all the possible facets of brick-making from the earth (the matter) out of a mould (the form). The dyad of matter and form presupposes the concept of individuation that renders it static, with no possibility of a dynamic becoming. Simondon proposes in its place to look at the concept *in medias res*, throwing out equilibrium and stability as the foundation for the individual and instead looking at individuation from a metastable perspective. Slowly, Simondon reveals the dynamism involved in the brick taking shape, the underlying event being the individual brick emerging from a metastable system. The mould does not perform the role of a stable limit on the earth, the substance of the brick. It is constantly at play: the boundary delimited by the mould fluctuates with the force of the earth settling, pushing on its structure. The matter and the form are in a state of fluctuation, of metastability. Simondon goes so far as to expose this process from a wider angle: the brick is never the same for the worker who makes it, even though the industrialist who employs the worker sees only one brick. This is related to the effort the brick-maker puts into every single brick, thereby further shaping their individuality. This is a preliminary illustration of the concept of *operation* that envelops the structure: here, the brick/mould structure is enveloped in the operation of brick-making. The operation is endowed with an ontological force that makes the structure, mediated by the conscious individual, a system.

Metastability is laboriously explicated through crystallization. Simondon describes the process of crystal formation, itself a model that, from then on, will be the *idée fixe* for the rest of his system. Subsequently, incrementally, Simondon expounds on the splitting of cells and the formation of organisms, featured in the second part of the first book – the individuation of the living being. A whole chapter is dedicated to coral reefs and questions about what constitutes an individuated being when corals are an amalgamation of beings with particular functions: some beings in the reef have the sole function of reproduction, others are the ones that eat, and others still defend the colony.

The second tome of the system starts with individuation at the psychic level, but follows the same model of crystallization. Finally, the end puts into play the question of what constitutes an individual in a society, a social-individual. According to Simondon, an individual is not an individual until he or she is in a transductive relation with other individuals in a society. Two processes are important to this statement. The first is transduction, a biological term from which Simondon isolated a theory of systematic information sharing. A transduction is 'the transfer of genetic determinants from one microorganism to another or from one strain of microorganism to another by a viral agent'.[73] The second process at work in his definition of a social-individual comes from his close study of corals: Simondon states that in a coral colony, which is an organism but not an individual, the true individual is the one that breaks away from the colony in order to start a new one elsewhere. The pure individual in society in this sense is the individual that breaks away from social constraints and norms – against society. However, Simondon does not have a mutineer in mind, rather he chooses the persona of an inventor: an innovator, a creator, someone who takes the plunge and learns how to swim, as Bergson would say.

Muriel Combes explains in her work focusing on Simondon's concept of transduction how Simondon replaces the mould with a *modulation*.[74] This switch makes it possible to think about the process of form-taking as an interaction between forces and materials. The whole idea of stability and static hylemorphism is therefore replaced by the notion of metastability: that is, the environment in which an individual can be in a process of becoming. Perfect stability is death. A metastability that can be most accurately predicted in all of its infinite detail in the process of becoming is a perfect being. These are the two extremes of the metastability–potentiality–individuation triad. At this point, it is apparent that we can have a monotonous philosophy of the one but this will be a multiplicity – a conjugated multiplicity of the system. Simondon then teaches us how a philosophy can move dynamically and juggle the one and the many in a reciprocal dynamism. Therefore, this crucial link between material, physical individuation and psychic–social individuation slides seamlessly, systematically between materiality and thought. It is a further elaboration on the concrete concept seen in Badiou; but in this context, of a process that makes possible a systematic continuation of the material in thought through analogy, the system is seen as fluid and virtual rather than rigid and repetitive.

This passage from abstract to concrete is based on Simondon's articulation of the possibility of actual, physical analogies in the midst of his philosophy. He asks if it would not be productive to develop an entire system of analogy based on the individuation of crystals:

> Perhaps it would be necessary to find in the familial link between forms, functional analogies that link up a great number of individuating processes belonging to very different domains; an aspect would be common to them all: the identity of the process of growth, that would be a creation of the ensemble organized according to an autoconstructive schema based on a growth dynamism and initial random data; a similar rule could be found in the growth of flowerage, in the development of a tree, in the formation of a colony, in the genesis of mental images, as if the dynamic dominance gave a structure to ensembles from a singularity.[75]

In this passage, Simondon clearly states that there is a schema at work that is repeated through various systems. Flowerage and mental images are based on the same schema: the schema is growth. And a link can be established between the biological vegetation and the geological crystals based on a similar function.

In his book on Simondon, Pascal Chabot describes the long history of crystallography. During the eighteenth century, crystals were hypothesized in terms of their formative mechanism. This new focus on the inner loci of the dynamic process of the crystal was instrumental in moving past the stage observing its exterior surface. The shift from the outer layer to the inner mechanism redefined the relationship of the science of crystallography to its object. Like most sciences before the eighteenth century, crystallography concerned itself with the issue of inventory and cataloguing of crystals extracted from mines and volcanoes.[76] In addition to the formative processes of crystals, the science also concerned itself with the earth's formation. Crystals were indicative of the process of development on both the physical and the metaphysical plane.[77] In the past, crystals were analogized to certain aspects of biology and the body: for example, the process by which crystals grow was compared to coagulation of the blood. Crystals were thought to coagulate at the centre of the earth because it was believed the temperature of the earth's core was very low.[78] At the beginning of the seventeenth century, Kepler, the man responsible for conceiving the planets' orbits as elliptical instead of circular, made another analogical leap in his idea that the crystalline shape of snowflakes was directly dependent on a force of action reflecting the soul of the earth.[79] For Buffon, a biologist of the Enlightenment and the author of the voluminous *Histoire naturelle*, crystals were a sketch of life because of the residue of organic molecules.[80] Furthermore, crystals were used as epistemological models to think about foetus formation and the soul.[81] For a long time, crystallization was thought to be the 'missing link' between physical matter and organic life.[82] This is a fundamental aspect of Simondon's system: as Chabot states, 'The crystal, paradigm of individuation, constitutes for Simondon the occasion to reaffirm the link between the phases of being and becoming.'[83] For Simondon, a deep reflection on crystals has clear reflexive and speculative consequences that spill out of the physical into the philosophical.

Analogy as a relation between two different objects only functions if it has some sort of ontological validity. This ontological validity is found in the scheme of the known being – a scheme that can then be slid onto the unknown term of the analogy. The main feature of Simondon's concept of analogy resides in the split between the operations vis-à-vis the terms of the analogy. For Simondon, what is most important in an analogy is that these two elements remain autonomous. The validity of Simondon's analogical method relies on two crucial elements. The first is that the analogy has an ontological dimension. The second is that the structure of the analogy is only known through dynamizing operations. From an epistemological point of view, the analogy is legitimized when 'the transfer of a logical operation' coincides with 'the transfer of an operation that reproduces the operational scheme of the known being' (since an analogy is a move from a known term towards an unknown that is understood to be the same because of the similarity of operation the terms share).[84] This coincidence of operation can be worked out in a material reality as well as an epistemological process.

The process of crystallization is a material manifestation of an operation that coincides ontologically with the generation of thought.[85] It must be understood that this operation does not function metaphorically. Rather, the mechanism of crystallization is repeated in the operation of analogy. And so, because crystal formations expand only with the basis of the model that offers itself as a platform for the expansion of other subsequent crystals, the method of thinking becomes as 'real' as the crystal. The power of analogy for discovery, for bridging 'upwards', is based on the model of 'crystallization in the domain of physical individuation'.[86] The analogy functions by analogy with crystallization. What matters here is that the operation be independent from the terms.

Simondon's demonstration of the affiliation in terms of operation between two processes can be explained as the process through which a crystal grows from a crystalline germ of microscopic size. Simondon wonders whether the process of thought might function through a comparable set of operations. What makes Simondon's particular use of analogy a potent method for thought is precisely the fact that it is explained in terms of an analogy with a physical process.[87] And just like the construction that appears out of the crystallization process – where each crystal spawns another identical to itself, as if it were a self-generating architectural edifice – the analogy is also compared to a 'bridge that crosses over a border. But this border is not abolished by the bridge: rational proportion does not destroy real differences.'[88] The bridge constructed over the gulf underlines the fact of the gulf.

Simondon's own use of analogy is ingenious because he establishes an order to his philosophy that equalizes the real differences between a human and a crystal – through an analogical short-circuit.[89] Simondon achieves this productive devaluation through the overarching process of individuation. As such, to be human or crystal – that is, a being – is a process that is delicately organized into a system. If the individual is never finite, and the being of this individual is in process, it is the same process: the very real process of crystallization. Simondon explains the physical aspect of this process through the notion of depth in binocular vision, where the form-taking operation is based on incompatibility and sursaturation, as in crystal formation.[90] The analogy of the crystalline process generates its own analogy in thought. The terms may not be fully superimposed, entirely compatible, but the difference is productive. The crown is to the king what the sword is to the warrior. But the crown is not a sword and the king is not always a warrior. The gulf is bridged but the gulf remains. What Simondon proposes by his theory of allagmatic is to study that gulf – the operation.

Anne Sauvagnargues, in her essay 'Deleuze. De l'animal à l'art', offers an insightful summary of the thesis guiding Simondon's system: Simondon asks when we can speak of One, whether one individual, one animal, one crystal.[91] The question is answered through being transposed onto the plane of the form and matter problematic, or hylemorphism, from *hylé* (matter) and *morphé* (form). Can the principle of individuation explain the genesis of the individual, the process of becoming one individual? And then, can individuation – that is, 'becoming individual' and 'individual that has become' taken together – be considered one? In other words, when the process of individuation, through which the individual is formed, is superimposed onto the individual that has become, do they match up?

The answer is no. From the very first principle in Simondon's system we are introduced to the productive incongruence that will be described as disparation. Based on the hylemorphic schema – the problematic of matter and form – the question of individuation cannot be answered. A rift opens up.[92] The incongruence between the individual and the process of individuation is key in Sauvagnargues's interpretation of Simondon: not only does it inaugurate the distinction between operation and structure, it also provides a material opening of difference. Deleuze writes about the disparities present within oppositions and the intensive depth that rises from them: 'These are the source of the illusion of the negative, but also the principle of the denunciation of this illusion. Only depth resolves, because only difference gives rise to problems.'[93] The reconciliation of the difference will not bridge the gap. The differenciation of the difference between the oppositions will emboss this gap as intensity. 'Oppositions are always planar; they express on a given plane only the distorted effect of an original depth. This has often been commented upon for stereoscopic images.'[94] The solution can be found in visual terms, as if the negative of the dark gulf brought it back to light.

Allagmatic exists as a word, albeit with a prefix, in the language of law, where it means to bring two parties together under a contract: synallagmatic. In effect, it means to form a couple, to bring two perspectives together. It comes from the Greek *Sunallagmatikos*,[95] which in turn comes from *sumallattein* meaning to bring together, to unify. Allagmatic could be defined, based on the Greek *allagma*, by the word 'change',[96] transformation. The allagmatic can be seen as 'the operative passage from one structure to the next'.[97] If Simondon is able to create a system spanning from the mechanism of crystal formation to the functioning of human society while passing incrementally through unicellular differentiation, the organization of animal societies, and human psychology, it is because he strings these elements together through the device of analogy. Allagmatic, at once removed from the objects contained in the terms of the analogy, gives these objects an ontological depth by stretching the frame so as to encompass what surrounds the terms of the analogy – its operation.

Simondon introduces the figure of the geometer in order to illustrate the operative aspect of the device. What is most striking about this example of the geometer is its graphic dimension. The tracing of the shape by the geometer illuminates immediately the visual aspect of the allagmatic process. The visual core of the example also emphasizes that the process must be understood visually. Finally, because of the way the example is laid out, its intricacies must be visualized in order for it to be grasped. Simondon uses the geometer's action to illustrate the frames of reality that make up a system. This example resembles that of the brick-maker and his brick. In the first instance, we are presented with the trace on the paper made by the geometer; in the second instance, we are asked to consider the geometer making the tracing as an integral part of the process of tracing a line. The passage reads as follows:

> The operation is the ontological complement of the structure and the structure is the ontological complement of the operation. The *action* contains the operation and the structure at the same time; also, according to the facet of the action upon which the attention is bestowed, it retains the operation element or the structure element while leaving behind its complement. Thus, when the geometer traces a line parallel to the straight line through a point taken outside of this straight line, the geometer is paying attention, in the totality of his act, to the structural element that alone interests his geometric thought, namely

the fact that it is a straight line that is traced and with a particular relation to another straight line. The structure of the action is here the parallelism of a straight line in relation to another straight line. But the geometer could also focus his attention to the aspect of the operation of his action, that is to say that the gesture according to which he traces, without worrying what it is that he is tracing. This gesture of tracing possesses its own schema. The system of which it is a part of is an operating system, and not a structural system; this gesture proceeds in effect from a volition that is itself a particular mental gesture; it supposes the availability of certain energy that finds itself released and ordered by the mental gesture through the interlinking of complex conditional causalities. The execution of this gesture puts into play an internal and external regulation of the movement in the operational schema of finality. Thus, geometry and allagmatic take divergent paths right from the beginning of their activity.[98]

Simondon's concept of the allagmatic reinforces analogy; we have to follow the example he provides. He invokes the image of a geometer, who, after having made some necessary calculations, traces a line on a piece of paper. After this line is drawn, a point is made in its proximity and another line is traced through the point. The second line stands parallel to the first. For Simondon this is an example of structure: it is oriented through the geometer's point of view, who is mostly interested in the very structure he drew on the page. Here, in order to avoid the different representational registers of analogical terms (if, for example, we chose to illustrate them as A. Warrior, B. Sword – C. King, D. Crown), the parallel lines on the page stand in place of the alignment of terms in a verbal analogy. What Simondon calls function, however, is the whole system of operations that revolves around the structure drawn on the page: the mathematical devices, the thought process, the hand tracing the line, and so on. It is the surrounding multiplicity, not just the terms of the analogy, that is part of the function. And so in an analogy, Simondon reminds us, we can rely not only on the terms (AB – CD), but on what puts one group of terms in relation to the other, which is the function. This function is charged with an ontological force.

Usually, only the structure is involved in an analogical exchange. Sometimes, however, both structure and function come together and exert a force on one another in order to make the system function. Such is the case of Descartes' *cogito*, which thinks itself thinking in the doubting structure that is chosen initially to deny the operation of thinking. In order to put things into a relation, the process is composed of the conversion of a structure into a function and back to a structure again. A fuller way to proceed is to abstract everything to the level of operations: the resulting allagmatic relation involves an independent ontological relation between the operator and the terms converted in this operation. Without this ontological relation, what we have left is simply a case of resemblances of ideas.

The inextricable ontological relation between operation and structure is shown by the geometer in the midst of performing the action of tracing 'a line parallel to the straight line through a point taken outside of this straight line'.[99] The line being traced according to the straight line and the point on the paper make up the structural aspect of the action. The second part of the action is the operation that involves not what is being traced on the paper but the general aspect of tracing. Simondon writes, 'This gesture of tracing possesses its own schema.'[100] The operating system consists of that which brings about the structure: '[I]t supposes the availability of certain energy that finds itself released and ordered by the mental gesture through the interlinking of complex conditional causalities.'[101] Both operation and structure are the parts necessary for the resulting action; both are complementary. It is the brick-maker seeing his brick taking shape.

Whereas analogy bridges terms in thought, the allagmatic process bridges terms on the principle of sight (they exist, then, because they can be perceived through the material organism of the eyes). Furthermore, the terms in an allagmatic process depend on the presence of an ontic being to carry out the operation. It therefore constitutes a material manipulation of the process.

The figure of the geometer is not wholly original when philosophers consider philosophy, especially when they ponder the problem of abstraction and concreteness, or the passage between theory and reality. Kant summons the geometer to illustrate the operation of analogy. This is taken up by Young Ahn Kang's excellent text *Schema and Symbol: A Study in Kant's Doctrine of Schematism*.

The passage in Kant's *First Critique*, in which the geometer is invoked, brings about the notion of self-reflexivity discussed here. First, the philosopher ponders the concept of the triangle and he fails to discover anything new within it. He analyses the concept of the straight line and the angle and is not able to bring to this concept anything that is not already in them. But a geometer will start with the construction of a triangle:

> Since he knows that two right angles are equal to the sum of all the adjacent angles which proceed from one point in a straight line, he prolongs one side of his triangle, thus forming two adjacent angles which together

are equal to two right angles. He then divides the external one of these angles by drawing a line parallel with the opposite side of the triangle, and sees that an external adjacent angle has been formed which is equal to an internal, etc. In this way he arrives, through a chain of inferences, though always guided by intuition, at a fully evident and general solution to the question.[102]

According to Kang, the cognition of a mathematical concept is not produced from experience or from figures. What is instrumental in this process is the material and visual source of the cognitive method thus made into a graphic method:

> In other words, a cognition of a mathematical concept is not produced by the confrontation with the figures and experience of things, but by the reading-off and interpretation of the properties of a concept through 'alphabets' or 'signs' (*Zeichen*) (point, line, plane, number or symbol).[103]

Kang seems to suggest that there is a mediating step in the production of concepts and that this step is graphic in nature – in fact, it is beyond language. This means that the geometer, as well as the mathematician, reach results through geometric constructions or symbols: 'by means of symbolical construction in algebra and quite as well as by an ostensive or geometrical construction or the objects themselves in geometry, at results which our discursive knowledge could never have reached with the aid of mere concepts'.[104]

Kant first chooses to determine the ground of possibility of the thing that is real when he is confronted with two different possibilities. He thus raises the a priori possibility of synthetic judgements in mathematics before considering whether the science of metaphysics is possible. Since mathematics exists and is real, but metaphysics as science – since we are talking about their possibility – is not, Kang explains that a question on the former will determine the ground of the possibility of the latter. Whether or not metaphysics as science is possible is not a question based on the modelling of metaphysics on mathematics, 'but rather ... [on] "disclosing" the source and ground of *a priori* cognition'.[105] The analogy is not made between the terms of metaphysics and mathematics. In the matter of metaphysics as science, the *operation* present in the structure of one question must be transposed onto the structure of another. In the second preface of *The Critique of Pure Reason*, immediately before the Copernican revolution in metaphysics is introduced, Kant explains that the 'true method of mathematics' is 'not to inspect what he [the geometer] discerned either in the figure, or in the bare concept of it, and from this, as it were, to read off its properties'.[106] It is rather 'to bring out what was necessarily implied in the concepts that *he* had himself formed *a priori*, and had put into the figure in the construction'.[107] Kang defines 'construction' as the 'act of determining the concept in mathematical cognition'.[108] Kang proposes, in effect, an alternative way of thinking about construction not framed in terms of material objects. But similarly, as the allagmatic device is based on visual perspectives and therefore needs the vision and the materiality of the eye to function, Kant's construction is made material through one very important element. The method is not derived from experience or from the boundaries of the figure traced by the geometer: what is material here is the fact that this transcendental act is performed by the subject, the geometer, the italicized *he*. The subject is part of the act of construction: 'This constructive act is not to "read off" the property of the concept from experience and figure, but rather to "read" (and a step further, to "interpret") it in accordance with the transcendental act of the subject.'[109] The place of the subject within this operation draws attention to an ontological dimension in the space of materiality. Therefore, in the allagmatic method, the ontic subject is a necessary element in the passage from one structure to the next.

These are the two geometer figures that link up the thread between both texts on a surface level. What is important here is that the figure of the geometer is the same one Simondon interpolates. And Simondon makes precisely the same argument. It is not solely about the things on the paper. The whole system surrounds the paper; the tracing and the one who perpetrates the action are involved.

Contrary to Kant, an analogy can be placed on a single univocal and material 'plane' rather than being an equivocal and metaphysical 'dualism' repeating the split of the empirical and transcendental. Deleuze's desire to eradicate the classical model of the double-bind analogical representation must be negotiated through the visual aspect of an *allagmatic materialism*. Analogy as a representational device operating through metaphors and symbols (where everything means everything else, as Deleuze and Guattari note in 'On Several Regimes of Signs'[110]) must be replaced by the spatial, orientative *operation* of the allagmatic. Spread on a spatial surface, we do not perceive something *as if* it were another, but instead, something *and* another at the same time. The function of the allagmatic collapses two things, makes them one, and also, through the stereoscopic process

System

of the material function of vision, provides depth, giving an ontological dimension to the objects that retains the difference in the repetition.

As an example of this superimposition, consider the Russian constructivist El Lissitzky as the allegorical image of the two geometer figures invoked by Kant and Simondon. Lissitzky is the geometer as constructor:[111]

> The collocation of the pair of compasses, graph paper, and cranium; the insertion of the Latin letters *XYZ* with their simultaneous evocation of universality and anonymity . . . the cool black, white, and gray palette of the photographic medium – each of these components emphasizes the apparent rationality and sobriety of Lissitzky as constructor.[112]

As opposed to the collage technique, in which images are juxtaposed, Lissitzky superimposes two different photographs, creating a photogram. In this 'photogram', Lisstizky is surrounded by geometric objects – compass, lines and graph-paper patterns. His eye, peering through the superimposed palm of a hand, captures the notion of the geometer's agency constituting a frame of the process of tracing a line – in this case, an unfinished circle springing from his head. The constructor is thinking what the eye is seeing, what the hand is doing.

A duality can be read into the picture:

> Although using the compass to indicate his trust in science and technology, by positioning an eye in the center of the palm of his hand Lissitzky also reminds the viewer that the artist's visual acuity was central to his new constructivist identity.[113]

But rather than the duality of art and science brought together through vision, it is the idea of the allagmatic that is illustrated: 'The sobriety of the assemblage is what makes for the richness of the Machine's effect.'[114] Lissitzky illustrates the process needed to create the photogram within the very work through a sober superimposition of several disparate images, in effect examining the face of a clock to expose its gears.

Through the superimposition of images, Lissitzky exposes the articulation within the notion of the allagmatic: the concept of disparation. Deleuze refers to disparation as a way of capturing the ontological ground of assemblage: 'Gilbert Simondon has shown recently that individuation presupposes a prior metastable state – in other words the existence of a "disparateness" such as at least two orders of magnitude or two scales of heterogeneous reality between which potentials are distributed'[115] – disparation, disparateness. This is the schism, the incongruity necessary for vision. As Yves Citton writes in 'Sept résonances de Simondon':

> It is the disparate nature of the image perceived by my left eye with that of my right eye that allows to accede to a perception of this third dimension which is depth; it is a tension belonging to these incompatibilities, to these *disparations*, that nourishes the emergences of new significations, and of the superior forms of individuation – and not their conversion to the flattening logic of homogeneity.[116]

Sobriety, sobriety. Paradoxically, it is through the eyes of the drunk that the concept can best be illustrated. Clément Rosset shows the inverted view, and plays with the opposition between sobriety and drunkenness: 'Drunks have the reputation of seeing double.'[117] Rosset describes the doubled view of a drunk by referring to Malcolm Lowry's *Under the Volcano*:

> Man possesses two eyes and consequently two real images that normally are superimposed on each other; when he is drunk, this superimposition is not made well, from which comes the fact two bottles instead of one dance in front of the drunkard's eyes. But this duplication of the real is a purely somatic phenomena, it does not affect the depth of the real in the perception of the drunk. On the contrary: the drunk perceives simply, it is rather the sober man who, habitually, sees double.[118]

It is on this principle that the allagmatic assembles two orders of terms, in the same way as an analogy; but whereas the bridge between terms in an analogy remains flat because the schism is never resolved – indeed is necessary for the analogy to function – the allagmatic gives the schism its three-dimensional reality. Rosset's example shows how upholding an illusion is important for its subsequent denunciation.[119]

Allagmatic is the theory of exchanges that results in the transformations of a system.[120] It is a theory of operations. In the present case of turning the allagmatic into a visual theory, the core of the operation is the blind spot, the incongruence that puts system into motion: 'An interval signifies in fact the possibility of a relation and a relation consists of an operation.'[121]

The bridging of two terms has to be seen as more than metaphorical. In Deleuze and Guattari's rich corpus, concepts such as the diagram (which relies on tracing and mapping), assemblages such as the wasp and the orchid, or images such as the archipelago and the spine all uphold within their duality an ontological core that renders these groupings viable concepts. These images, *qua idea*, should not be confused with mental representations, illustrations or metaphors. Instead, they must be read as a 'virtual differentiated complex. This intensive and virtual difference actualizes itself by differenciating itself (with a c) when it individuates itself. Such an individuation comes to be a stabilizing liaison, which resolves the difference in the initial potentiality.'[122] This is crucial to understanding Deleuze's meaning when he talks about a non-representational image of thought.

The stabilizing union modelled on Simondon's 'disparation' thus solves the problem of two flat, two-dimensional images, each on the wall of each eye, giving rise to a third dimension. The three-dimensional image is the idea that solves a problem as a process and comes to be. The incongruence is a negative space. But the negativity of this space is productive when considered as part of the whole ensemble since it is necessary for the resulting figures in the positive space to exist. If the negative space is read in its positivity, it is read as a figure of the virtual which cannot be positively presented: the virtual exhausts itself in the actualization. The negative space is an abstract representation of something that is unrepresentable: the virtual. This is what is at stake when the operation, rather than the terms in an analogy, is manipulated – when the *blind spot* of the 'disparation' is not seen as a lack, but provides the three-dimensional depth and, in doing so, provides an ontological fullness to analogy as allagmatic. This *blind spot* is a negative space until it is stared at enough to become positive, and then it provides an inkling of an unrepresentable dimension.

Brian Massumi, in his essay 'The Diagram as Technique of Existence', explains how the blind spot within the field of vision needs to be overcome for the eye to see:

> How could we literally see a continuous surface-surround of space when our very own nose sunders our field of vision in two – not to mention the holes poked in both halves by the blind spot of each eye? Bridge it over. . . . We see unity of form in excess of our eyes.[123]

The eyes are in constant motion in order to compensate for the blind spot: 'If the jerking stops, vision blanks out.'[124] Massumi's description of the physical actions involved in the covering over of the incongruous schisms within vision mimics the image of the directionality involved in the analogical operation: 'The continual variation draws the protofigural lines of the ambient array across the gaps between the rods and cones, across the nose hole, and across the blind spots. The discontinuities are giddily bridged by a continuity of movement.'[125] But Massumi is able to clearly shed some light into the void to reveal the mechanism at work underneath the texture of reality: 'The bridging yields a complex of moving lines of light *continuing across* invisible abysses of darkness. Protobridges of continuity, self-standing, over a void of vision.'[126] Into the void, Massumi throws in the notion of the virtual.

A further and crucial operation takes place in the ontologizing process of the analogy turning into an allagmatic. Each term, in order to be put into relation, has to be endowed with an ontological charge. It is in the process of perception that such a thing occurs. An especially apt theory is the process of disparation that deals with the stereoscopic capture of phenomena by vision. Didier Debaise[127] explains that disparation occurs when 'twin ensembles are not totally superimposable'.[128] This process is manifest in the way that vision functions. An image appears on the right and the left retinas, and it is then doubled. One object is captured by two images in a single system. But since there are two images, they are necessarily at two different locations; they cannot be completely the same. The fact that both identical images are captured in an ensemble 'allows the formation of a unique ensemble of superior degree'.[129] This new and unique ensemble is able to capture all the elements of both images even if they are in different places (and therefore not totally superimposable) through the intervention of a new dimension. In the case of vision, as Simondon's example continues, this new dimension is provided by stacking up different levels of depth, which results in a third dimension.[130] The incommensurability of the two individual images, because of their disparate locations in space, creates a rift. But this is a productive rift. The rift between the two images is necessary because it is only through this schism that a third dimension can enter the system. Debaise explains that an underlying or transcendental unit is what makes the link between both flat images possible. But this link is manifest in its absence; the blind spot operating in the disparation makes the images three-dimensional. It is a 'relation through differences' that takes place. A tension arises from the differences between the flat images and resists any evening out of the relational difference.[131]

The operation surrounding the structure of an analogy in the concept of the allagmatic has been extrapolated and its ontological depth extricated through disparation. The ontological depth emerging from an analogy and augmented into the allagmatic takes on an independent existence as the methodological mechanism in the formation of a philosophical system based on visual image. One way to demonstrate the methodological validity of the function is to examine how it performs along aesthetic lines.

In 1957, Robert Rauschenberg painted his *Factum I* and *Factum II*. The titles of the works infer, like a synallagmatic, a legal term based on the notion of fact and act. They parody the notion of gesture and acting. Rauschenberg's works illustrate the process of stereoscopic vision through the ontological gap that divides them and provides them with individual spatial positioning (as dispersed as their locations, in New York and on the other side of the country, Los Angeles, allow[132]). *Factum I* and *Factum II* are split geographically, but they are not fully superimposable. Rauschenberg's two combines are meant to parody the Abstract Expressionist idea of original creation. Along these lines, the works consider the operative process of artistic production, not simply the transcendental notions of subject matter.

However, beyond the fact that they are a commentary on uniqueness and simulacrum, originality and reproducibility, they are emblems of the allagmatic. We can imagine *Factum I* and *Factum II* as the separate images projected into each eye:

> An image appears on the right and the left retinas and it is then doubled. One object is captured by two images in a single system. But since there are two images, they are necessarily at two different locations; they cannot be completely the same.[133]

But both images together, form an ensemble that registers more deeply. The subtle differences within the reproduction of their content (which led John Cage to comment on the blind seeing) has led to speculation about differences within their repetitions[134] – the simple fact remains that they cannot be superimposed. The third dimension of depth that results from their incompatibility is the denunciation of illusions. They show the artificiality of the real by showing the flaws in the single (flat) image-as-illusion of the original Abstract Expressionist gesture. Furthermore, Rauschenberg enacts the motion and takes into consideration the outer frame of the operation. But the differences between *Factum I* and *Factum II* dissipate according to their spatial location and provide a three-dimensional blur sticking out like an anamorphosis, underlining the operative touch of the artist's hand.

The concept of the allagmatic is an operative theory that puts images on a single plane and inserts depth into the space of difference. This depth injects an ontological dimension into a simple comparison, rendering images into concepts. The allagmatic upholds the material ground of the analogy that sutures Simondon's system and the notion of assemblage in Deleuze and Guattari's philosophy. Its manifestation in visual works of art only begs the question of whether it can be applied to other forms of expression – whether, for example, it can fill the blind spot Deleuze sees in the works of 'modern novelists'.[135] If the allagmatic can become a critical theory, it will have to do so with a sober strategy that nevertheless giddily bridges the flower and the cosmos.

Now that the function surrounding the structure of an analogy in the concept of the allagmatic has been extrapolated and its ontological depth extricated through disparation, it is time to prod the depth of the function itself. The ontological depth that emerged from an analogy and intensified into the allagmatic takes on an independent existence as the methodological mechanism in the formation of a philosophical system based on visual images. These images carry the weight to stand on par with concepts forming the system. One way to demonstrate the methodological validity of the function is to examine how it performs along epistemological lines.

In order to see how a function can have an epistemological bearing, we need to consider the notion of process, since it clearly underlines the dynamic aspect of a function. Guattari described the concept of *process* with the terms that also describe the concept of function examined below:

> *Process* [Processus]: continuous series of facts or operations that can lead to other series of facts and operations. A process implies the idea of a permanent rupture in established equilibria. This term is not used in the sense of schizophrenic processes in classical psychiatry, which always implies an arrival to a terminal state. Rather, it echoes what Ilya Prigogine and Isabelle Steingers [sic] call 'dissipative processes'.[136]

What is crucial in this definition of a device that compares operations to operations instead of terms to terms is the fact of the rupture, the schism present in this process. This is what gives the device a dynamic impetus. The space of differenciation not only serves to provide a three-dimensional ontological depth, it also serves to give it a dynamic dimension: the disparation provides the possibility of seeing an object in three dimensions. Furthermore, it also destabilizes the terrain of the system and puts the objects in a state described as 'far from equilibrium' – in other words, unstable but productive.

But these ways of analogizing through the process of the allagmatic can be clearly illustrated through processes that are part of concrete material systems, effectively connecting systems to diagrammatic functions.

Manuel DeLanda opens this productive concept of function and populates it with vivid examples. In 'Deleuze, Diagrams, and the Genesis of Form', he explains the manifestation of interesting spaces in the pages of *Difference and Repetition*. These spaces are characterized by their functionality, and DeLanda can extend them very diligently to form a multilayered epistemology in Deleuze's work, an epistemology energized by the notion of function. DeLanda explains Deleuze's use of 'spaces of energetic possibilities (technically referred to as "state spaces" or "phase spaces") and of the topological forms (or "singularities") that shape these spaces'.[137] These topological manifestations are forms of function, but the function is ontologically charged and has the possibility of actively linking elements of different intensity. The elements in question – exemplified by DeLanda as particular instances of geology, genetics and societies – are linked through different functions in intensity through analogy and not just through common terms. The link is through an analogy divested of its matter, not the representational level of analogy. An analogy linking the functionality of elements instead of their terms of similitude is a diagram of analogy. In fact, DeLanda calls these topological spaces 'phase diagrams', which, he announces, 'are, indeed, the very first type of diagram used by Deleuze'.[138] The reason these 'phase diagrams' are significant in the context of the allagmatic is that instead of being simple analogical connectors, they have a material manifestation. They are incarnated in actual material occurrences and therefore solidly bind together assemblages. He writes:

> On the other hand, given phase spaces and singularities become physically significant only in relation to material systems that are traversed by a strong flow of energy, Deleuze's philosophy is also intimately related to the branch of physics that deals with material and energetic flows, that is, with thermodynamics. Chapter five of *Difference and Repetition* is a philosophical critique of 19th century thermodynamics, an attempt to recover from that discipline some of the key concepts needed for a theory of immanent morphogenesis.[139]

DeLanda provides two different models of organization that will stand in for function: the sedimentary and the meshwork. DeLanda enumerates sedimentary organization in geology, genetics and society versus meshwork organization in the same domains, thus demonstrating an analogy erased in favour of function. These instances of geological sedimentation, genetic evolution and social stratification are not just *like* one another. Rather, the function of sedimentation is the same as the function of evolution and social stratification. A diagram is drawn between these dissimilar noumena. What matters is this function, this diagram, this overarching gesture.

This functional arc between geology, genetics and society is drawn and cemented by the presence of another diagram supporting its actual trajectory: the meshwork diagram. Let us explore the implication of a functional diagram in further detail. Geology is not like genetics. The mechanism of sedimentation in geology is the mechanism of sedimentation in genetics. It is the same object that is present in a different place. Architectural theorist Sanford Kwinter explains the existence of incorporeal, nonspatial manifestations: 'Now integration, organization, and coordination are each abstract nouns without demonstrable correlates in the physical or chemical world. Yet this does not mean that they are immaterial – far from it! – only that they are *incorporeal*.'[140] This incorporeal mechanism can be translated onto Deleuze's own system: *sedimentation* would be *filtering* (similar to Badiou's monotonous repetition in Deleuze's philosophy and the structuring mechanism of contraction and constraint). *Meshwork* would be the *environment* in Deleuze's system: the environmental sections that are represented and that are at work in such places as the waxing and waning images of wasps and orchids and, as we will see later, islands and bones. DeLanda writes:

> It should be clear by now that talk of the 'stratification' of abstract machines is simply another way of discussing the actualization of the virtual, or in other words, that the theory of diagrams developed in *A Thousand Plateaus* was already present in Deleuze's early work. Indeed, I would go so far as to say that this theory was developed in greater detail in *Difference and Repetition*, and that it is this book that constitutes the main reservoir of conceptual resources needed to approach diagrammatic thinking.[141]

DeLanda tabulates two concepts from Deleuze and Guattari's corpus in order to offer them up as examples of processes in the emergence of structure: strata and self-consistent aggregates. These are respectively compared to the models of the tree and the rhizome. They are both, each in the form of the process of the structure and its model, abstract machines since they are networks of forces expressed into actuality. The abstract machine is, as Kwinter explains, just that – abstract, because it is not part of an actual reality – but is still a machine because of its function: 'they are fully functioning machines, that is, they are agencies of assemblage, organization and deployment'; they are things that have been devised to do other things on their own.[142] Kwinter then explains how reality functions through abstract machines: it is as if they were sewing the fabric of the actual around themselves, around and in us at all times.

> Reality ... is comprised both of matter and the organization of that raw matter into deployable objects or complexes. The argument, stated simply, is as follows: to every organized entity there corresponds a micro-regime of forces that endows it with its general shape and program. Every object is a composition of forces, and the *compositional event* is the work of expression of an abstract machine.[143]

DeLanda provides the developing embryo as a concrete example of this process: 'The DNA that governs the process does not contain, as was once believed, a blueprint for the generation of the final form of the organism, an idea that implies an inert matter to which genes give form from the outside.'[144] Rather, the genes are part of a process, DeLanda states, and function through a constraining mechanism. They arrange the matter into a form (hylemorphism). They do so virtually; in other words, a particular diagrammatic process works matter into an actual form instead of simply deploying an already specified form and awaiting its manifestation.

> The modern understanding of the process pictures genes as teasing form out of an active matter, that is, the function of genes and their products is now seen to be merely constraining and channeling a variety of material processes, occurring in that far-from-equilibrium, diagrammatic zone in which form emerges spontaneously.[145]

This process of function can be captured diagrammatically through three models of strata, explained as follows by DeLanda. The first is geological: (a) pebbles of different sizes are sorted, that is, filtered, by the current of the river; they are guided by the flow of the river and when they arrive at the bottom of the waterbed, the small pebbles fall together and as do bigger ones; (b) after the process of sedimentation, both small and big pebbles are cemented together where they fell: 'certain substances dissolved in water ... penetrate the sediment through the gaps between pebbles.'[146] The second is evolutionary: (a) the sorting process in genes occurs over time according to selection, survival, climate, geography and parasites; (b) this process is cemented when a gene pool is closed off: a species emerges that cannot reproduce with others. And the third model is social: (a) members of a society are sorted according to different mechanisms that hierarchize the social spheres; (b) these relations are cemented by a codification of the network.[147] Each of these different spheres of reality – geological, evolutionary and social – is analogous, but the process at work is the same: ontologically different from reality but still real in its function. The three elements are allagmatically put in relation with one another, they actually *are*, and are not just representations of each other.

I will now survey the three models in another direction. DeLanda's scheme includes three models of the meshwork network: The first is geological: volcanic eruptions give rise to 'a complex of heterogeneous crystals which *interlock* with one another' in igneous rocks through the process of the magma cooling down instead of the double process of sorting and cementing. The second model is evolutionary: the meshwork network in this case is the example of the ecosystem; food and energy are complementary to prey–predator and parasite–host relations which, in turn, depend on vegetation, digestion and microorganisms at work. The third model is social: money and the market place are a way of immediately relating individuals and collapsing time and distance, which the sorting mechanism of codification put in place through hierarchizing and cementing.

These two organizational models, of sedimentary and meshwork, are complementary, but their function is what brings them to a single actual level that springs from a single actual level of virtuality. The process is the diagram that constrains multiplicities, sorting and cementing while at the same time putting them all in a far-from-equilibrium state of meshwork networks.

What is interesting in the whole idea of diagrammatic process can be witnessed at the level of the example that DeLanda provides to define the process. In order to explain what a stratum is, DeLanda has to explain how a stratum functions. A stratum is, by definition, how it functions. This definition of the strata (rocks, water, etc.) is exactly how a Deleuzoguattarian stratum (tree-model) functions. The concept of the strata and an actual, physical stratum do have something in common. But their commonality is not the representation of one term (the physical strata) by the other (the conceptual strata). Rather, it is the function that makes them, not just similar, but actually the same. They are the same, their being based on the grounds that reality (what is actual) is constructed by the abstract machine, that is, it is based on functions. The analogy between the real object and its philosophical concept slides seamlessly. Behind the fabric of reality, behind the actual, is a multiplicity of processes from which spontaneous forms emerge like volcanic islands on the tumultuous sea.

Conclusion

The three notions discussed in this chapter connect with the notion of the diagram on various levels. An assemblage is a multiplicity made up of heterogeneous elements. It brings these elements together and fosters relations between them. A diagram, within an assemblage, abstracts to the level of pure function of different systems and creates the possibility of a passage of the abstract traits between systems. The assemblage is an integral part of the mechanism of the diagram. The abstraction into function of specificities is made by constraint. This is why this notion is important in the larger process of connectivity within an assemblage. And, if we are to start thinking about connectivity and abstraction, the analogy is a good place to start. Except that in order to move from one system to the next, to create sympathy between elements that not only differ in form but also in their level of concreteness, the allagmatic is a necessary concept to use in order to facilitate this passage. All of these terms – assemblage, constraint and allagmatic – are linked by their organizing function. Each of these terms organizes differently. The assemblage brings together multiplicities. The constraint abstracts and makes repetition of traits possible. The allagmatic creates a concrete link between heterogeneous terms. And all three terms are linked to the method behind Deleuze's philosophy. The assemblage is the minimal unit of Deleuze's expansive and encyclopedic corpus. Constraint, as Badiou has shown, serves as the mechanism which articulates the baseline of Deleuze's philosophy. And the allagmatic allows the passage between connected images – it traces the line between a concrete object and its conceptual image (the concept of the rhizome and the rhizome of an orchid). The connective and relational function of these three terms are an integral part of the diagrammatic process and they are at the basis of the exploration of the many facets of the concept of the diagram.

Chapter 2

Black Line, White Surface

In our progress towards the revelation of the diagram, we now pause on the subject of illustrations. The illustration is the object in which the concept of constraint is located and from which structure emerges. The concept of structure is then first brought up in this section as a way of classifying knowledge. The dyad of text and image gives rise to an entire dimension. Taking a cue from Deleuze's explanation that the informal diagram is swallowed up in the gap between the visible and the articulable, I interpret visible and articulable into the textual and the visual – or the text and image.[1] I believe that the text and image dyad, rather than that of the visible and articulable, is more materially and hermeneutically accessible and helps us see a representational manifestation of the diagram. From these two elements, the textual and visual dimension that emerges is that of the diagram.

The Graphics of Classifying

The feature shared by the text and image is the black line on a white surface. We can see how the simple, sober line is instrumental to classifying knowledge according to Michel Foucault: it filters out excessive elements from reality and translates the essential elements to the flat surface of the page. In effect, Foucault theorizes the gap between the textual and the visual, a dimension taken up by Gilbert Simondon in his treatment of education, Roland Barthes in his interest in the visual language of the *Encyclopédie*'s plates, Manuel DeLanda in his description of constraint in botanical taxonomies, and Stephen Werner in his treatment of the aesthetics of visual information in the *Encyclopédie*. These writers reveal the depth of the line in their treatment of visual language that is revelatory to the underlying aesthetics of Deleuze's diagram.

Foucault in *The Order of Things* captures the mechanics of systems formation and describes the epistemological shift that occurs in eighteenth-century botany through a modification of the spacing between the visual and the textual. The terms 'visual' and 'textual' are not yet defined in any category. These terms designate the essence of something put down on paper, but also the semiotic dimension of any text that can be seen or read. These terms are aesthetic, ontological, and trace an epistemology. But they need to be open in their definition because they form a contraction in an assemblage. They uphold several dimensions together and point, from their respective dimensions, to a diagrammatic, unrepresentable dimension. And so, in the 'Classifying' section of *The Order of Things*, Foucault charts the reliance of systems on graphics. In a typically Foucauldian manner, an *adroit* concentration of terms spawns a formula that defines natural history as 'nothing else than the naming of the visible'.[2]

Classical botanists step into the modern era of natural history by ceasing to read things in nature as signs and nature itself as signifying something. They confine themselves to the observable surfaces of things and describe them as the things they really are. Based on his formulaic definition, Foucault proposes that the function of natural history is not to deal with flora and fauna, but solely to shorten the distance between language and things. It was not uncommon, prior to this shift, for taxonomies to double as cookbooks, in which were listed not only the physical attributes of an animal, but also sauces that would harmoniously complement the animal's meat if it were cooked and served as a meal. One only has to revert to the preface of the volume in which Foucault expresses his enchantment with Borges' fictional Chinese encyclopedia to understand the taxonomical chaos that existed before the implementation of the graphic element. And so, smells and tastes of plants are discarded because they are considered too variable and unreliable and are replaced with more rigid elements, such as surface visibilities and, to a certain extent, tactile observations (rough versus smooth).[3] Foucault succinctly summarizes:

> The area of visibility in which observation is able to assume its powers is thus only what is left after these exclusions: a visibility freed from all other sensory burdens and restricted, moreover, to black and white. This area, much more than the receptivity and attention at last being granted to things themselves, defines natural history's condition of possibility, and the appearance of its screened objects: lines, surfaces, forms, reliefs.[4]

The elements to underline here are the black and the white that colour the lines and surfaces, which, in turn, interact with forms and reliefs.

This argument is reiterated by Simondon in *Du mode d'existence des objects techniques* when he lauds the graphic quality of Daubenton's eighteenth-century didactic book on the husbandry of sheep. The visual aspect of the book – the graphs and illustrations – detaches itself from the rhetorical level of the text, which, Simondon concedes, is revolutionary enough to allow a lay person, instead of only a man of letters, to follow the instructions laid out. Daubenton is a comparative anatomist of the Enlightenment who, with Buffon, compiled *L'histoire naturelle*. On his own, though, he wrote a manual for the use of shepherds. Simondon mentions that the book's engravings are as clean and expressive as those of the *Encyclopédie* and are an essential element of Daubenton's book. According to Simondon, the book *Instruction pour les bergers et pour les propriétaires de troupeaux* brings to the established didactic genre 'a new life with the use of a clear graphic symbolism'.[5] He adds that its graphic quality makes the book accessible even to the illiterate. Simondon isolates the graphic element in the encyclopedia as the essential trait of the systematization of knowledge: 'It is from the schema', Simondon writes, 'that technical encyclopaedism gathers all its sense and power of diffusion, becoming truly universal'.[6] It is through the *planche*, or its illustration, that objects of knowledge participate in the visible world.

According to Simondon, encyclopedias must be understood in the context of an ontology of technical objects. In effect, they are learning tools. He develops an axiomatic theory of education, specifically looking at how children's capacities for learning differ from those of adults. Children must be taught, whereas adults can learn by themselves. The encyclopedia is a device facilitating auto-didacticism and, for society, it is an engine of change from immaturity to maturity.[7]

The graphic element that stands against the text in the work of Daubenton offers a possibility of auto-didacticism; the adult takes the task of education into his own hands. The graphic element is thus an opportunity for the dissemination of knowledge. Like Foucault, Simondon notes that the emotional variables that are part of language and rhetoric are schematically simplified as they are filtered into graphics, allowing for an objectivity of information. For Simondon, technology demands a mode of expression other than oral. The difference between the two modes of expression – oral and graphic – resides in the fact that the former uses known concepts and is able to convey emotions. Oral expression is not as successful as graphic in transmitting 'schemes of movements' or 'precise material structures'.[8] Therefore, 'the adequate symbolism for the technical operation is visual symbolism, rich in its game of forms and proportions.'[9]

This is a watershed moment for Simondon: the instant in history when 'the civilization of the word' retreats and the civilization of the image comes on the scene.[10] The latter is far more universal in nature than the former, which does not function through a signifying code. The civilization of the word is exclusive because the people who understand a particular written or spoken language are part of a group privy to a mediating code; on the other hand, '[A]ll that is needed to understand schematic expressions is to see'[11] – or, in the French, '[I]l suffit de percevoir pour comprendre l'expression schématique.'[12]

Roland Barthes is also enchanted by the *Encyclopédie* and its visual language, extolling them in the 1964 essay 'Les planches de l'"Encyclopédie". Barthes, as a contemporary of Foucault and Simondon, is the scholar who most developed and popularized the concept of structuralism. His reading of the encyclopedic illustrations offers an important point of comparison to Foucault's reading of structure, since Barthes deals solely with the graphic element of the encyclopedia. He treats this semiotically; he reads the images as a text, treating the visual as textual. This 'reading' of the image – which was so crucial in the 1960s with the advent of an image-based culture – offers yet another perspective through this particular coupling on the duality of the visual and the textual. Barthes' analysis of the *planches* of the encyclopedia relates very clearly to the spatial organization of text and image on the page, since he reads them as emblems or mottos. Barthes, like Simondon, sees an origin in the encyclopedia of contemporary media images. He explains how the encyclopedic diagram detaches the human object from the manifold of nature. In clear contradistinction to the word, the technical object represented in the illustrations of the *Encyclopédie* reiterates this process of clarity by illustrating the object in clear lines, in clear clean environments – an 'aesthetic of bareness'.[13]

He explains the classifying aspect of the encyclopedic image by focusing on the etching of Noah's Ark, in which each pair of animals is depicted as peering out of framing windows, thus compartmentalizing each animal species. Barthes conjectures that the possession of the world, which is part of the classificatory mandate of the *Encyclopédie* dictated by an 'inventorying effort', stems mythically not from Genesis, where Adam named the animals in the Garden of Eden while still basking in the grace of God, but from the Flood, when man was compelled to name each kind of animal and organize them into species.[14] This constraining circumstance of an immanent flood (a catastrophe, *effondement*) is an event that forces thought, and, in this case, thought in the form of classification. Reprising the problem of objectivity that Foucault wrote about, this 'will of the inventory . . . is never neutral' because it is not simply a will to inventory in order to record and take notice, but a will to possess.[15] And so each animal species is separated and lodged apart from its neighbouring species.[16]

Barthes isolates the 'human' quality of the encyclopedic image because the encyclopedic plate 'constitutes a structure of *information*'.[17] Whereas Simondon specifically distinguishes the information that comes out of the image from spoken language as being more democratic, and whereas Foucault sees these eighteenth-century diagrams as a new and separate step in the epistemology of language, Barthes seeks to make the diagrams human by approximating this 'somewhat iconographic' informational structure to 'real language'. Barthes fits the 'language' of the encyclopedic image into a structuralist linguistic model. This informational structure of the images reproduces two dimensions of the real language:

> [W]e know, in fact, that all discourse involves signifying units and that these units are ordered according to two axes, one of substitution (paradigmatic), the other of contiguity (or syntagmatic); each unit can thereby *vary* (potentially [*virtuellement* in the French original]) with its parents, and *link* (in reality) with its neighbors.[18]

The encyclopedic plate is divided into different parts: at the top, for example, the scene depicts the inside of a cork factory, while on the lower part of the plate, a close-up depicts only the hands working on the corks. Barthes' assessment is established by the division of the categories in language, as they are represented in the spatial organization of the encyclopedic diagrams. There, the upper and lower parts of the illustration play the role of linguistic articulations. Barthes, like Simondon, sees the language articulated by the diagrams as a 'complete, adult language'.[19]

For Barthes, interestingly enough, the encyclopedic diagram, in its cybernetic function, behaves like an autopoetic system – from the Greek *poesis*, to make, to produce, to construct, a self-producing system: 'Here we find prophetically formulated the very principle of cybernetic ensembles; the plate, image of the machine, is indeed in its way a brain; we introduce substance into it and set up the "program": the vignette (the syntagm) serves as a conclusion.'[20] Barthes, but also Diderot, describes this imagistic articulation as the process of drawing for the encyclopedia. For them, it is a way to 'perceive the elements without confusion' by following the routes of reason, whereby 'the image is a kind of rational synopsis: it illustrates not only the object or its trajectory but also the very mind which conceives it.'[21] The image not only represents an object but is a manifestation of the intellectual processes of the producer of the image vis-à-vis the representation of the object.

The superfluous is taken out of the equation and the botanist now observes a strict structure in order to formulate a system. The structure constrains the elements that are taken into consideration in the classifying process and therefore systematizes the observable world through negation: 'By limiting and filtering the visible', Foucault writes, 'structure enables it to be transcribed into language'.[22] This structuring operation is an inherently graphic operation.

In *The Order of Things*, classifying – the process of filtering observations through a structuring process and organizing them into a system – occurs in a space that is not merely a process of analogous translation (i.e. representation). Instead, this movement from the observed into the system occurs in a graphic space, a space that is opened between the visual and the textual. Foucault describes this process: 'The area of visibility in which observation is able to assume its powers is thus only what is left after these exclusions: a visibility freed from all other sensory burdens and restricted, moreover, to black and white.'[23] In fact, according to Foucault's assessment of eighteenth-century botany, this whole process hinges on black and white drawings, whose very restrained graphic elements mirror the black and white lines of written text, and thereby gain a similar level of weight and authority. Graphics thus includes both writing and drawing.

We have thus far seen three critical instances of black and white illustrations fashioning knowledge and its capture and dissemination. We can now give these illustrations another dimension and consider them not as a link to knowledge, but as an integral part of knowledge and thought. In other words, we can now add to the illustrations by giving them a supplementary dimension as diagrams. If the illustrations were closer to tracings, the diagram pushes them past mappings. The diagram is equal parts tracing and mapping. Tracing operates through constraint: it reproduces artificially what is 'out there', as we have seen, in the classical root-book style. Mapping, on the other hand, is a rhizomatic process, moving freely and unrestrained into 'unexplored countries', making relations based on the positive principle of seriation. Therefore, mapping itself operates through the element that Simondon isolates in the encyclopedia, namely, relationality between differing objects; but instead of being *re*productive, it is simply productive.

DeLanda, in *Intensive Science and Virtual Philosophy*, describes the notion of constraint on another plane of operation, one relating to the construction of Deleuze's philosophy and his negating process of filtering out certain elements to construct a positive system:

> Besides the avoidance of essentialist thinking, Deleuze's speculation about virtuality is guided by the closely related constraint of avoiding *typological* thinking, that style of thought in which individuation is achieved through the *creation of classifications and of formal criteria for membership in those classifications.*[24]

In the same way, two opposing principles can function simultaneously on the same plane. And so, even though according to DeLanda, Deleuze avoids typological thinking, typological thinking is in fact based on constraint. Deleuze, then, constrains typology out of his philosophy. By doing this, he adheres to the function that typology contains; by constraining it out of his system, he adheres to it on the functional level without relying on the term, the typology, that contains it.

And so, at the same time, DeLanda finds the 'classical' process of constraint in the very composition process of Deleuze's system; he asserts that the principles at play in the way Deleuze figures his system are those directly inspired by eighteenth-century botanical taxonomies. It is not a simple point of comparison but is actually a process common to instances of negating, constraining and filtering out:

> For the purpose of discussing the constraint: guiding Deleuze's constructive project, one historical example of typological thinking is particularly useful. This is the classificatory practices which were common in Europe in the 17th and the 18th centuries, such as those that led to the botanical taxonomies of Linnaeus.[25]

DeLanda later explains how these taxonomies functioned through the observation of resemblances, the recording of identities, the configuration of analogies in order to judge them, and finally the establishment of hierarchies through oppositions. He tells us that these taxonomies were 'fixed and continuous, regardless of the fact that historical accidents may have broken that continuity'.[26] After all, this is the only element that Deleuze filters out of his use of constraining classificatory principles. Time does not figure into eighteenth-century classifications, according to DeLanda.

Anne Sauvagnargues agrees with this last point. Yet, she directly opposes the initial statement presented by DeLanda; namely that Deleuze dispenses with typological thinking. In 'Deleuze. De l'animal à l'art', Sauvagnargues writes, 'Deleuze explores the epistemology of human sciences and privileges the pre-Darwinian variations of Geoffroy Saint-Hilaire: less evolutionist and historical than geographical and typological.'[27] Sauvagnargues suggests that by concentrating instead on space, we will be able to establish a virtuality that reveals classification and systematization through the visual device of the sketch. When the focus shifts to the organization of the organism, as opposed to its classification, time will figure into it again, especially when contrasting Cuvier's animal classification to Geoffroy Saint-Hilaire's method based on abstracting and folding.

As a permutation of illustration on the road to defining the diagram, we have to describe the blueprint as a concept. The essence of an architectural blueprint is abstracted to reveal its function. Using the plates of the *Encyclopédie* as an architectural blueprint, we have to wonder what we could build if we were to follow the lines of the plates as though they were instructions for constructing the object depicted. What if the representation on the plates is not of an object, such as a harpsichord, but an activity, such as farming? What if we follow the lines depicting an activity or a concept as if they were meant to be followed in the building of a house? The gap between the actual and the virtual is underscored by these questions, as is the notion of materiality. What is the materiality of an activity or an idea if it had to follow a plan in order to make it real? That is the *concept* of the blueprint we are dealing with here.

Stephen Werner writes on the elegant aesthetics of the clean black and white lines that constitute the plates in the *Encyclopédie*. In his book, *Blueprint: A Study of Diderot and the Encyclopédie Plates*,[28] the concept of the title is given a three-dimensionality that resembles the operational parameters of Deleuze's diagram. The simple smartness of the lines in eighteenth-century prints may not have an obvious Deleuzean resonance, but it is this simplicity and this sobriety of style that is so precisely Deleuzean: '[W]hat is needed . . . to . . . harness the Cosmos is a pure and simple line accompanied by the idea of an object, and nothing more.'[29] Clean lines in botanical diagrams are what make Foucault think of the possibility of a structural change between empirical and representational dimensions. Sobriety is needed to isolate a function in order to categorically move an object from dimension to dimension. As Deleuze and Guattari write: 'Sobriety, sobriety: that is the common prerequisite for the deterritorialization of matters, the molecularization of material, and the cosmicization of forces.'[30] It is the sobriety of the line of the plates that makes them so versatile for Werner. He starts to shift the concept of the blueprint from the simple blueprints he finds in the *Encyclopédie* by discussing architecture and buildings. This concept expands into the terrain of other plates that, because of their clean, simple lines, are meant to be read as objectively as plans for a house – even though they depict human activities, such as cork-making, or the instruments of an art, such as music or medicine. The plates as a whole begin to be read as a blueprint that catalogues the building of a modern society through the machines, manufacturing trades, and leisurely bourgeois depicted in some scenes.

As Werner writes:

> The portrait of a France casting off its roots in agriculture, small family enterprise, or manufacturing processes centered on wood and beginning to enter the preindustrial age of turbines, cotton factories, steel mills, and spinning looms is clearly one image stamped on the plates in this blueprint manner.[31]

The blueprint, as far removed from its original designation as the model of a house, is employed because it designates clarity and function; it is a drawing whose purpose is to depict an object in such a particular way that the person who follows the line of drawing will be able to build it. Deleuze and Guattari offer the formula: 'The sobriety of the assemblages is what makes for the richness of the Machine's effects.'[32] Werner explains it thusly:

> But the technical plates of the *Encyclopédie* also reveal another side of blueprints. It takes them out of the orbit of the mimetic, or the copying of a known and easily described subject, into modes of representation of a far more problematical and uncertain nature. However finely drawn a blueprint, or perfect its detail, an engraving of this kind can never provide a complete portrait of its subject. This state can only be achieved when a blueprint has been put into use, and a building or machine constructed. Until such a time, its final or definitive shape exists only in outline.[33]

Werner turns the blueprint into a concept that can be applied to different types of plates by taking heed of Barthes' advice to look behind nature and to look at things from varying angles, especially from a change in scale: so that a flea, the example Barthes takes from the plates of the *Encyclopédie*, is blown up by the microscopic lens of the page, turning an insect into a mythic monster. What turns a blueprint into the concept of the blueprint is the function that is abstracted from the original object and then applied to a different one within the limited scope of the isolated elements constituting the concept. This function makes the blueprint versatile. This blueprint concept is able to peer behind nature and behind the lines of a print; it is so versatile that it can take the virtual as its material:

> This 'virtual' side of the blueprint is very much present in the technical plates of the *Encyclopédie*. They endow the *Encyclopédie* with a style of representation that sets it even further apart from the mass of eighteenth-century reference books and compendia. The style is one of process: the gradual emergence and freeing of images embossed on the plates in the manner of a photographic negative requiring a laboratory or darkroom to bring them to light.[34]

If we can use the eighteenth-century drawings of plants to discuss text and image dualities within the context of structuration through constraint, then how would a rhizome be depicted in black and white? In the discussion above comparing rhizome to tree, the vegetal examples were used to examine the possible ways of linking together elements of knowledge through assemblages. In this context of black-on-white illustrations, we find Deleuze and Guattari describing the assemblage as 'a complex of lines'.[35]

The line, for Deleuze and Guattari, is a conceptual kernel. It draws the limit of a philosophy, moving away from representation in the same way that figurative art progresses into abstraction:

> We can identify a first state of the line, or a first kind of line: the line is subordinated to the point; the diagonal is subordinated to the horizontal and vertical; the line forms a contour, whether **figurative or not**; the space it constitutes is one of striation; the countable multiplicity it constitutes remains subordinated to the One in an always superior or supplementary dimension. Lines of this type are molar, and form a segmentary, circular, binary, arborescent system.[36]

The line is at the basis of the diagram. Through their conceptual virtuosity, Deleuze and Guattari can summarize the models of the tree and the rhizome through lines and their dynamism. The line that is subordinated to the point is the line that represents the classical tree, the arborescent system. There is a second type of line that is akin to the rhizome model:

> The second kind is very different, molecular and of the 'rhizome' type. The diagonal frees itself, breaks or twists. The line no longer forms a contour, and instead passes *between* things, *between* points. It belongs to

a smooth space. It draws a plane that has no more dimensions than that which crosses it; therefore the multiplicity it constitutes is no longer subordinated to the one, but takes on a consistency of its own. These are multiplicities of masses or packs, not of classes; anomalous and nomadic multiplicities, not normal or legal ones; multiplicities of becoming, or transformational multiplicities, not countable elements and ordered relations; fuzzy, not exact aggregates, etc.[37]

It is no small feat to have summarized a philosophical system and a process of organizing thought through two types of lines. Two lines are all that is needed to compose a system. The lines that make up a diagram – if by diagram we mean an illustration like the plates in the *Encyclopédie* – simultaneously constitute another diagram, this one a diagram-concept. This latter diagram transcends the ink on the page and the semiotic configuration of the figures. It carries a depth in its dark streak. It is another dimension. This line carries traits that can compose the possibility of thought.

The Decoy in the System

What is this depth that emerges from the zone between the visual and the textual? Jean-François Lyotard explains its ontological nature in *Discours, figure*. First, he questions the notion of system, and more precisely, the system of language. Then he focuses on the visual and textual analysis and the depth that emerges between these two elements. And finally, he shows us that the essential element of the duality is the line. With his treatment of the line, Lyotard reveals the basic element of the zone between visual and textual.

Lyotard opens the rift between the visual and the textual and frames it not in terms of a scientific objectivity but rather in terms of an ontological concern for truth. The notion moves the duality of the visual and the textual onto a space: the possibility of a spatial dimension carries its own ontological depth. It forms the groundwork for thinking about the diagram as a method of thought and organizing a system.

The site located between the visual and the textual seems to have as its point of origin a botanical aspect, as Foucault's discussion of this duality demonstrates. Botanical and encyclopedic illustration can be used as a springboard into this rift. Lyotard gives us an opportunity to take this rift, change the negative space into a positive fullness, and treat the rift as a thread, though with a marked variation: he takes up vegetation critically and figuratively in *Discours, figure*,[38] in which he calls the sylvan world the 'absolute frame of reference of all analogies'.[39] The vegetational thread takes a turn in this section and leads us to a different register. If Foucault's and Simondon's vegetal examples come from an order of botany as a descriptive science, Lyotard's example comes from Paul Claudel and is more in the order of horticulture. The softer side of vegetation is fitting here since we will be penetrating the notion of the reality of the figure as well as its depth.

In the beginning of *Discours, figure*, Lyotard criticizes the notion of reading the real: 'Ce livre-ci proteste . . .'[40] He condemns Claudel's synesthetic notion of a listening eye, a metaphor that suggests that what is visible is readable, audible and intelligible. Lyotard sees in this logic something regressive since it revives the medieval notion of the book of life, where nature is a text to be deciphered, read and interpreted. By reading nature as a text, its fullness and depth is denied. The signifier constantly dissolves the operating thickness of the real. The given (*le donné*) cannot be taken as a text because it has a depth that is constituted by a difference.[41] Lyotard shows that Claudel is a proponent of nature as a text. Claudel describes a scene where, in the frame of his vision, the foliage of maples is harmonized with pine trees. He then proposes to comment on this 'forested text'.[42] Lyotard wonders if that which speaks only when the eye has found it can really be a text. Since one cannot really walk into a text and move around in it or in front of it as in a forest, a text can be entered like a forest only in metaphor. On the other hand, the sylvan world is arranged spatially as a painting.

Discours, figure has the virtue of dealing precisely with the aesthetics of systems, be they philosophical, scientific, or, more commonly, linguistic. The latter includes all other systems, as dictated by the structuralist zeitgeist of the time. The object of Lyotard's hunt in *Discours, figure* is the *real* in the system. To be more precise, in a self-referential manner Lyotard focuses on the action of seeking the real *of* the system rather than the real *in* the system. The system becomes an ideological trap that, by capturing the real, blurs it. His focus then shifts to aesthetics. By infiltrating the system with an aesthetics and making it integral to the functioning of the system, the very concept of aesthetics becomes blurry.[43] And so Lyotard grounds himself on a slippery concept of aesthetics that allows for an assessment of the truth content of systems, which he performs at the textual level of the book. Lyotard does not propose to read figures in terms of discourse, despite what the title of the book would have us believe. Rather, just as discourse and figure are separated by a comma in the title, they remain separated, complementary but unbridgeable. In a similar manner as Deleuze's disjunctive synthesis, the comma functions as the 'and' in a stutter. Lyotard does not adhere to the semiotic programme of trying to 'read' figures. He does not read images discursively, but shows how they come into being empirically and how they can be produced through the very ideology that forms and regulates systems.

And so, just as the title of *Discours, figure* announces, the method with which Lyotard proceeds through his treatise is an oscillation between two terms. A third term arises between them like froth, or rather like a blur – an anamorphosis. The third term is the object that cannot be directly seen – in the same way that we cannot directly look at the Pleiades – and it cannot be erased; it remains stellar detritus, like the light of a supernova still seen in the earth's sky even though the star is long extinguished.

From the outset, *Discours, figure* announces that a philosopher must also be a painter, and Lyotard implants a duality that could stand in as the motto for this chapter. The figure of the painter/philosopher emerges from another duality: that of the visual and the textual. Sometimes these dualities dialectically merge briefly, but like oil and water, they remain separated. That is because the space between the line and the letter is an insurmountable zone, needing the light of both to give it form and, because both are needed, making it obvious that neither is enough. We can shake these elements vigorously, step away, and perhaps for a few moments be fooled into believing that they will actually hold together, before they dissolve again and open up the unbridgeable fissure.

Lyotard's unrepresentable fissure between the line and the letter should be compared to the space of structure between the real and the representation in Foucault. Lyotard introduces an element of contrariety into the objective scientific construction presented by Foucault. He scrutinizes the presence of truth and illusion in already formed systems through the visual/textual duality. He reintroduces a sensory element into the system that the botanists in Foucault's example were filtering out.[44] And so, pursuing the vegetational thread, Lyotard announces his own project of reflection on the system:

> It is not that we could ever apprehend the real itself, as we pick a flower after having cleared it from the surrounding herbs. The decoy and the real come together not as contraries in a system, but at least as a *thickness* that has its recto and its verso together.[45]

Black Line, White Surface

A further sketch of Lyotard's view of the mechanics of a system must inevitably follow the visual traits that he uses in this account.

The real is indeed not something to be plucked like a flower; it is an aberration that emerges in the space between signification and knowledge. It emerges through clashing, as a distortion. The term that Lyotard uses in French is *détonner*, which can mean both something that sounds out of tune, a distortion, or something that clashes visually as colours might. By clashing, the real makes itself felt on the surface of discourse. The translation from French to English carries further difficulties, embedded within the term *vrai*, which can be translated as *truth* or *real*. The former has an ontological dimension and the latter a materialist dimension. I chose to use the latter since it is more compatible with Deleuze's theories. But the real only makes itself felt by its effects and these effects are not always truth itself but sometimes illusions. The recto and the verso of the depth emerge on the surface of the system.

The real emerges as a depth[46] on the surface of the system in the way that shading is added to a line drawing. It makes the object drawn seem three-dimensional, real, floating above the surface of the page. Of course, it is still just an amalgam of strategically placed lines. But these are positioned as calculated decoys: an amalgam of lines that are not sticking out of the page at all – they remain on the surface of the page – but appear three-dimensional. They are illusions,[47] aberrations; but by coming off the page, they also clash with the flatness, the order of discourse, and therefore offer a possibility of capturing the real.[48]

Finally, Lyotard proposes a programme to deal with the recto and the verso of systems in drawings. He writes:

> What we have to do is not to discern the real from the false: both of them are defined in terms of the internal consistency of a system or the operational process of an object of reference. Instead, what we have to do is learn to discern between two expressions: one that is there to outplay the gaze (in order to capture) and another that is there to surpass it, to give the invisible to see.[49]

Both sides of the real undergo a three-part operation that (a) starts with the dream-work, described by Freud in the chapter of the same name in *The Interpretation of Dreams*; (b) is reversed by the diagrammatic 'floating attention' of the artist's work; and (c) finally turns the product of the dream-work into an oeuvre.

These visual terrains are best approached through the drawing and theories of the line of French Cubist painter and art theorist André Lhote and Swiss Expressionist and Bauhaus art teacher Paul Klee. In the span that separates these two artists, the concept of the line is stretched out and, consequently, distorted. Lyotard divides this concept along the boundaries of their opposite views. Lhote is a proponent of the primacy of drawing and its ideal function of signification; Klee, on the other hand, despite his materialistic theories of art, is open to an oneiric dimension of art.

In *Anti-Oedipus*, Deleuze and Guattari treat Lyotard's *Discours, figure* as a very important book, considering it 'the first generalized critique of the signifier'.[50] They explain Lyotard's main concepts in this book – the figurative and the figural – in relation to the notion of the signifier. Lhote's function in the text is obvious from this point of view, since he is the proponent of the signifier. Deleuze and Guattari infuse their explanation with directionality when they state that the signifier is surpassed in two different directions: (a) towards the exterior by figurative images, and (b) towards the interior by the pure figures that compose these images. The latter are what make up the concept of the figural that comes between the interstices: between the signifier and the signified. If Lhote believes in the primacy of the line, unsullied by the chiaroscuro effect that gives the image an illusion of false depth, the figural smudges the certainty he adheres to, clearing a path between the signifier and the signified. But it is the signifier, in its semiotic span, that gathers the textual and the visual together, only to have the figural to distort them. In the plastic arts, the figural is made of two dimensions that are based on lines: (a) 'active line and the multidimensional point', and (b) 'multiple configurations formed by the passive line and the surface it engenders'.[51]

These two sides of the figural open up an interworld within the flat surface of the painting, as Deleuze and Guattari have Klee say. The interworld,[52] this dimension that emerges at each stage of a duality, is what Deleuze and Guattari name the flux-schiz and the break-flow.[53] Deleuze and Guattari find in this space of the purely figural an emerging 'matrice-figure'. This is a diagram composed of desire that can regiment a creative and positive process: it becomes the nimble function that unfurls the scrambled and distorted limits of a codified system into a joyful multiplicity.

According to Deleuze and Guattari, Lyotard fails to develop this process to its full potential. Rather, he constantly falls back on structure and familiar territories where terms are simply transgressed: they are never fully abstracted into an allagmatic function because he reintroduces lack and absence, the negative, into desire. Deleuze and Guattari sternly warn against bringing back the signifier in the matrice-figure, the diagram, and making the negative obey – in this case, the negative as the tracing process instead of the productive mapping function. The negative that Lyotard pulls out of the figural must be made productive instead of positive (positive would only make it rely on a negative for its identity as positive). Deleuze, in *Difference and Repetition*, does away with the negative: 'The negative is an illusion because the form of negation appears with propositions which express the problem on which they depend only by distorting it and obscuring its real structure.'[54] The problem of the negative works within the zones of determined levels and within the structures through which the figural weaves; it is an illusion, a false depth. The distortion that happens here is already organized; it is not the productive distortion as paradox that exposes the site between the textual and the visual. Deleuze continues, tainting the passage with a shadow that testifies to the importance of the chiaroscuro as a philosophical device: 'Once the problem is translated into hypotheses, each hypothetical affirmation is doubled by a negation which amounts to the state of a problem betrayed by its shadow.'[55] But the shading is wiped out from the real, here read as nature: 'There is no Idea of the negative any more than there are hypotheses in nature, even though nature does proceed by means of problems. That is why it matters little whether the negative is understood as logical limitation or real opposition.'[56] The obscured zones of the chiaroscuro, like the depth in the darkness of the line, have to be made productive, like the silence of the vacuole that makes expression possible.

The Double Snare

Like Lyotard, Foucault was also interested in Klee's artistic work. Hence, his treatment of Klee in *Ceci n'est pas une pipe*, a monograph primarily dedicated to René Magritte. First, by following Foucault's analysis of Magritte's works, we see exactly how the philosopher complicates the zone between the visual and the textual in an aesthetic context. Second, by revealing the 'floating space' in Klee's work, Foucault is able to give us a glimpse of an aesthetic view of the diagrammatic space. Thirdly, Foucault shows us how it all comes back to the element of the line. And, finally, the line, specifically Klee's manipulation of the line, reveals an important device in Deleuze's theories, clearing the terrain for the concept of the faciality and then the diagram.

In Foucault's *The Order of Things*, Linnaeus, the eighteenth-century botanist considered to be the 'father of taxonomy', takes residence in the space between the visual and textual and gives the duality a new depth.[57] As Foucault writes:

> [Structure] permits the visibility of the animal or plant to pass over in its entirety into the discourse that receives it. And ultimately, perhaps, it may manage to reconstitute itself in visible form by means of words, as with the botanical calligrams dreamed of by Linnaeus.[58]

Linnaeus' dreams contaminated Foucault's thoughts and were finally manifested, according to the philosopher, in Magritte's drawing titled *Ceci n'est pas une pipe*. One version is a drawing from 1926 and the other a drawing published in Alain Jouffroy's *L'Aube à l'antipode* in 1966. The first version is that of the famous pipe filling the frame with the text below indicating that it is not a pipe. Both float above an undefined background – or are drawn on the surface. In the second version, an easel stands on the floor holding a frame with the pipe and the writing below it. Floating above the easel within the frame is another pipe, larger and drawn in hachure. These are not to be confused with Magritte's *Treachery of the Image* (1929), an oil painting. Foucault concentrates on drawings and not paintings because the former have more elements with written text: paper, black-on-white lines or letters. Foucault analysed the Belgian painter's drawing in a short book bearing the same title as the artwork. Foucault's text is crucial because it engages the problem of the gap between text and image directly – and clearly does so in the terrain of art. According to Foucault, Magritte's drawing is 'as simple as a page borrowed from a botanical manual: a figure and the text that names it.'[59] But the simplicity of the drawing is complicated from the start when botany, text and figure delimit the constellation.

The coexistence of textual and visual elements on the same plane sets up a decoy mechanism. The mechanism that regroups these elements is a calligram, such as a poem whose letters are arranged to visually illustrate the subject matter it treats in writing. Foucault writes:

> Pursuing its quarry by two paths, the calligram sets the most perfect trap. By its double function, it guarantees capture, as neither discourse alone, nor a pure drawing could do. It banishes the invincible absence that defeats words, imposing upon them, by the ruses of a writing at play in space, the invisible form of their referent.[60]

In the case of Magritte's *Ceci n'est pas une pipe*, the calligram is at play in the dimensions of (a) a drawing whose subject matter is writing (as the pipe that is drawn is in fact not an actual pipe) and (b) writing that is a drawing (as the legend beneath the drawing is itself a *trompe-l'oeil* since the message is not really written but painted).

The calligram of *Ceci n'est pas une pipe* is dual: the pipe is and is not a pipe and the writing below is and is not really writing. Foucault describes the first part of this double trap, this writing at the bottom of the drawing that serves as a caption or a legend. It is not written, we have to keep in mind; it is drawn so as to *represent* writing. It is, as Foucault says, 'handwritten in a steady, painstaking, artificial script, a script from the convent, like that found heading the notebook of schoolboys or on a blackboard after an object lesson'.[61] Its shape is the shape of writing. The discursive part of this shape refers to the shape of writing, stating that the very shape that signifies discourse is not a pipe.

The second part of the calligram is the drawing of a pipe. Foucault imagines the lines that constitute the shape of the pipe to be composed of microscopic words or letters so small that we can only perceive them as lines: 'We might imagine it brimming with small chaotic letters, graphic signs reduced to fragments and dispersed over the entire surface of the image. A figure in the shape of writing.'[62] Magritte's calligrams capture the interplay between illusion and truth, the duality that Lyotard treats in his work, and become a diagram of Lyotard's model of the depth in the system; 'A double trap, unavoidable snare: How henceforth would escape the flight of birds, the transitory form of flowers, the falling rain?' asks Foucault, obviously seduced.[63] Easy, says Lyotard: both the visual and the textual are pointing to one another, reflecting on each other since they cannot be trapped in a structure, described as a phenomenon, or dialectically subsumed in a system. This reflection of the textual on the visual and vice versa needs language, without which it will be mute vision. Conversely, it must be pushed to a distance by vision, without which language would be just a thing unable to express itself. For Lyotard, it is not (as it is for Foucault) a question of knowledge, but a reflection on knowledge – and hence his discussion of truth and illusion. Through his treatment of Magritte, Foucault is representing a paradox, or, more precisely, a visual paradox.

Further explorations of different elements in painting are found in Foucault's assessment of the surface of Klee's paintings. In Lyotard, this space is established more deeply than in Foucault, since Lyotard looks between the structure and the system rather than between the observed object and its organization into language. We feel, after Lyotard's treatment of depth, that we have fallen into the use of the depth metaphor.

Bergson's plunge into the depth of philosophy comes to mind, but in this case, it is the surface of painting that is penetrated. This depth can be imagined, if we stick to Lyotard's forest imagery, as penetrating the landscape and finding oneself surrounded by trees. Again, in the context of writing, we are exposing another metaphor. If modernist art focuses on the surface elements of painting – such as colour, frame and flatness – this is translated in writing into a stark avoidance of plunging into the depths of metaphors. Yet, it is precisely these metaphors that reveal the artificiality and materiality of language and, in this case, language in a written form. These metaphors are used here not without self-reflexivity, but they are necessary and instrumental precisely in the revelation of the diagrammatic dimension: the material, real, virtual.

So what does the surface of Klee's paintings reveal? What occurs on the space of the canvas? In his treatment of Klee, Foucault describes the artist's paintings in terms of a 'floating space',[64] indicating that the dimension involved is not flat; rather a surrounding, light space is conjured. This space is composed of a simultaneity of 'page and canvas, plane and volume, map and chronicle. Boats, houses, persons are at the same time recognizable figures and elements of writing.'[65] In this passage enumerating the elements of Klee's paintings, Foucault himself made a diagram of the artist's paintings by putting on one plane certain characteristic elements that recur in his work. The page and the canvas are a hybrid here, just to start. The page and the canvas, when they are assembled in this way, reveal how Foucault summarizes both drawings and paintings without separating them into different classes of objects. He is attempting to get to something else altogether, something beyond the paint, page and canvas. The diagrammatic space of the virtual that Foucault isolates is in turn described by Christine Buci-Glucksman: '[T]he displacement of vision introduces the diagram of the idea, a non visual, mental cartography composed of the conjunction and disjunction of fluid or suspended space.'[66] Buci-Glucksman thus takes us back to the notion of cartography, which ties in into Foucault's map. The paratextual elements and diachronic symbols of Klee's paintings turn them into actual maps of a virtual dimension. The characteristic floating space of the diagram applies to Foucault's attempt to describe the infrastructural or topographical elements animating the space of Klee's work, and might offer a fragile solution to the problem of the space between the visual and the textual. By characterizing his space as fluid or floating, Foucault and Buci-Glucksman make Klee into a diagrammatist and give his pictorial space a materiality – if only a fluid, floating one.

Klee's signature arrow is the graphic trait that indicates the direction the viewer's eye is to follow, as in *Southern Gardens* of 1936, where a red arrow pointing downwards resembles a red tree the painter meshed within the landscape. The painting *Unstable Equilibrium* of 1922, whose title recalls DeLanda's treatment of the question of Deleuze's diagram through the thermodynamic notion of far-from-equilibrium, depicts vertically stacked squares. The lines of these are crossed by black arrows pointing left and right, towards the edge of the picture frame. Two larger red arrows, mingling with the square shapes, each point upward and downward. *Wandbild aus dem Tempel du Sehnsucht Dorthin*, 1922, portrays the simply rendered tall buildings of a city; the black surfaces of their rooftops launch beyond the edge of the roof and end in arrows that point in the direction relative to the angle of the tilt of each building. These arrows all point to another dimension, but they also indicate a dynamism. Deleuze describes this dynamism as the teeming matter of the Baroque. It is a dimension that renders marble and stone fluid and floating, like a curling wave or a horse's mane. And the closer one gets to the material, the more apparent it becomes that, on an infinitesimal level, the matter is dynamic and fluid. In order to indicate direction into that matter, Deleuze relies on Klee's schemas. Deleuze, in *The Fold: Leibniz and the Baroque*, uses Klee's pedagogical drawings of dynamic lines to illustrate his concept of the fold.

Deleuze refers to three figures at the beginning of the chapter titled 'The Folds in the Soul'.[67] The first is a figure that traces the inflexion: an elongated *s*, inverted and on its side. If the two points at either end of the *s*-line were to continue in the same pattern and touch, they would form the mathematical symbol for infinity; however, they do not. The second figure is the same inverted, sideways *s*, but with a thinner line dancing in and around the thicker line, forming zigzags, loops and curves. This figure is supposed to demonstrate the fact that there can be no exact figure or figure that is not mixed. In the third figure, straight lines jut out from the *s*-shaped line, giving it depth, a third dimension. The striations or rays can be read as elongations of the thickness of the line or a third dimension schematically added. But even if Klee's curved lines are folded, they remain black and white, static on the page; Deleuze's fold cannot be represented statically. It is dynamic and multidimensional. Rather, Deleuze relies on the energy of Klee's lines, like the black arrow of light, to point to a materiality that is imperceptible yet present, virtual but real.

The figure of the active line serves as a diagram in the book, pointing in the direction one is to follow in order to dive into the static yet fluid matter of the fold. The line indicates a folding and gives the illusion of travelling into space, yet it is also a flat graphic design on the surface of the page. It would be like tracing a square on a page to represent a cube and subsequently elongating the square through a series of lines and saying that, just as the square represented a cube, the subsequent cube represents a fourth dimension. Klee's dynamic lines are coordinates that locate the fold. The line is a multidimensional indicator of space: in its entire sobriety, the line is the flexible element capturing the visual and textual. Here, it is capturing the rhizome – the rhizome as diagrammed by the line.

Coming back to the rhizomatic model, Mireille Buydens sees the rhizome as a horizontal stem, or rather a line that runs across a surface, instead of the root of a tree that plunges into depths. She writes:

> The *line* (linear model) is a privileged figure in Deleuze's thought, from theoretical foundations to aesthetic positions. Supple, malleable, open to all torsions of will and of chance, it is opposed to the punctal model or the form proceeding through organic imbrications and superpositions of constituted and closed entities (the point, or the form as a system of relayed points).[68]

Buydens extrapolates from Deleuze's writings that the line is anterior to the drawing it ties together. To capture the line in the contour that it traces, she writes, is to crystallize it in its contrary. The same could be said for the rhizome: What better element than the line to illustrate it? According to Buydens, the form is a dead line.[69] Even though her reading is contextualized within a discussion of the contingent in Deleuze, if you look at it diagrammatically, the line as she explains it is an Ariadne's thread that can lead us to the virtual as long as it is not actualized.

As we have seen in *Discours, figure*, the line for Lhote is a semiotic device, working as an arbitrary sign at the level of the page, signifying something other than itself, the signified. In this way, it does not try to sculpt a false illusion of depth or a third dimension through perspective; the line remains pure. For Klee, on the other hand, the line traced on the page is flat; Klee avoids perspectives that are illusory, sculptural. His line carries a space in its depth, a force he is able to control after he has explored the depth of his psyche. Therefore, he does not rearrange the lines to represent space on the page, but rather, he represents the forces present on the surface of the page: the arrow seems to float because it is a flat object painted on a figurative depiction of a play of perspectives. The intersecting lines make different points of perspective apparent, which creates a tension. A jarring confusion arises when the viewer tries to decipher the rebus, which consists of a letter without any obvious reference surrounded by a landscape. Through the intersection of the line and the letter, the sign that underlines the flatness of the picture plane rises to a dimension which, in turn, releases its own depth. This is the material depth that allows Deleuze to navigate between the virtual and the actual.

Deleuze paraphrases Klee's diaries, stating that the atom of the fold is the inflection. Therefore, by grounding himself on the material level of the line – the positive, the scientific and the systematic – he can launch himself into a depth in the real: that is, the virtual. Yet the inflection already has a non-determined quality that defies any sort of grounding. It exists as part of the line; but according to Deleuze, it can never be pinned down. Even from a topological point of view, the inflection is something ungraspable, like the virtual. Deleuze writes:

> Thus the inflection is the pure Event of the line or of the point, the Virtual, ideality par excellence. It will take place following the axes of the coordinates, but for now it is not yet in the world: it is the World itself, or rather its beginning, as Klee used to say, 'a site of cosmogenesis', 'a nondimensional point' 'between dimensions'.[70]

Here Deleuze is obviously discussing, through his own theories, Klee's concept of the interworld, in fact giving it a material concretion. DeLanda explains this virtual dimension as traced through points and lines thusly:

> As is well known, the trajectories in this space always approach an attractor *asymptotically*, that is, they approach it *indefinitely close but never reach it*. This means that unlike trajectories, which represent the actual states of objects in the world, attractors are *never actualized*, since no point of trajectory ever reaches the attractor itself. It is in this sense that singularities represent only the long term tendencies of a system, never its actual state.[71]

An interworld is this new nature that is not present *in* nature but is a natural world emerging from the artist's drawing. He is able to pierce this space through his reliance on a graphic concept that permits him to create a figure in the system, a floating space, and make the painter into a philosopher. It is the double snare of the painter–philosopher: a painter–philosopher of unrepresentable dimensions.

Line to Traits

The line is an important part of a representational diagram. It is also an analogue of the abstract trait that is involved in the diagram. The line, seen through particular philosophical and artistic perspectives, reveals a predisposition towards the abstraction necessary to be a fundamental part of the concept of the diagram. In order to trace the path from the line to the trait, we have to take into consideration several different elements that explain the multidimensionality of the line. First, we will see how a comparison between Paul Klee's and André Lhote's notion of line according to Lyotard steers us towards a particular view of the line. Klee sees the line as negative – but his is a productive view of the negative line, which we will explore in the second step of considering the idea of the trait. Third, the line – and by extension, the artistic work – expands to include the painter. This shows us the range of the line: it can in fact be part of the system beyond the page. In order to fully understand this, we will look at Heidegger's treatment of the various dimensions of an image. The particular image used by Heidegger will reveal how the line and the trait are exposed in Deleuze's concept of faciality.

Klee's approach to painting led him to develop a theory of art based on the possible variations of the line. The line is a point in motion that carries its own force. Slight modulations in the line's trajectory create volume. Klee draws and paints not only delicate, fantastic cityscapes but also formidable flying machines upon which ride strange creatures; and letters and various diacritical signs and symbols often adorn his abstract landscapes.

The Swiss painter established himself as an articulate and prolific modern art theorist while teaching at the Bauhaus with Moholy-Nagy and Kandinsky. As a careful pedagogue who published his course lectures, he explained his art in clear detail and kept a long and subsequently published journal of his artistic thought process. His paintings mix pure geometric forms with calculated colours and graphic signs, such as letters, arrows and musical clefs – relished by philosophers coming out of, and still influenced by, structuralism and semiotics. Furthermore, he never succumbed to strictly reducing his theories into a rigid method, but instead maintained his playfulness and open-ended aesthetic explorations, as do the post-structuralists in the face of structuralist dogma.

Deleuze's relationship with painting is crucial for his philosophy, since he believes that philosophy, like painting, is an analogous relationship between art and thought. Although he published books on Bacon and Fromanger,[72] Deleuze never wrote a full length study of Klee; nevertheless

Black Line, White Surface 89

Klee's importance for Deleuze's philosophy is felt throughout his writings. Klee features prominently in *A Thousand Plateaus*, and his art and theories are used to elucidate such concepts as assemblage.[73] In *What Is Philosophy?* Klee is the gateway to infinity through the materiality of his art.[74] For Deleuze (and Guattari), Klee demonstrates that the passage to another dimension (diagrammatic) necessarily starts at a material surface and that the elements that lead us there are very minimal (point and line). It follows then that the most important endorsement of Klee is in *The Fold: Leibniz and the Baroque*, in which Klee's three curvaceous variations on the line become an emblem of sorts for the theory of the fold in the matter – again this depthless dimension that is paradoxically contained within the flat surface.[75]

Indeed, Klee's paintings are not just maps or tracings; they are both. And if they are tracings, then they are tracings of a virtual materiality. And if they are maps, then they are mapping a space spreading within the painting as material object. *Arrow in the Garden*, 1929, delicately depicts decorative horticultural elements in muted soft colours and thin, quiet lines; towards the middle of the picture plane a small black arrow is floating, superimposed on the garden elements. It is a minimalist map, fitting for a whimsical subject like a garden. *Villa R.*, 1919, depicts a country house from a point of view that is slightly above the central subject; a disproportionately large letter R dwarfs the house and flattens the perspective. The textual element, because of its uncanny appearance in the landscape, creates a vivid visual shock. *Italian City*, 1928, is a painting that gives a cross-section of an abstracted city: beige and muted ochre-coloured cubic shapes float in space, as if they were about to be reattached by a computerized special effect. The eye swoons before the multifaceted configuration. The play of perspectives makes the painting a diagram because it shows dimensions that seem to come out from a space that is not traced on the canvas. These three paintings, with their spatial themes and depictions of somewhat architectural subjects, are important because they tie spatial, cartographic and textual notions together into a thematic fabric.

Similar to this is the depiction in the 'frontispiece' to Deleuze and Guattari's very important plateau 11 – '1837: Of the Refrain' – which features Klee's *Twittering Machine* of 1922. The machine in question in the painting is suggested by a handle in the lower, right part of the picture plane. Starting at this handle and reading from right to left, the handle continues with a straight horizontal line that then juts upwards at a sharp angle and turns left to produce two lines from this point of origin. One line dissolves in a sinuous wave and crosses the other thin horizontal line, which continues discreetly to the edge of the painting and shoots up again at a right angle. On the wavy line, stick figures, slightly feathered or furry, emit shapes from their tulip-like heads and cone-shaped mouths: teardrop shape, paisley shape, curved line and arrow head. These shapes look like sounds: full, lilting, whistling and sharp. The very delicateness of the shapes in Klee's paintings is in harmony with Deleuze and Guattari's call for sobriety that comes later in this plateau. The machine is also an amalgam between the machinic (inferred by the lines) and the organic (bird-like creature twittering). The play of perspectives and the denuded lines illustrate a diagram (a few lines to explain a process), and the concept-diagram is suggested by the various dimensions that the painting delves into from the perspective implied through the angles and shapes of the lines. Finally, *Twittering Machine* is like a plate of the *Encyclopédie*: as whimsical as this machine may be, it is isolated on the page, a blueprint to make your own twittering machine.

Before we turn to consider how Klee's lines are important for Deleuze, we need to look at Lyotard's revelation of the space Klee opens up in his aesthetic by comparing him to another painter, André Lhote. The purpose of drawing a line between Klee and Lhote on the one hand and the critiques of Deleuze on the other is to see how Deleuze's philosophy illuminates Klee's paintings. But, more importantly, it also allows us to see how Klee's paintings inform Deleuze's philosophy – and, more precisely still, how Klee's theories on painting inform Deleuze's writings once these are filtered through the art of Klee.

In *Discours, figure*, Lyotard contrasts Klee's artistic theories to those of André Lhote, who, while greatly influenced by Cézanne, was a staunch Cubist dogmatist. Lhote was an implementer of severe classical rules. So classical in fact that he considered everything that came after the Renaissance as degenerative rather than as innovative. From that point of view, Lhote seems to serve as a straw man, advocating a systematic coherence and purity against Klee's playful eluding of the rules. Lyotard writes that

> [Klee] furnishes to the object and the line a whole other terrain of communication, that is neither the recognizable text of visible appearances, nor the geometrical writing of the plastic screen, but the site (or non-site) generated through procedures such as the systematic evasion of rules of perception and of conception, the displacement of objects out of their space of origin, the simultaneity of succession, the co-affirmation of the contrary, the condensation of distinct constituents, the affinity of things considered strange.[76]

In the elements listed by Lyotard, we can see what he has in mind: Klee is the practitioner of difference.

It is not without irony that Lyotard juxtaposes the expressionist with the Cubist Lhote. Lhote too believes in the line, but without the depth and psychological dimension with which Klee endows it; Lhote seems to fail to grasp the full potential of art. He makes art a system of communication that only communicates semiotically, and while denouncing the illusion that art can fall into if it tries to model itself on reality, he does not seem to realize the illusion of the false depth of a purely semiotic system that purports to be objective. He misses the fact that objectivity is only as illusionist as the subject makes it out to be. Lhote, instead, is a draughtsman who adheres to the strict rules of signification and therefore never eludes the systematic space of discourse. But while he thinks he is escaping from its trap through his ascetic adherence to the line, he falls straight into it. For Lhote, the line is the primary element of art. But it is a line that can only function as a signifier on the flat surface of the page, like a letter. It is a black graphic sign whose sole function, according to Lhote, is to divide the white picture plane. Anything deeper than that and the draughtsman loses himself in a subjective depth and fools the viewer with the illusion of a false transcendence.[77]

For Lhote, the Renaissance was an age of aesthetic corruption and degeneracy, when drawing gave up its signifying functions in favour of an illusory depth. Before that, Lhote contends, the artist never pierced the surface of the picture plane with the suggestion of depth, through a chiaroscuro, for example, or through a modelled figure instead of a figure shaped by lines. By constraining himself to the height and length of the picture plane's real and material boundaries, the artist thus avoids a false depth and uses lines in a series of oppositions that result in a signifying system, to be read by the viewer instead of taken in sensuously. And this is where, while believing he avoids the decoy of depth, Lhote ensnares himself, since he is unable to think past the inconsistencies that are, from a post-structuralist point of view, always already ingrained in a cohesive system of signification.

Klee also discusses the duality of black and white and its inversion, but instead of comparing painting to the graphic sketch, he compares it to photography. Klee inverts the order of black and white, especially in the context of portraying light. While tradition would have light depicted by bright colours, Klee radically opts for the depiction of light with a thick black arrow. Whereas traditionally bright colours would automatically signify lightness in the scheme of the picture plane, Klee's black arrow does not represent the light beam as it is seen 'out there', but rather the coordinate force of light and its directionality. He rationalizes this move scientifically by pointing to photography. Before the picture is developed, light is actually black on the negative, and therefore, in nature – 'out there' – are actual instances when light is black:

> To represent the light through brightness is nothing but the snow of yesteryear. . . . Now I try to render light simply through a deployment of energy. From the moment that on a presupposed white I treat the energy in black, it too must drive to a point. I will bring to mind here the absolutely rational blackness of light on photographic negatives.[78]

Not only is Klee doing exactly what black and white are supposed to be doing in terms of sobering objectivity and documented authority, but he is actually appealing to reason. The rationality of light as black in effect reverses the order and, through his assertion, points to a virtual, in-between world, what Sauvagnargues, in a different context, would call a 'virtual plan of composition' or 'virtual diagram'.[79] This is the paradox of the black and the white as points of reference in a scale of judgement of the truth and the false. The loudest discrepancy is claimed when either end of the spectrum seems to be consistent with what it represents: light represented by white is more false than light represented by black. This paradox devalues the hermeneutic operation of trying to decipher what things mean according to a codified convention. In Klee's graphic universe, one cannot operate according to accepted truths, which are reversed but not less true. True and false, positive and negative, are erased in this paradox between the black and white.

Brian Massumi explains this duality of truth and false in his guide to *A Thousand Plateaus*,[80] in which he demonstrates that the diagram is false and true at the same time. It is false because the diagram constrains its objects into a homogeneity in order to bring an unrepresentational heterogeneity into a representational, actualized whole for a moment. But it is true because this process of constraining into a homogeneity is one of resistance and protest; it affirms the affect that shatters threads of origins and disorganizes the expected order.[81] The black and the white of the graphic representation map out the direction into a depth through the distortion of expected values.

The only sense that could be attributed to 'negative' here would be the black and white film before development. On the negative, the black area will appear as white when doused with lights and drowned with liquids. 'But since the concealed things unceasingly accumulate, and grow larger like a black snowball, the liar is always betrayed.'[82] The black snowball captures the paradox of the logic of truth and false in a swift snapshot. It is worth noting that in the context of autopoetic systems, there is always a target of ultimate equilibrium towards which the system is geared as it tries to establish its equilibrium. This is what Klee's arrow is pointing towards – something outside the picture plane, the *hors-champ* that Deleuze discusses in the context of film and open systems: 'For the essences dwell in dark regions, not in the temperate zones of the clear and the distinct.'[83] The essences – that is, the virtualities – inhabit a systematically developing environment; it is the depth of the sombre zones that gives the illusion of a false depth. But by doing so, in an easy paradox, this depth reveals a real, non-representational depth that is set up by the system all the way to its actualization.

In *What Is Philosophy?* we are told, 'One no longer paints "on" but "under"'.[84] Deleuze and Guattari announce a new dimension that can be reached though painting. The virtual state of nature is never to be actualized in Klee's line, as an arrow pointing to a target, a target that is not outside the picture plane. Rather, this nature is located underneath it or 'in-between', as DeLanda suggests. Still focusing on lines and graphics, DeLanda defines the multiplicity through the vectorial line, the line that Deleuze considers the 'ideality *par excellence*', the diagram of the virtual:

> A multiplicity is a nested set of vector fields related to each other by symmetry-breaking bifurcations, together with the distributions of attractors which define each other of its embedded levels. This definition separates out the part of the world (trajectories as a series of possible states) from that part which is, in principle, never actualized.[85]

Figural space is not marked by coordinates indicating up and down, left and right, foreground and background, and so on; instead, it is a space of metamorphosing unconscious forces. And since its spatial configuration is uncharted, it needs the direction of the black arrow to turn the space into a diagram. Figural space defies 'good form', ready categorization or visual convention. In contrast to figural space is the figurative space that indicates the possibility of deriving a pictorial object from its real model, which occurs through a continual translation.[86] This opposition between figural and figurative space allows for a further distinction, which Lyotard makes through his description of textual space. This space is where the graphic signifier is inscribed. In other words, textual space for Lyotard only contains written representation. But figural space 'oscillates between two poles' – those of the line and the letter. Both are arbitrary, both turn the space (read: the painting or text) into their own object, and both are dialectically interlinked; this is how they both manifest that which is not there. By using both these spaces in one site where they are dialectically mixed, Klee is not penetrating the surface of the picture plane by creating an illusory depth, but rather plunging into the depths of the line itself while staying at the surface of the picture plane and using the line in the same purely significative way that Lhote would.

Let us come back to the black arrow through which Klee tries 'to render light simply as an unfolding of energy'.[87] This energy is dragged out through the directionality that the arrow signifies, not the light that a light colour might have signified. But the rationale for this comes from the painter and is not dictated through conventions of forms or the rules of a system of representation. The space that is opened is not a depth in the painting; it is a depth in the painter. The painter becomes the non-site of the dialectical intersection of the two graphic aspects of the figural that makes the depth of the system. Lyotard writes, 'The task for Klee is not to bear witness that the intelligible is the regulator of the sensible; it is to turn the painting into an object.'[88] He explains that the painting as object will not be created to be interpreted or submitted to hermeneutic scrutiny. Rather, the object will be on par with the materiality of the objects in nature, yet still slightly different:

> This object was not produced by nature. Far from conforming to its plan, it is denaturalized or transnatural. It attests that the creation exceeds the created nature, and that the artist is a place where it continues to produce its fruits.[89]

The diagram on the picture plane *makes rhizome* with the painter outside of it in a very material way, in the sense that the painter is the ground out of which the rhizome grows.

Black and white, negative and positive, the photographic metaphor is also important because it shows us how fluid images are and how abstract this dimension is. Heidegger invokes the photograph in his explanation of Kant's schema in *Kant and the Problem of Metaphysics*. The *graph* at the end of 'photo' is revelatory here, making Heidegger's choice of example coincide with the graphic element of representation: 'a photography remains only a transcription of what shows itself immediately as "image".'[90] We have an image and we have the photograph, the transcription of this image. Heidegger manipulates the concept of the photographic image in a series of frames, demonstrating the many levels at which the photograph is 'immediately' an image. In fact, the photograph already doubles the sense of image: 'This thing here, this photograph which is at hand, immediately offers a look as this thing. It is image in the first and broad sense.'[91] We have an image, then the photograph of this image. And the photograph itself, regardless of what it represents, is already immediately an image: an empirical object, a photograph. Slowly, then, Heidegger develops in sequential frames several states of the image, each frame holding an image at various degrees. The function of the photograph is to provide an image other than itself: 'But while it shows itself, it wants to show precisely that from which it has taken its likeness.'[92] That is why Heidegger says that in order to possess an image we can either immediately intuit a being or get or take a photo.[93]

When Heidegger, focusing more closely and opening another frame, gives an example of what this photograph could represent, the sequence of frames opens up in another direction – this time in the opposite direction, towards the empirical thing. The photograph as an example of image is crucial because within the photograph we find collapsed its representative function of providing images. Heidegger demonstrates this through an inherent attribute of the photograph: the reproduction of the representation as copies. The photograph reproduces an image that is already a representation, not the true image of the thing, since the thing is captured by the concept just as the photograph captures an image of the thing. Heidegger invites us to take a death mask as an example of the thing the camera snaps and represents as a photographic image:[94]

> The copy can only directly copy the likeness and thus reveal the 'image' (the immediate look) of the deceased himself. The photograph of the death mask, as copy of a likeness, is itself an image – but this is only because it gives the 'image' of the dead person, shows how the dead person appears, or rather how it appeared. According to the meaning of the expression 'image' hitherto delimited, making-sensible means on the one hand the manner of immediate contemplation of a likeness in which the look of a being presents itself.[95]

Heidegger soon brings the proliferation of frames of representation to a halt:

> But what do these 'looks' (images in the broadest sense) of this corpse, this mask, this photograph, etc., now show? Which 'appearance' (ειδος, ιδεα) do they now give? What do they now make sensible? In the one which applies to many, they show how something appears 'in general'.[96]

The multiple frames of examples through which Heidegger conjugates the meaning of the image serve to demonstrate its multidimensionality. In fact, this is how the dynamism of the image makes its sense fleeting, especially when it stands at the crux of the object represented and the representation of the representation: 'This unity applicable to several, however, is what representation represents in the manner of the concepts. These looks must now serve the making-sensible of concepts.'[97]

The frames are collapsed into one, and the image, in its multidimensional aspect can begin to yield its conceptual character, in effect reflecting the multidimensional form of the Kantian schema itself:

> This making-sensible can now no longer mean: to get an immediate look, intuition from a concept; for the concept, as the represented universal, cannot be represented in a *repraesentatio singularis*, which the intuition certainly is. For that reason, however, the concept is also essentially not capable of having a likeness taken.[98]

The singular is transposed from its empirical status to an intellectual one. It creates a depth, a reversible unfolding. In effect, with his example, Heidegger shows us that we can never get at a true image of a thing regardless of the number of frames in which we capture its traits. Through a multilayered example of representation, Heidegger shows us the non-representational aspect of the dimension of the diagram. With these multiple snapshots of a face – the face of the deceased, the death mask, the photo of the death mask and the image of the photo with the aforementioned representations – Heidegger's example of the elusive nature of the trait serves as a transition to Deleuze's concept of faciality.[99]

The face is a '*white wall/black hole* system'[100] – as in a death mask in a black and white photograph, or the close-up in a film. The black and white elements of this system can be considered as constituting an abstract machine: the system's traits can be transposed, or deterritorialized into other situations, and function diagrammatically. '[T]he black hole/white wall system is, to begin with, not a face but the abstract machine that produces faces according to the changeable combinations of its cogwheels. Do not expect the abstract machine to resemble what it produces, or will produce.'[101] Like the diagram that is ever-malleable, the function that puts the face and not the face together is the abstract machine faciality system at work. The face can be linked to the landscape according to its traits: the face is the snow, the eyes are the blood that falls on it. This can be seen on the flat surface of the painting:

Black Line, White Surface

> Even when painting becomes abstract, all it does is rediscover the black hole and the white wall, the great composition of the white canvas and black slash. Tearing, but also stretching of the canvas along an axis of escape (*fuite*), at a vanishing point (*point de fuite*), along a diagonal line, by a knife slice, slash, or hole: the machine is already in place that always functions to produce faces and landscapes, however abstract. Titian began his paintings in black and white, not to make outlines to fill in, but as the matrix for each of the colors to come.[102]

The abstract machine, already present virtually on the surface, is 'sometimes . . . developed on a plane of consistency giving it a "diagrammatic" function, a positive value of deterritoriality, the ability to form a new abstract machine'.[103] At the foundation, the trait on the canvas is ready to be a landscape or a face, 'to invent the combinations by which those traits connect with landscapity traits that have themselves been freed from the landscape and with traits of picturality and musicality that have also been freed from their respective codes.'[104] Traits are the basis of the abstract machine, decomposing and recomposing, making connections and links. These traits will be further explored below.

And so we have come full circle: the traits of faciality are the decoy in the depth of the grass. From faciality we can turn to portraits.

Some Traits of the Diagram

The diagram, as the dimension in which abstracted functions intermingle between two heterogeneous systems, proceeds by an atomization of matter into traits. But what is a trait from an aesthetic perspective? First, we will draw out a definition of the trait. Second, we will see how the information dimension vital to the configuration rises from Deleuze's trait. Third, we will compare the trait to a blind spot in the system on which exchanges between heterogeneous formations hinge. This will be laid out on a cinematic terrain with lacunae and risings of self-reflexivity that map out the connections between two types of reality. And finally, we will suggest characteristics pertaining to the emergence of a diagrammatic zone.

The diagram is the abstract machine, not just part of the definition of 'abstract machine'. But what is the operative element in this machine? The answer to this lies in the last collaboration between Deleuze and Guattari. In the chapter in *What Is Philosophy?* where they discuss the plane of immanence, they also consider the diagrammatic trait – a crucial notion since it could be considered the germ of the diagram. The diagrammatic trait was introduced earlier in the text, clustered into a duality with the intensive traits. The plane of immanence, the main subject of this chapter, supports the concepts in Deleuze and Guattari's image of philosophy; but, in an inverted proportional manner, it is the concepts that make the plane of immanence appear: 'Both the creation of concepts and the instituting of the plane are required, like two wings or fins.'[105] Intensive traits are absolute dimensions while diagrammatic traits are absolute directions.[106] The difference in translation is noteworthy since the English translate *trait* as 'feature'. The English translation reads: 'Intensive features are never the consequence of diagrammatic features, and intensive ordinates are not deduced from movements of directions.'[107] The French original, however, employs the word *trait*: 'Jamais les traits intensifs ne sont la conséquence des traits diagrammatiques, ni les ordonnées intensives ne se déduisent des mouvements ou directions.'[108] Why is the word 'trait' so telling in this definition? Both kind of trait are complementary and necessary to each other, but independent. Are diagrammatic traits diagrams? Is there a difference between them? Diagrammatic traits could be seen as absolute diagrams. If a diagram is a map and a tracing, both surveying unknown countries and constraining into a structure what is present in fact, a diagrammatic trait is a diagram of a diagram.

First, we must consider the word 'trait'. The fact that we were considering 'drawing' and 'sketching' in Lhote and Klee earlier is no coincidence. 'Trait' in English comes from the Middle French word that means to pull or draw – the stroke of a pencil or of a brush. It is also a facial feature or a line. This appears in Francis Bacon and the diagram inside the face: the notion of the Sahara desert splitting in half a figure's head.[109] In French, the word *trait* is synonymous with *ligne* (line), *barre* (a stroke or to bar something, as in to constrain something), *marque* (a mark), or *rature, hachure*. The hachure is an accumulation of short lines used for shading and denoting surfaces in relief – as in map drawing – drawn in the direction of slope. The hachure is short, broad and close together when the slope it depicts is steep, and it is long, narrow and far apart when the slope is gentle. And so a hachure that denotes topographical elements on a map denotes depth and height on a flat surface – on a plane. Moreover, *trait* can mean *portée*, as in the maximal distance that a projectile can travel, an intellectual effort, or a force or intensity. *Trait* is also *javelot* or *lance*, which would bring us back to our image of the black arrow of Klee pointing to a direction outside a frame. Since this last definition is an assemblage of three elements – a distance travelled, an intellectual effort and an intensity – we can see how

Black Line, White Surface

the semantic field of this definition chimes with notions we were exploring within the purview of the line. The definition of *portée* brings the notions of space and intellect together with intensity. The trait is not only a drawn line, or an ensemble of lines giving depth to a surface or indicating height in a geographical sense, but also the graphic signs of three-dimensionality, as in the chiaroscuro to which Lhote's flat plane drawing was contrasted. The trait is also that which is involved in the absolute directionality within a system and which gives orientation to thought. If a diagram can be considered a schema or a sketch, then the *trait diagrammatique* is the ontological element of this sketch. It is a sketch of a sketch.

It is important to note that a trait cannot be isolated[110] and that it is part of a duality at least. This brings us back to the double-sided truth of the system. Philosophy, according to Deleuze and Guattari, is constituted by the integral part of the plane of immanence, which is in turn necessary for the creation of concepts. The discussion of the declination of the meaning of the word 'trait' as a necessary element of orientation in thought yields a map of the plane of thought. As we become aware that the plane itself is an image of thought without being its representation, we see the arch that we have traced: in enumerating the meanings of 'trait', we presented the facets of the concept of the trait. And as we traversed the stages of meaning, representation and thought, we also realized that an important factor of this process is the presentation of the stages of this process.

Hence, Deleuze and Guattari come back to art: 'The history of philosophy is comparable to the art of the portrait.'[111] The portrait, por-*trait*, comes from the Middle French *pourtraire*, *portraire*. The word comes from the Latin *protrahere* (to draw forth, to reveal, to expose), which is composed of *pro* (forth, before) and *trahere* (to draw). This etymology therefore demonstrates that trait is the proper translation for *trait* and not feature. Feature covers one part of the elements of portraiture, that is, the facial characteristics, but does not cover the atom essential to portraiture: the stroke of pencil or brush that is part of the process of painting. Trait, then, is as pluridimensional as *dia*. It is movement and intuition; it is direction and depth.

In *A Thousand Plateaus*, the trait is at the crux of Deleuze and Guattari's many concepts, or rather, their many strategies to provide an image of the creation of philosophy:

Each freed faciality trait forms a rhizome with a freed trait of landscapity, picturality, or musicality. This is not a collection of part-objects but a living block, a connecting of stems by which the traits of a face enter a real multiplicity or diagram with a trait of an unknown landscape, a trait of painting or music that is thereby effectively produced, created, according to quanta of absolute, positive deterritorialization – not evoked or recalled according to systems of reterritorialization. A wasp trait and an orchid trait.[112]

The duality of the wasp and orchid open a constellation of concepts, such as territory, geography and the block. The block, as the solidification of a duality, is not without movement, as the montage technique demonstrates in the fluidity of the cinematographic arrangement. According to Deleuze, one cinematographic example, in which this definition of the diagram is crystallized in a cartographic superimposition, can be found in Resnais' *My American Uncle*: '*My American Uncle* will be a grand attempt at diagrammatic mental cartography, where maps are superimposed and transformed, in a single character and from one character to the next.'[113] Resnais' film is interesting from a diagrammatic perspective: the American uncle from the title is the unrepresentational image around which the narrative of each character revolves. The uncle is the figure of an abstract notion – for example, failure, as one character explains. The uncle went to America to seek riches but failed and ended up homeless on the streets of Chicago. It is around these blind spots that the lives of three characters revolve, mapping a terrain based around something that is not there. The film is an excellent example of a diagram because it is said to be something else: a map.

As a map, the diagram has the function of moving thought through space:

> Perhaps, when we read a book, watch a show, or look at a painting, and especially when we are ourselves the author, an analogous process can be triggered: we constitute a sheet of transformation which invents a kind of transverse continuity or communication between several sheets, and weaves a network of non-localizable relations between them. In this way we extract non-chronological time.[114]

The continuum that makes experience possible is the way objects persist in the mind through time. But Deleuze redistributes the a priori – subject, time, reason – from the Kantian model to a structuralist, flat, horizontal, geographical model. *It is the subject here that is a functional stratum.* Thus, the depersonified, reified subject is reconstituted geographically as spatially located matter.

Black Line, White Surface 101

But also, within the movement of analogy in Simondon's allagmatic model, the central function of the analogy is the ontological empty space: the *blind spot* of the allagmatic operation that fills the operation with a three-dimensional depth and makes it real. It is a diagram representing the dimension between the terms of an analogical operation: an ontological diagram, a diagram of ontological fullness. It is incorporeal and real *because* it is incorporeal. Deleuze's *Cinema 2: The Time-Image* provides a description of the diagram in which it seems located in something that is of human shape. In Resnais, it is what makes an ensemble of transformations from one plane to the next. A diagram is needed because it is a pluralistic, multidimensional and flexible machine; it does not trace a single formation (*skhêmatismos*)[115] from one state to the next; it instead traces an ensemble of transformations (*metaskhêmatismos*).[116] It thus enables multiple transformations to be traced while allowing for the transformation of a network of dependent relations. The diagram captures different places at different points in time across different planes. Because of the diagram, there can be a redistribution of functions and a fragmentation of objects. A recodified object can move from one strata to the next and retain its shape. The diagram then is not simple restructuring; instead of moving from one plane to the next, it goes through a continuum of planes. It is as if Foucault's plant in *The Order of Things*, the one that is translated from reality onto the page, were fragmented into traits that make up the shape of the plant. These traits then become part of a system of knowledge. But, by heaping the traits one on top of the other, by creating a relief, a mound on the page, the diagram would allow the flower to suffer another transformation: to leave the page and to become a flower again, or another flower, or a smell that triggers a memory.

The object in the system gains a thickness; it comes out of the page or out of the screen like in Woody Allen's *The Purple Rose of Cairo*, the character of a popular movie steps out of the screen and into the movie theatre. It is the well-known device of self-reflexivity which communicates back to the viewers, making them aware of the apparatus that articulates the illusion happening on the screen. Another, more apt, example is *La Jetée* by Chris Marker, in which this effect comes about quite differently – perhaps more clearly because the film is so aesthetically minimal. The main character, travelling back and forth in time (from a dystopian future, to his past, our present) to find out the circumstances of human kind's decimation, falls in love with someone in the past. The film is made of still black and white photographs with a voice-over tying the narrative together. The viewer watching the still pictures appearing on the screen, one after another, becomes used to their forward motion. In the middle of the film, however, the love interest – in a scene that has been showing her, through various still shots, waking up in bed – is suddenly animated. In one of the still shots, her eyes open and she smiles. She transcends the stillness of the photographs that form the juxtaposed narrative. The dimension that opens with the blinking of her eyes in bed in the morning while birds sing is haunting.

In another sequence of photographs, the man and the woman are at a natural history museum. The stills show them pointing at various displayed, mounted animals – like two people discovering an exhibition on a leisurely afternoon. After looking at a myriad of animals – sharks, giraffes, rays – they end up in the bird exhibition. A multitude of toucans perch in a grid-like pattern, ordered behind glass windows. In one image, the woman's hand, her forefinger extended, points to a toucan, her finger resting on the glass that separates her from the stuffed birds. The reflection on the glass is of the large windows presumably behind her; but as a reflection, the windows appear between her finger and the bird. Pointing towards the bird, the woman is at the same time pointing to the sky reflected on the glass beyond the window behind her. It is an elaborate network bringing to mind the hand pointing to the animals in Barthes' description of Noah's Ark. But the reference in *La Jetée* comes from an earlier part of the Bible: the man and the woman are a post-modern Adam and Eve pointing to animals that are already dead – and doubly so, because this whole scene takes place, in the narrative logic of the movie, before the end of the world. The woman seems to be pointing to the sky where the bird rightly belongs. But the bird is dead, the sky is just a reflection, and the whole is framed within a film about time travel which, if the story is followed to its ending, is structured on a perpetual loop. The hand is actually pointing beyond the limit of the reel.

The film's materiality carries its own time machine within the celluloid. Deleuze states: 'When we read a book. . . . When we look at a painting. . . . If we made it. . . . We become a plane of transformation, we have a function, we are a diagram, a body without organs'; it is not that we are part of an intricately woven network, but that the intricately woven network is us.[117] Massumi, explaining the subject position in Deleuze and Guattari's philosophy, sets the open equation (. . . + y + z + a . . .) against the equation of representation ($x = x = $ not y)[118] in order to compare traditional philosophy's double identity 'of the thinking subject, and of the concepts it creates and to which it lends its own presumed attributes of sameness and constancy'[119] to a philosophy of difference characterized by a 'conductivity that knows no bounds,[120] which he illustrates in the following way:

> A concept is a brick. It can be used to build the courthouse of reason. Or it can be thrown through the window. What is the subject of the brick? The arm that throws it? The body connected to the arm? The brain encased in the body? The situation that brought brain and body to such a juncture? All and none of the above. What is its object? The window? The edifice? The laws the edifice shelters? The class and other power relations encrusted in the laws? All and none of the above: 'What interests us are the circumstances.'[121]

The problem of the real comes into the floating space between the visual and the textual under the umbrella of the diagram. It is best illustrated in the following way: if image and text are put on the same playing field (both consist of black lines, or traits), where neither is valued over the other, then we can represent each by a neutral object, say a plate of glass. These two plates of glass are stacked one on top of the other and no space exists between them. Of course, there is a space, but it is imperceptible. In order to bring it to prominence, we infuse the space with water, an equally neutral substance. The plates of glass cannot be stacked on each other anymore; the water can be as neutral as it desires, but it exercises such a force that it will push the plates of glass. Furthermore, the image observed through the glass panes, though once clear, is now grossly distorted and must be organized through reason for it to make sense. It appears now that the see-through glass and the tasteless water are not so neutral anymore. A diagram forces things to be put together. Only the separate parts are neutral; when they are put together, they are in a problematic relation with one another. It makes the observer of the world realize that everything – even the most natural, unadulterated elements of experience – is put together, constructed, and has to be thought through to be experienced.

This is what Massumi means when he says that the diagram is both true and false at the same time, and that what makes it false in fact makes it true. This paradox can be illustrated by prominent politicians in the public eye. What is more desirable: a politician who is crooked in his dealings but honest about it, or a leader who has the false veneer of honesty and uprightness but who keeps his deceptions secret? You know where you stand with the first one, but where you stand is in deception. You might initially trust the second one, but feel more cheated when you finally find out. But both are politicians, and you cannot really hold it against them because dishonesty is their nature.

But returning to the panes of glass and the water, the layers that they illustrate, and the distortion that ensues when they are put together, we can say that their distortion, at least, is very clearly a distortion. What Massumi writes could be understood as a caption to this image:

> The diagram is false, in that it contracts a multiplicity of levels and matters into its own homogeneous substance. But it is true, in that it envelops in that substance the same affect, and because it reproduces the in-betweenness of the affect in the fracturing of its own genesis.[122]

A diagram necessarily *functions*. It functions even when its meaning is unclear, because it underlines the manufacturing of meaning. Meaning is manifest between two poles of clarity and opaqueness. As architects Ben Van Berkel and Caroline Bos put it, '[A] diagram is a diagram because it is stronger than its interpretations.'[123] Massumi, again, drives the paradox that is strung along the lines of deferred desire: once you have what you wanted, it is not the same thing that you wanted because it is something that you now have.

> The expression of meaning is true in its falseness to itself, and false in the trueness of its content. Translation is repetition with a difference. If meaning is becoming, it is a becoming-other. It is the alienation of the same in the different, and the sameness of the different in its alienation from itself.[124]

A diagram is a mechanism of capture that sees the bird it caught in its hand wilt away and turn to dust. Only then does it realize that what it really wanted to capture was not the bird at all, but its free and light flight path, its invisible song, the ruffled sound of its feathers – in short, traits. 'The (non)relation is a *separation-connection*.'[125] The process of the diagram follows its mandate to bring together and widen the gap between heterogeneous systems.

The panes of glass stack up and become more opaque with the different layers of interpretation of the diagram. No matter how clear the device is at first, at some point the light has difficulty getting through. The bottom of the ocean is dark, after all. And so the explanation of the diagram, at this point, can contain three such panes. Foucault would be located on the first, as he conceives of the diagram in relation to the elements of power, architecture and light in the Panopticon, which, by itself, *symbolizes* the concept of the power. Deleuze, on the second layer, isolates the diagram in

Foucault as the material manifestation of the aformal, the unrepresentable. One of these manifestations of the unrepresentable is in the layer (think of the water) between the visual and the textual, between what is said and what is seen (I am combining the visual with the seen and the textual with the said, even though there is between each coupling another insurmountable layer, if only from an ideological point of view).[126] On the third level we can situate Badiou, commenting on the previous two. He sees Deleuze's description of the diagram isolated in Foucault as a diagram in itself: 'Deleuze, under the name of Foucault (or under the constraint of the case-Foucault), indicates, therefore, that seeing and speaking, things and words, constitute registers of being (or thought) that are entirely disjointed.'[127] Apart from bathing the diagram in a distinctly ontological current, Badiou demonstrates that the interpretation of the diagram is itself distorted by the diagram that results: the 'diagram-Deleuze' in this case, distorts the 'diagram-Foucault', or 'Foucault-case.' This is the ontological aspect of the diagram itself; it is in-the-hands-of because of the very insurmountable space that it locates as a diagram.

These questions can be elucidated by Guattari, who gets his definition of the diagram from Peirce: 'Denotation disappears in the face of the process described by Peirce as "diagrammatization".'[128] Massumi seconds this when he describes Peirce's diagrammatic operation of tracing lines on a blackboard.[129] Peirce demonstrates on a blackboard, which he designates as the diagram of everything possible, that a series of white traits breaking the darkness of the black space is already an assertion of existence. He also argues that there is a guiding hand in the multiplicity of white lines breaking the black spaces, as they pile up to filter out an oval shape in the darkness; it is the multiplicity of straight lines that forms a circle. The process is akin to the multiple traits that make up a hachure denoting a relief on a flat plane. It is a question of perspectives, yes, but it is also a question of scale. It is a question of the teeming letters on the lines of the drawing. On a macroscopic level, it seems that a circle is drawn by an uninterrupted line, but if we look at the line through a microscopic lens, we see that the circular line is itself made out of millions of tiny straight lines. It may not be exactly the intentionality that we are used to in a subject that ideologically ignores the forces that shape him, but it is a form of agency on a different scale.

In *Difference and Repetition*, Deleuze underscores the question of distinct elements by showing how the whole concept of the ground is made autonomous: 'The rising ground is no longer below, it acquires autonomous existence; the form reflected in this ground is no longer a form but an abstract line acting directly upon the soul.'[130] The use of the abstract line is an integral part of

Deleuze's description here. Darkening the borders, the abstract line contrasts the represented object from its background, puts it at the forefront. At the same time, it makes the mechanism of drawing obvious. Here, it is the soul that gets the abstract line treatment, putting a ghost into evidence, attempting to trace the untraceable, pointing out the monster:

> When the ground rises to the surface, the human face decomposes in this mirror in which both determinations and the indeterminate combine in a single determination which 'makes' the difference. It is a poor recipe for producing monsters to accumulate heteroclite determinations or to overdetermine the animal.[131]

This passage demonstrates taxonomic elements, and how determined elements of a particular animal can create monsters. We can think of Geoffroy Saint-Hilaire, who in fact compiled volumes of cases of monstrosities. The particularities here are the drawing analogy and the biological analogy, which both make for an illustration of the philosophical ground. In *Difference and Repetition*, Deleuze demonstrates how a diagram functions practically as a philosophical construction:

> It is better to raise up the ground and dissolve the form. Goya worked with aquatint and etching, the grisaille of the one and the severity of the other. Odilon Redon used *chiaroscuro* and the abstract line. The abstract line acquires all its force from giving up the model – that is to say, the plastic symbol of the form – and participates in the ground all the more violently in that it distinguishes itself from it without the ground distinguishing itself from the line.[132]

Deleuze's diagram is presented as a philosophical tool to capture the unrepresentable. The concept, not yet named 'diagram', is already present here, but will need Foucault's help, as well as that of Guattari and Peirce, to be more fully developed and named as such. This development will allow Deleuze to use drawing analogies to illustrate his abstract philosophy. It will be a useful tool for figuring out a system.

Conclusion

The line travels throughout this chapter and changes shape. At first, it is the line as illustration, outlining things and translating them into a system of knowledge. It transforms objects into flat drawings and brings them side by side with text. Then, it appears that between the visual and the textual, the line traces a boundary. This boundary between the figure and the discourse is an incommensurability from which a depth emerges. In effect, it underlines another reality within the system of knowledge. After that, we focus on the line, combined with the text, on the plane of art and we see it yielding a new dimension, something palpably out of reach. The line is divided: it either separates the white plane in a linear fashion or it shows a potential, a virtuality within the space of the work of art. The line is much more than illustration, it brings attention to the notion of the image and representation. It is finally atomized into traits. A trait, as the minimal diagrammatic unit, brings out the non-representational diagram into relief. From the line as a way of filtering out the real and classifying it within a system of knowledge to the multiplicity of the traits that create the illusion of depth on the page, the incorporeal diagram gains in thickness. It is still out of focus but it can be located.

To close this section on the black and white elements of the illustrative diagram that is positioned somewhere between the visual and the textual, I would like to invoke the monogram. The word refers, on one hand, to a cipher composed of interwoven letters representing the name of the person who owns the object to which the monogram is stitched. On the other hand, it is applied to a picture in lines only, such as an outline or a sketch. Here, *mono* designates the only or the single, as in monotonous, and *gram* comes from *graphein*, to write or carve. A monogram, then is an outline and a character, as in a calligram, and occupies the visual and the textual, the line and the letter.

Kant uses the monogram to describe the way that his concept of the schema functions. In the chapter 'Of the Schematism of the Pure Concepts of the Understanding', Kant compares the schema to the monogram because of the nature of the image that describes the schema.

> We can say no more than: the **image** is a product of the empirical faculty of productive imagination; the **schema** of sensible concepts (such as of figures in space) is a product and, as it were, a monogram of pure *a priori* imagination, through which and according to which images first become possible.[133]

In the following chapter, we will be seeing exactly what kind of strange image the schema is. But here what is interesting is the necessity of this visual and textual anchor when describing the process through which empirical elements are brought to our understanding. The schema is at the crux, we could say, of a strange dimension that Kant is not fully able to describe. This is why he uses approximate terms, which in themselves are defined by their approximate nature. The monogram could be a tribute to elasticity.

At the end of *The Critique of Pure Reason*, Kant recapitulates the look of his philosophical system, which he calls an architectonic because of its carefully planned construction. In the chapter *The Architectonic of Pure Reason*, he focuses his attention on the schema of his architectonic. Again, the word monogram comes up to provide the schema with an analogous term. We can see that the monogram is a contracted image of a thing: it only has its traits and its outline, but not all of the details that come into the making of the thing it represents. We can draw a link between the monogram as the outline and the sketch and the general structure of the architectonic.[134] The link between the plan, as sketch, and the diagram will become apparent in the following chapter. There the diagram will be compared in more detail to the schema in order to show that the diagram is an integral part of spatial thinking.

Chapter 3

Gilles Deleuze's Diagram (Complicated by a Comparison to Immanuel Kant's Schema)

The relationship between Gilles Deleuze and Immanuel Kant is a difficult one, and is made more complicated by a comparison between the twentieth-century diagram and the eighteenth-century schema. We can level this comparison somewhat by focusing on the space that brings these two concepts together rather than on the time that separates them – namely, by considering the geography and architecture of the philosophical systems in which these concepts are embedded.

The diagram is a duality composed of tracing and mapping. As described by Deleuze and Guattari in *A Thousand Plateaus*, tracing is a process of graphic translation. Tracing operates through blind repetition, through a process of constant skipping back onto the outline of the object it traces. Tracing functions by constraint: 'It is instead like a photograph or X ray that begins by selecting or isolating, by artificial means such as colorations or other restrictive procedures, what it intends to reproduce.'[1] Mapping, on the other hand, exposes undiscovered spaces, expands the terrain on which thought habitually dwells, and extends the boundaries so as to spill out into unexplored regions. Deleuze and Guattari concede that tracing and mapping must be superimposed to form a process of simultaneous constraint and expansion. By definition, the diagram does not obey the programme set by tracing; but far from being inconsistent, it rather varies and adapts to diverse conceptual situations within Deleuze's (and Guattari's) corpus. For example, in *A Thousand Plateaus*, the abstract machine is part phylum, part diagram.[2] In Deleuze's *Foucault*, however, the diagram is the name given to the informal dimension of the matter and function: the diagram is the abstract machine and not just part of the definition of 'abstract machine'.

On the other hand, the function of Kant's schema – of converting, through subsumption, empirical objects of intuition into concepts of pure understanding – is possible because of the central[3] position it occupies within the architectonic. The schema is unlike the nomadic diagram. It is the 'third thing': 'The schema bridges the divide between pure concepts and pure intuition in including universality (a condition of pure concepts) and sensibility (the basic condition of intuition).'[4]

But rather than pitting the peripheral against the central, let us see instead what the concepts look like together.

The Diagram

The concept of the diagram has been most successfully incorporated into contemporary architectural theory. In addition to interpreting Deleuze and Guattari's philosophical concepts with an integrity and enthusiasm rarely matched in other disciplines, architectural theorists have broached the status of the concept of the diagram. Viewing it as more than just an apt object through which to explore the classic duality of plan and building, contemporary architectural theorists are interested in the virtuality, potentiality and multiplicity they can squeeze out of this loaded concept. Architectural theorists are also interested in the material, constructivist and machinic-productive aspects of Deleuze and Guattari's work. It seems difficult to discuss the diagram without recourse to architecture because the nature of the diagram – especially its capacity to saddle both the virtual and the actual – follows the trajectory of the possibility of a plan to be realized as a constructed building. Ben Van Berkel and Caroline Bos, a Dutch team of architect and art historian, have examined the diagram in Deleuze and Guattari's writings and have isolated three instances where the concept's separate facets are revealed. With the caveat that their analysis of Deleuze and Guattari's diagram is specifically architectural, Van Berkel and Bos underline the fact that these are not three instances of different diagrams, but of tonalities, or moods, within a single concept. Each instance is like a different shade of one colour.

These tonalities are, as the architects write, 'associated' with Michel Foucault, Francis Bacon and Marcel Proust. The association with Foucault, who developed his own concept of the diagram, can be seen in Deleuze and Guattari's later theory, which is partly his, partly their own, and a mixture of both. With regard to Bacon's discussion of diagrams, Deleuze's far more developed concept augments the original sense of the word as it was used by the painter and translated by the philosopher.[5] And the association with the Proustian diagram, a concept that has no obvious source in Proust's texts, must be extrapolated from Deleuze and Guattari.

The first facet, or tonality, of the concept is its antiprogrammatic element: Deleuze, contra Foucault, sheds the notion of programme. By discarding the programmatic nature of the diagram, Deleuze focuses on function instead of instances.

The second facet is that of being anticliché: 'It involves the insertion of an element that contains within dense information something that we can latch onto, that distracts us from spiraling into cliché, something that is "suggestive".'[6] The architects explain that in their own blueprints they use various materials from the outside, such as pages from technical manuals or photocopied reproductions of art works or simply random images. This anticliché use of the diagram is akin to what William S. Burroughs practised as the cut-up: random texts folded in together and then edited for flow, leading to nonsensical yet suggestive results. The anticliché diagram operates as something distorting the controlled programme. These diagrams are 'infrastructural', write Van Berkel and Bos, 'they can always be read as maps of movements, irrespective of their origins.'[7] Since they include a liberating element of randomness, they are 'not selected on the basis of specific representational information'.[8] Such a diagram functions as a germ, with something from the outside disturbing a preprogrammed flow, like a knot in a wooden plank – 'essentially used as a proliferator in the process of unfolding'.[9] This second manifestation of the diagram is also exemplified by Francis Bacon's splotching of paint on the surface of figurative paintings. This squirt of paint carries a depth of information inside its core. The result of a quick hand gesture, the splash is another manifestation of the disturbance created by the photographs and snapshots Bacon consulted before applying the paint to the canvas. Just as, while in the middle of painting a portrait, Bacon distracted himself from the figure he was painting with a photograph of rhinoceros skin, the paint flung from the brush took the painting into a different direction.

The third facet of the diagram in the lineage is operational: the concept functions like a black hole. It makes something do something else. It carries some sort of directionality. It involves a technique. It does not blur, but directs and systematizes. This third facet is associated with Proust and involves a junction between music, literature and psychology. It is best summarized in *Swann's Way*, through the scene in which Swann is intently listening to Vinteuil's refrain while waiting in the urbane parlour to meet

Odette. Listening to the refrain, Swann 'had before him this thing that is not pure music anymore, but that is drawing, architecture, thought, and that allows us to bring music to mind'.[10] It may be incorporeal, but it is not less real for it.

In this chapter, I focus more sharply on the first, or antiprogrammatic, facet of the diagram, which grew and evolved throughout the work of Deleuze and Guattari but originated in a review article Deleuze wrote about Foucault's *Discipline and Punish* and later reworked in the pages of *Foucault*.[11] There, the diagram is understood in non-representational terms. Deleuze uses it to give a name to an indefinite list of non-formed, non-organized materials and functions that are neither formalized nor finalized. Foucault uses the term in *This Is Not a Pipe* – a book in which he analyses Paul Klee's work. Klee's work is of interest in this context because in his geometrically abstract yet figurative landscapes, signs like arrows and letters of the alphabet often inhabit the same space as houses, rivers and skies. The space of the picture plane is both three-dimensional (because of the abstracted yet discernible perspectival allusions) and flat (the letter 'R' lying on the canvas as if on a page). From this milieu springs the question of a new dimension – an informal dimension:

> In the same way, analyzing Paul Klee, Foucault says that the visible figures and the signs of writing combine, *but in a different dimension to that of their respective forms*. In this way we must also leap into a different dimension to that of the stratum and its two forms, a third informal dimension that will take account both of the stratified composition of the two forms and of the primacy of the one over the other. What comprises this dimension, this new axis?[12]

Deleuze captures this dimension with the word 'diagram'.[13] But the non-representational aspect of the diagram in *Foucault* has a decidedly representational origin in *Discipline and Punish*. It is in the section on the Panopticon that the diagram is mentioned with regards to prisons. Deleuze underlines the fact that it is the *only* time the word is used in the book:[14]

> But the Panopticon must not be understood as a dream building: it is the diagram of a mechanism of power reduced to its ideal form; its functioning, abstracted from any obstacle, resistance or friction, must be represented as a pure architectural and optical system: it is in fact a figure of political technology that may and must be detached from any specific use.[15]

Gilles Deleuze's Diagram

As we have already seen, the Panopticon, a prison system designed by Jeremy Bentham, allows for maximum surveillance of those imprisoned within its walls through the device of a central tower from which a guard can survey the totality of the cells arranged in a circular wall around him. This is the architectural aspect of the prison. The optic aspect ensures that the guard in the central tower is hidden in the shadow of the construction and cannot be seen by the prisoners in the surrounding cells who, in turn, are in full view: their cells are pierced by the light that comes from the top of the structure and the cell windows. 'Visibility is a trap', Foucault writes.[16] Foucault emphasizes the fact that the Panopticon is not an oneiric building, thus securing the notion that the diagram should not be taken for something imagined, a fantastical product of the mind. It might be incorporeal, but that does not make it a phantasm. Foucault dissolves the walls of the structure into a diagram: an abstraction of the mechanism of power. By abstracting it from its materiality, he clears away all the obstacles and resistance that matter can put up and arrives at a pure architectural and optical system. Architecture and optics are the duality of the diagram of power, and, in this specific case, they form part of a double dissolution of the structure of the building. The model of the Panopticon functions by wielding visibility and invisibility through light. If the prison represents power, the diagram 'reduce[s] power to its ideal form'[17] – ideal as in abstracted, or more accurately, as part of the way Deleuze formulates the virtual: abstract without being ideal. The diagram is abstract enough not to have a specific use.[18]

Even though Deleuze insists that Foucault uses the word 'diagram' only once in relation to the Panopticon, it does appear earlier in *Discipline and Punish* in the context of the visual structure of a military camp. There, it is a *dispositif* that constrains visually: 'The camp is the diagram of power that acts by means of general visibility.'[19] The diagram seems to appear in Foucault's book in places where visibilities are explained. This is a fortuitous example since it shows that the diagram of visibilities appears in two different systems, the prison and the barracks. Deleuze compresses the two terms into his abstract machine in order to explain the non-representational, abstract, but real aspect of the diagram:

> The *diagram* is no longer an auditory or visual archive but a map, a cartography that is coextensive with the whole social field. It is an abstract machine. It is defined by its informal functions and matter and in terms of form makes no distinction between content and expression, a discursive formation and a non-discursive formation. It is a machine that is almost blind and mute, even though it makes others see and speak.[20]

The trait of abstraction guides the path of the abstract machine to join with the diagram on the surface level of the text. The dimension opened through this operation is the zone present in Deleuze and Guattari's philosophy, which can only be grasped, with excitement and excitation, by putting a finger on something that is not there – by opening our eyes as wide as possible so as to see through and around what remains invisible.

Deleuze on Kant's Schema

It is within the pages of *Foucault* that Deleuze compares Foucault, the philosopher, to Kant. He draws a correlation between the Foucauldian diagram and the Kantian schema.[21] First, he explains the incongruity between the visible and the articulable in Foucault's theory: the visible as determinable and the articulable as determination. Light, the visible, is receptive; language, on the other hand, is spontaneous. In establishing the analogy, Deleuze posits Kantian intuition as receptive and understanding as spontaneous, intuition as determinable and understanding as determination. Deleuze writes, 'Kant therefore had to invoke a third agency beyond the two forms that was essentially "mysterious" and capable of taking account of their coadaptation as Truth. This was the *schema* of imagination.'[22] This bridge is then compared to the 'non-place' of the disparity between the visible and the articulable. This non-place, this new dimension, is, as we have seen with Klee's help, the diagram. Deleuze ties up the analogy neatly, linking Kant's 'mysterious' agency to Foucault's 'enigmatic' incongruence: 'The word "enigmatic" in Foucault corresponds to mystery in Kant, although it is part of a completely different whole and distributed differently.'[23] Even if the analogy is balanced by these terms, it appears that the notions of the enigmatic and mystery enfold the comparison into a haze of difficulty:

> Foucault's diagrammaticism, that is to say the presentation of pure relations between forces or the transmission of pure particular features, is therefore the analogue of Kantian schematicism: it is this that ensures the relation from which knowledge flows, between the two irreducible forms of spontaneity and receptivity. And this holds in so far as the force itself enjoys a spontaneity and receptivity which are unique to it even though they are informal, or rather because they are informal.[24]

Architectural theorist Sanford Kwinter, in turn, establishes an analogy between Deleuze's diagram and Kant's schema. The schema and the diagram are both machines or contraptions, or, as Kwinter suggests, 'synthetic explanatory devices (though they are no less real for that)'.[25] They are not transcendental, but synthetic, artificial, assembled – like machines. The schema and the diagram fulfil a function: they are material devices. Their materiality is not, however, of the visible and solid kind we are used to. The function of these devices is to 'open up a space through which a perceptible reality may be related to the formal system that organizes it'.[26] This schema/diagram negotiates machinically between reality and an abstract system that organizes it. Kwinter insists the diagram is not a mechanism operating through 'reduction', that is, taking away from the manifold of reality in order to make its object fit into an organized system. The process rather occurs through 'contraction', a function that Kwinter explains by referring to the medieval use of the term as a 'complication of reality'.[27] This function does not take away from the object, it does not reduce it or subtract from it; rather, the function folds the object. It makes it smaller so that it can traverse the process and then, once it has taken place in the system, be unfolded: 'This is important because once complicated or enfolded, every worldly thing harbours within itself the perpetual capacity to explicate or unfold.'[28] This concept redefines the whole notion of space and engenders 'a whole new set of problems'.[29] It certainly poses some degree of difficulty. Kant already called this notion of the schema 'the most difficult point'.[30] The diagram, therefore, can be understood as a difficult complication.

The comparison between diagram and schema must be envisaged keeping in mind that Deleuze's relationship with Kant is a precarious one. Deleuze saw Kant as a worthy opponent, an enemy of sorts, and also as a meteorological phenomenon, calling him the 'fog from the north'.[31] However, Deleuze does have an interest in Kant. 'K' stands for Kant in the *Abécédaire*, where he is called horrific but fascinating – and clearly great. The French philosopher compacted not just one but all three of Kant's critiques in a monograph that is not even one hundred pages in length. Deleuze was already practising the enfolding in a smaller space of an expansive architectonic. Furthermore, he summarized the philosopher's notion of time through four poetic formulas.[32] But Kant's schema keeps coming back in his writings. And the schema is a possible source of origin of the concept of the diagram, a relation strongly evinced in Deleuze's comparison between Foucault's diagram and Kant's schema.

But another line must be drawn between the concepts, in addition to Deleuze's comparison. The schema's function within Kant's architectonic must be spatialized and then made geographic. The purpose of this exercise is to make it compatible with Deleuze's diagram, which already has geographic and cartographic elements. Apart from the spatial imagery that Kant injects into his philosophical texts, he does not make a direct link between the schema and geography as Deleuze does with his diagram. This is why I enlist Martin Heidegger in our comparison of Kant and Deleuze, despite the fact that Deleuze's relationship with Heidegger is also strained. Deleuze writes about Heidegger in *Difference and Repetition* and mentions him in passing in other works. While he obviously does not deny Heidegger's important place in philosophy, he does disapprove of his 'mistake'.[33] Nevertheless, Heidegger's analysis of Kant's schema is invaluable, especially when coupled with the phenomenologist's notion of space leading to a philosophy of the earth – a philosophy that can be compared to Deleuze and Guattari's geophilosophy.

In *What Is Philosophy?* Deleuze and Guattari formulate a philosophy of geography. And even though *The Deleuze Dictionary* does not carry any entries for either geography or geophilosophy, these notions are of great consequence for the team's philosophical system. Deleuze and Guattari not only draw out the concept of geophilosophy and make the earth the foundation of thought, but they describe thought itself, with the plane of immanence where concepts form archipelagos, in terms of geographical landscapes. Even Kant, who they caricature at the beginning of the book in a paratextual sketch, finds redemption through geography.[34]

Geophilosophy is an attempt to think outside the categories of subject and object: 'Subject and object give a poor approximation of thought. Thinking is neither a line drawn between subject and object nor a revolving of one around the other. Rather, thinking takes place in the relationship of territory and the earth.'[35] Deleuze and Guattari create a clear relation between Kant and the earth. Or rather, they cast Kant as a figurehead at the bow of their theory of the earth. Immediately following these introductory sentences of their chapter on geophilosophy, they continue: 'Kant is less a prisoner of the categories of subject and object than he is believed to be, since his idea of Copernican revolution puts thought into a direct relationship with the earth.'[36] In *Kant's Critical Philosophy*, Deleuze demonstrates how Kant was bound by the categories:

> It would seem that Kant runs up against a formidable difficulty. We have seen that he rejected the idea of a pre-established harmony between subject and object; substituting the principle of a necessary submission of the object to the subject itself. But does he not once again come up with

the idea of harmony, simply transposed to the level of faculties of the subject which differ in nature?[37]

Deleuze does not doubt the originality of the transposition Kant performs, but he does not deem it original enough to demand an accord between the faculties when the *Critiques* in general demand one also.

If the chapter on geophilosophy begins with this particular problem in Kant, do Deleuze and Guattari propose to solve it with a spatialization of Kant's philosophy, making the earth the common accord? If so, the solution will not signify an end but rather mark the beginning of a new journey, since this earth as ground is not stable but demands constant movement, transposition: 'The earth is not one element among others but rather brings together all the elements within a single embrace while using one or another of them to deterritorialize territory.'[38] Deleuze and Guattari's concept of the earth is the grounding of the categories, but it is a malleable ground: 'Yet we have seen that the earth constantly carries out a movement of deterritorialization on the spot, by which it goes beyond any territory: it is deterritorializing and deterritorialized.'[39] The earth as the ground for pure intuition (practical) is a teeming ground: '[I]t neither moves nor is at rest.'[40]

Deleuze and Guattari present their own philosophy in geographic terms. Consequently, the single embrace of the earth is also internalized into thought: the geographic is the image of thought.[41] It comes as no surprise that in *Difference and Repetition*, the discussion of Kant's schema is generated in close proximity to a discussion of ideas as islands. With the aid of the geographic element of the island, Deleuze establishes the essential difference between ideas and concepts. In this definition of the concept in spatial and temporal terms, Deleuze mobilizes the notion that the schema plays an active role within the mechanism of the concept:

> Are not these spatio-temporal determinations what Kant called schemata? There is, nevertheless, an important difference. A schema is indeed a rule of determination for time and of construction for space, but it is conceived and put to work in relation to concepts understood in terms of logical possibility: this is so much part of its nature that it does no more than convert logical possibility into transcendental possibility. It brings spatio-temporal relations into correspondence with the logical relations of the concept. However, since it remains external to the concept, it is not clear how it can ensure the harmony of the understanding and sensibility, since it does not even have the means to ensure

its own harmony with the understanding without appeal to a miracle. Schematism possesses an immense power: it can divide a concept and specify it according to a typology. A concept alone is completely incapable of specifying or dividing itself; the agents of differenciation are the spatio-temporal dynamisms which act within or beneath it, like a hidden art.[42]

Can we not get closer to a diagram with Deleuze's explanation of the schema? The typological aspect constrains the concept in a similar way that the tracing constrains the mapping component of the diagram resulting in a device that is neither at rest nor in motion.

Deleuze explains the active mechanism of the Kantian schema in detail in a lecture in 1978, in which he describes two operations of knowledge for creating a correspondence between concepts and space-time. Concepts and space-time are heterogeneous, Deleuze explains, and so the correspondence between them will have to be a synthesis, an act of the imagination: 'Kant gives a fundamentally new meaning to the act of imagination, since it is the act by which spatio-temporal determinations will be put into correspondence with conceptual determinations.'[43] Deleuze explains that according to Kant, imagination does not produce images; instead, it is 'the faculty by which we determine a space and a time in a way that conforms to a concept, but that does not flow from the concept which is of another nature than the determination of space and time'.[44]

Two such correspondences exist between concepts and space-time: one is reproductive and the other productive. The reproductive imagination is the synthesis which forms a concept based on existing space and time: 'the concept is the form of the object which I qualify according to the diversity whose synthesis I have affected: it's a table, it's a house, it's a small dog.'[45] It is present in the here and now. The productive imagination is called the schema. It is not in the here and now because it is conceptual first: 'The schema: you have a concept, and the problem is to determine the spatio-temporal relation which corresponds to this concept.'[46] If synthesis is to be able to recognize a dog or a table or to think of one's friend, schema is to have a concept of the line that will allow us to trace a line – instead of thinking of our friend, we go and visit our friend: '[W]hile the synthesis went from the space-time intuition to the concept carried out by a rule of recognition, the schema on the contrary will operate by a rule of production.'[47] The opposition between synthesis and schema, between reproductive and productive, resembles the difference between tracing and mapping or diagramming: one repeats, the other discovers.

Deleuze makes the concept of the schema productive; to be able to recognize tables and trace lines is all very well, but what do we do when we are confronted with a lion? This is where Deleuze shows how his concepts of territories, rhythm and refrain are in part based on the schema.[48] Fundamentally, the question consists in asking what the rules are that govern the production of a lion:

> You can make yourself a concept of a lion; you can define it by genus and specific difference. You can define it in this way: big animal, mammal, with a mane, growling. You make a concept. You can also make yourself lion images: a small lion, a big lion, a desert lion, a mountain lion; you have your lion images.[49]

In his lecture on Kant, Deleuze seems to be balancing this notion: 'What would the schema of a lion be? I would say in this case, not in all cases that the concept is the determination of the species, or its [sic] the determination by genus and specific differences.'[50] Deleuze speaks of 'spatio-temporal attitudes [allures]', and the animal's territory, the path that it takes through its domain, and the frequency with which it takes them.[51] All these very real things are not going to give us an image, a concept of the animal; we will not be able to recognize the lion. These elements – the way that the territory is crossed, the sounds that are made, the traces that are left, the way the space is inhabited – are, for Deleuze, constitutive of a productive aspect of the animal: 'it's the way in which it produces a spatio-temporal domain in experience in conformity with its own concept.'[52] It is as if the Panopticon was determined by its light and window spaces instead of its walls. Or better yet, it is as if its walls were dissolved but the power relation due to visibility was still in place. In the case of the lion, these are the diagrammatical signatures on a territory of the animal, what the animal is when we do not see it: lurking and hunting, playing and surviving, tending to its territory. These elements are the statistics, the lines and the legends compiled and traced on a map: 'I would say that the schema of an animal is its spatio-temporal dynamism.'[53] In a more concrete example, '[t]he schema of the spider is its web, and its web is the way it occupies space and time.'[54] And so, from Deleuze's lecture, it becomes apparent that this device is related to space – but not any rudimentary notion of space. The schema is related to space as territory: the space an animal occupies with its abstract elements. It seems evident to Deleuze that Kant's schema is not too far from a constitutive geography.

Can we link the system according to the same abstraction with which we turn space into a territory, distilling an animal into a number of signs that constitute the limits of the animal's territory instead of the animal itself? After all, both the diagram and the schema are elusive and mysterious even within the context of the philosophy that supports them. Can the traits of a system be its metaphors, images and models: that is, the graphic traces of the philosophy contained in a system? Just as the lion's footprints, odours and trajectories are present in its territory but it is not, so we can find very real traces that indicate a philosophy without being the philosophy directly. The philosophy is not there, but its territory can be traced through the resulting images: these constitute the territory of the philosophy, its diagrammatic image. Van Berkel and Bos describe this process in their architectural diagrams; they trace the trajectory and the statistical displacement of pedestrians in a city to guide their conceptualization of a plan.

How do we direct Kant onto the plane where geography and philosophy meet, the plane occupied by Deleuze and Guattari? We must consider the geographic images of Kant's philosophy. But we must do so in the context of the totality of his system, since the constellation of geographic images directly refers to his philosophy as a whole. I will address this issue in Kant so as to shed light on how aesthetic images function in Deleuze and Guattari's system.

Stephen R. Palmquist addresses this dynamic of images in relation to systems.[55] He considers metaphors as models that, far from simply being ornaments in the text, are very important vis-à-vis the overall philosophical argument articulated in the ensemble of the system. Palmquist refers to Max Black's book *Models and Metaphors*, in which he explains the model as a 'sustained and systematic metaphor',[56] and underlines its function within an overall system: 'For models, like metaphors, furnish, "a distinctive mode of achieving insight, not to be construed as an ornamental substitute for plain thought".'[57] Black's notion of metaphor within a philosophical system is that of a filter – an organizing and constraining mechanism. The metaphor is the lens that allows the context in which it is used to be interpreted differently than initially conceived.[58] Palmquist's research focuses on geometric figures, such as circles and crosses, according to which he 'maps' Kant's work. Palmquist's use of the word 'mapping' to designate the activity of surveying a philosophical system underlines the depth of the concept: it designates the full activity of considering figures of thought as integral to the process of constructing a system and the fact that a system in its entirety is necessary to understanding discrete ideas. For Palmquist, this mapping[59] of the system according to figures results in a diagram: 'We will find that when Kant's System is mapped onto such figures, the resulting diagram, like a metaphor, "selects, emphasizes, suppresses, and organizes".'[60] According to Palmquist, Black anticipates the attack of sceptics on the productive aspect of metaphors and models by arguing rhetorically that 'recourse to models smack[s] too much of philosophical fable and literary allegory to be acceptable in a rational search for the truth.'[61] While Black seems to be using 'fable', 'literary' and 'allegory' to denigrate a particular philosophical practice, his use of the terms seems to be jumbled. This is why Tom Conley is crucial to the analysis of the duality of images and the whole of the philosophy containing them, as he counteracts the criticism of the sceptics anticipated by Black.

Conley's strength is to approach Deleuze's text and style of writing as an aesthetic object to be critiqued. He applies Deleuze's own theories to his works. Conley explores Deleuze's texts and images, the shape of his books, and how these further convey, through images, the philosopher's theories.[62] He brings aesthetic instances of Deleuze's writings into relation with the manner in which the text is arranged: that is, its topography. In fact, he maps out Deleuze's corpus and describes it spatially. It is no wonder Conley is also one of the few writers to have considered the concept of the diagram in depth. Because he writes about Deleuze's whole books as aesthetic objects, the diagram Conley isolates from these texts is considered in relation to the whole of Deleuze.

Specifically, Conley provides a convincing argument for the integration of images and metaphors in Deleuze and Guattari's philosophical text:

> The book acquires the appearance of a creation in the line of Alciati's *Emblematum liber*[63] or, perhaps, a piece of storyboarded philosophy that opens up visual and discursive 'lines of flight' within and through its typography. It asks the reader to look at paratactic patterns of images and texts as one might study different areas of an abstract painting.[64]

Conley argues that this allegorical model is actually an integral part of Deleuze and Guattari's philosophical articulation of ideas; it seems that instead of functioning as an allegory, the emblem inserted into *A Thousand Plateaus* functions as the anticliché diagram of Francis Bacon. It disturbs the text, and creates new conceptual possibilities through this *incongruence*. Palmquist, however, stops short of endorsing models as a way of actually producing philosophy: 'But, as long as we remember that conceptual models can only "furnish plausible hypotheses, not proofs" . . . and must be supported by more literal accounts, it will be safe to experiment with their explanatory power.'[65] My premise, however, goes one step further. I argue, in effect, that models, or diagrams, are an integral part of a system's organizational and ontological fabric. The metaphorical models I have in mind are not circles or crosses, but architectural elements that are part of Deleuze and Guattari's philosophy, as well as Kant's and Heidegger's. In what follows, the emblem for the diagram will be the house.

In *What Is Philosophy?*, Deleuze and Guattari draw up a description of a diagram of a house. More precisely, it is a description of isolated elements of a house. This amalgam of architectural elements comes together to form a theory of art based on the principle of the frame. Architecture, they write, is the 'first art of the frame'.[66] The reason this is a description of a diagram of an abstract house made up of framing devices is because it contains 'a certain number of enframing forms that do not determine in advance any concrete content or function of the edifice'.[67] This architectural incarnation of the diagram presents an image of a device that exists in its virtuality, in a state far-from-equilibrium before an actualization. The house they describe is 'floating', its parts detached. This is not a stable house. It is incorporeal:

> The wall that cuts off, the window that captures or selects (in direct contact with the territory), the ground-floor that wards off or rarefies ('rarefying the earth's relief so as to give a free path to human trajectories'), the roof that envelops the place's singularity ('the sloping roof puts the edifice on a hill').[68]

The citations are from Bernard Cache's *Earth Moves*, a book from which Deleuze draws when, in *The Fold*, he explains the curvatures of a line, the basis of his theory of folds. Here, the model of a house is parcelled into sections and opens up completely: its virtual structure that is not yet actualized is not placed on a ground and does not stand vertically on a surface. Instead, it is in motion and, because of its deframing components, opens as a system linking the sensations it captures to the cosmos:

> Interlocking these frames or joining up all these planes – wall section, window section, floor section – is a composite system rich in points and counterpoints. The frames and their joints hold the compounds of sensations, with their own appearance. These are the faces of a dice of sensation. Frames or sections are not coordinates; they belong to compounds of sensations whose faces, whose interfaces, they constitute.

Gilles Deleuze's Diagram 123

But however extendable this system may be, it still needs a vast plane of composition that carries out a kind of *deframing* following lines of flight that pass through the house-territory to town-cosmos, and that now dissolve the identity of the place through variation of the earth, a town having not so much a place as vectors folding the abstract line of relief.[69]

This is an image that may seem familiar: an architect's rendering of a building on a computer screen – animating its potential, disconnecting walls, calibrating the views from different angles and dynamic close-ups that simultaneously show the inside and the outside of the structure. Furthermore, similarly to Heidegger's temple, the house catches up to the earth. The earth is the house's ground in motion that brings all these floating elements together in its single moveable embrace.[70]

Heidegger Has a Plan

Diagrams – like the ones described by Van Berkel and Bos as distracting geographical and architectural elements that we can latch onto – break into the text in Kant's *First Critique* as metaphorical representations of his philosophical system. As the house is on the earth for Deleuze and Guattari, so it is for Kant and Heidegger. Heidegger depends, if not on geography, then on a notion of the earth, and, if not on architecture, then on a notion of building and dwelling in order to structure his path towards the ontological source of Being. However, the device that projects the earth into its representation as geography and collapses building and dwelling into their representation as architecture is the schema, a device Heidegger makes analogous with the notion of sketch.

Architecture is the first art of the frame. It frames the earth because of its contact with the ground. Both architecture and geography are spatial moulds because of this. Therefore, we do not stray by exploring geographic images through the contrivance of architecture.[71] When discussing his architectonic, Kant writes about the following edifice[72] with an attention to building materials:

> If I regard the sum total of all cognition of pure and speculative reason as an edifice for which we have in ourselves at least the idea, then I can say that in the Transcendental Doctrine of Elements we have made an estimate of the building materials and determined for what sort of

edifice, with what height and strength, they would suffice. It turned out, of course, that although we had in mind a tower that would reach the heavens, the supply of materials sufficed only for a dwelling that was just roomy enough for our business on the plane of experience and high enough to survey it.[73]

The architectural elements serve as a figure for the spatial organization of the structure of philosophy. In this passage, the word 'survey' appears. Again, it seems to hint at the visual and spatial characteristics of the architectural organization. The spatial organization is reinforced vertically through the architectural structure, which allows the possibility of surveying from the height of a tower as part of an empirically grounded structure. The structure may be empirically grounded, yet it reaches the heights of understanding. The trajectory taken by the schema is enacted as a device that allows for movement between the empirical ground and the realm of understanding. Kant removes himself from the metaphorical building and turns his attention to its graphic representation:

Now we are concerned not so much with the materials as with the plan, and, having been warned not to venture some arbitrary and blind project that might entirely exceed our entire capacity, yet not being able to abstain from the erection of a sturdy dwelling, we have to aim at an edifice in relation to the supplies given to us that is at the same time suited to our needs.[74]

Kant changes the focus from the material to the plan itself – from the building to the representation of the building. The plan is instrumental in the design of the building: it is the understanding as the end point of the conceptualization of the empirical.

In *The Critique of Pure Reason*, in the section 'Of the Schematism of the Pure Concepts of the Understanding', Kant describes the schema. The schema in itself, however, is not a clear concept; it is 'a hidden art in the depths of the human soul, whose true operations we can divine from nature and lay unveiled before our eyes only with difficulty'.[75] The device is powered by imagination, as Kant states, 'This representation of a general procedure of the imagination by which a concept receives its image, I call the schema of such a concept.'[76] It permits the movement of thought from empirical intuition to pure understanding, as it is through this device that concepts are formed. The problems that arise around the schema have to do with the notion of image.

Hannah Arendt, an unlikely reference for the treatment of Deleuze and Guattari, has a succinct formula for the schema. She also provides insight into Heidegger's texts on the issue. Indeed, Arendt,[77] building on Heidegger's own explanation of the Kantian schema through the concept of the image exemplified in the model of a house, bases her explication of the schema on an architectural example. 'The schema', she writes, 'through imagination, allows for the movement from the intuition to understanding'.[78] In her definition of the schema, Arendt isolates the movement in the device. The schema is a dynamic device, the movement of which covers the terrain between intuition and understanding. The orientation of this movement is directed from concrete to abstract levels of representation, hence the importance of imagination in concept creation in terms of images: 'And the way imagination produces the synthesis is by "providing an *image for a concept*". Such an image is called a "schema".'[79]

This image cannot be witnessed empirically: 'it is not given even to "the eyes of the mind".'[80] The schema is not an image as representation, but rather is like an image.[81] It *functions* like an image; in other words, it is a process. It is not a representation because representation implies a final result; again, the schema is a process. An image then, is figuration, visualization, iconicity – which implies that it is not closed or figurative, it is not a copy or a tracing. But there is another meaning to image: it is a framed totality. It is designated and denominated. In her architectural example, Arendt conspicuously discusses these two levels of representation as either drawing or building a house:

> Whenever one draws or builds a house, one draws or builds a particular house, not the house as such. Still, one could not do it without having this schema or *eidos* before the eye of one's mind. . . . Yet, though it exists in thought only, it is a kind of 'image'; it is not a product of thought, nor is it given to sensibility; and least of all is it the product of an abstraction from sensibly given data. It is something beyond or between thought and sensibility; it belongs to thought insofar as it is outwardly invisible, and it belongs to sensibility insofar as it is something *like* an image.[82]

When revising Kant's schema, Heidegger first establishes the strategic location of the section on schematism within the overall structure of the *First Critique*:

> The very fact of this allusion to the systematic place of the Schematism chapter within the ordering of the stages of the ground-laying betrays

the fact that these eleven pages of the *Critique of Pure Reason* must constitute the central core for the whole voluminous work.[83]

The schema, as described by Kant, is what permits the movement of thought from empirical intuition to pure understanding, as it is through this device (an incorporeal machine) that concepts are formed. We've seen above, however, that the schema itself – 'the hidden art in the depths of the human soul' – is not a clear device.[84] There is a reason why Kant describes the schema as an art, and a reason why graphics are mobilized to describe the look of the schema itself. In order to describe this mysterious device, Heidegger first starts by defining the schema as image in the guise of the very familiar notion of the sketch.

The notion of sketch is important in the discussion of the schema and the diagram. It carries a rich etymology that makes it profoundly apt in the context of this discussion. 'Sketch' in German is *Skizze*, a term that comes from the Italian *schizzo* meaning a splash or a squirt (these last two terms are akin to what Francis Bacon is doing to his paintings when he inserts 'diagrams'). 'Sketch', as the French *esquisse*, comes from the Greek root *skheim* (the word for schema) or *ekhein* (as in 'to have', 'to hold').

Kant's representation of the architectonic as a house is echoed by Heidegger, as he proceeds to find different ways of representing the schema. Moving from two to three dimensions, Heidegger seeks to offer a more complex model of the schema. He traces a trajectory starting from the plan[85] in the context of construction. In fact, the house does not move the discussion from a purely representative artistic object to an empirical one. The house is pertinent to the discussion of the schema because of Heidegger's conflation of image with construction and building. A house described with words also serves as a sketch of a house since it falls under the span of *graph*:

> We say: this house which is perceived, e.g., shows how a house in general appears, and consequently it shows what we represent in the concept house. In what way does the look of this house show the 'how' of the appearing of a house in general? Indeed, the house itself offers this determinate look, and yet we are not preoccupied with this in order to experience how precisely this house appears. Rather, this house shows itself in exactly such a way that, in order to be a house, it must not necessarily appear as it does. It shows us 'only' the 'as . . .' in terms of which a house can appear.[86]

Heidegger uses the house as an example of an object that is transformed by the Kantian schema into an object of understanding. He demonstrates the discrepancy between the object and its concept. As an integral element of schematization, the sketch – in essence approximate: pliable, elastic and nimble – allows for the conversion of an object into the general concept.

The model of the house multiplies the possibilities of an image. Heidegger models his discussion on the spatial schema Kant describes. The house represents the visual possibilities of a general concept of a particular object. The mental image of the house is not stable, but unlike the frames of representation multiplied in his explication of photography, the house as an actual object breaks out into frames that in their instability permit the empirical structure to be transposed into a concept. And so Heidegger writes:

> What we have perceived is the range of possible appearing as such, or, more precisely, we have perceived that which cultivates this range, that which regulates and marks out how something in general must appear in order to be able, as a house, to offer the appropriate look.[87]

As a visual representation of an object of space, the structure of the house is torn apart and reconstructed in the sketch. This occurs because the sketch is a peculiar kind of visual representation; it is a process and not a final 'picture'. What it holds, it can only hold in its parts, but these parts are infinitely more complete than a whole. A final representation of a house standing on a hill will only represent its façade and roof or two intersecting walls, depending on the point of view of the draughtsman. A sketch, because it is a process, can show an X-ray view of the structure, depict the floors separately, and perhaps give us the dimensions and measurements, cross-sections, and a map of where it is situated.

The sketch shatters the totality of the structure in order that it can be conceptually grasped: 'This initial sketching-out [*Vorzeichnung*] of the rule is no list [*Verzeichnis*] in the sense of a mere enumeration of the "features" found in a house. Rather, it is a "distinguishing" [*Auszeichnen*] of the whole of what is meant by [a term] like "house".'[88] Despite the fact that Heidegger qualifies the sketching-out as initial, the concept of the sketch is introduced only at the end of the sequence in the example. The sketch offers a view of the whole of the house as a conceptual image: a rapid sketch of the frames that make up the structure of the now broken down house, abstracted to the point where the house can be grasped in its totality. The collapse of the standing house, flattened to the level of the sketch, is an inverted *building* of the house as a concept. The sketch in itself builds a house – not a solid one, but its conceptual schema: 'The formation of the schema [*Schemabildung*] is the making-sensible of concepts. How is the look of the immediately represented being related to what is represented of it in concepts?'[89] The question posed by Heidegger constitutes the hidden art of the schema, and as both Heidegger and Kant mention, it is a hard question to answer.[90]

Sketching is thus essentially the building of images through ripping open and creating rifts. To recapitulate an already clear point, the house exists as an empirical object; tearing this structure apart, breaking the object into fragments, is actually building a concept of it.[91] In other words, we take apart the empirical and build it as a concept:

> Now if, however, as the Transcendental Deduction indicates, pure intuition (time) stands in an essential relation to pure synthesis, then the pure power of imagination carries out the forming of the look of the horizon. But then it does not just 'form' [*bildet*] the intuitable perceivability of the horizon in that it 'creates' [this horizon] as a free turning-toward. Although it is formative in this first sense, it is so in yet a second sense as well, namely, in the sense that in general it provides for something like an 'image' [*Bild*].[92]

This schematic building, through the imagination (an integral component of the mechanism of the Kantian schema), if already visual and spatial, requires a crucial element in order to achieve the 'second sense' of image that Heidegger mentions: that is, time.

But before we get to this essential question, it is necessary to study an example from Heidegger's philosophy in which, on the surface, sketch (as outline), space and ripping open are operational in Heidegger's own concept building. First, Deleuze nominates Kant as the founder of phenomenology, locating the foundation of this philosophical discipline in the distinction between appearance and appearing. Appearance, a Platonic term, is fraught with sensory illusions and must be left behind for the loftier truth of the essence. Kant, Deleuze writes, breaks with this paradigm by introducing the notion of apparition:

> There is phenomenology from the moment that the phenomenon is no longer defined as appearance but as apparition. The difference is enormous because when I say the word apparition I am no longer saying appearance at all, I am no longer at all opposing it to essence. The apparition is what appears in so far as it appears. Full stop.[93]

This comment is important because it aligns Kant's notion of apparition with an empirical notion of vision. This is taken up by Heidegger's phenomenological stance when he comments on the notion of appearing as the spatial form of representation: 'appearing in the first and authentic sense, as the gathering bringing-itself-to-stand, takes space in; as standing there, it creates space for itself; it brings about everything that belongs to it, while it itself is not imitated.'[94] This statement chimes with Heidegger's pronouncement on *Dasein* in *Being and Time*: 'In the literal sense, Da-sein takes space in.'[95] The second sense of appearing is contrasted to the first as a space that is already prepared, a space that is not taken in. As such, it 'steps forth from an already prepared space, and it is viewed by a looking-at within the already fixed dimensions of this space. The visage offered by the thing, and no longer the thing itself, now becomes what is decisive.'[96] While in the first instance, it was not imitated, in the second instance, it is the visage the thing offers as representation that is decisive. Heidegger then states the following formula: 'Appearing in the first sense first rips space open. Appearing in the second sense simply gives an *outline* and measures the space that has been opened up.'[97]

When he articulates the concept of appearing, Heidegger uses space as a way of delimiting the concept. Since it is in visual terms that appearing is important to the distinction between *idea* and *phusis*, Heidegger dresses appearing in space. The footnote to this passage reads, 'Heidegger is contrasting the verb *aufreißen* (to rip open) with the related noun *Aufriß* (an outline, diagram, architectural projection, or perspective view).'[98] *Aufriß* carries the connotation not of a mere sketch, but of a sketch animated in time, a schema. The outline, taken in, from the Kantian outside spatial to the internal temporality, creates an internal dynamic space. This is not an outline but a sketch insofar as it is diagrammatical – a static space internalized and put into motion through time. Provided that the concept of the sketch we are dealing with here is not mere representation but the closest we can get to the image of the unrepresentable, it is wise first to see what Heidegger does with the concept in terms of artistic representation in 'The Origin of the Work of Art'. Here, the concept functions by being grounded more deeply than in space: on the earth.

It would be simplistic to try to elucidate Kant's concept of schema through Heidegger's notion of art simply because Kant called his schema the 'hidden art'. But because Heidegger discusses the grounding of art in terms of a sketch or a schema, Kant's notion of the schema must be approached through art. The duality of art and schema is present in both philosophers' work but in very different contexts. Whereas Kant uses *art* as a *metaphor* to describe the elusive concept of the schema, Heidegger plays on the word schema – that is, *sketch*, which also means *rift* – in order to define *art*. The arrow points in the opposite direction in the case of each philosopher.

The concept of the rift as sketch and fissure is a paradoxical one, but luckily it carries a set of instructions: because the rift opens and brings together, splits apart and unifies – it must function in space and it is a spatial concept. Heidegger's concept of space, as described in both 'Building, Dwelling, Thinking' and *Being and Time*, is animated by such paradoxical dynamism and is the solution I will propose for the duality of Heidegger's concept of rift that opens up as it collapses distances. Finally, if the space used to describe this paradoxical movement is endowed with any kind of dynamism, it must be because time is part of the equation. This dynamism emerges through the notion of rift in two consecutive manifestations: first, rift as sketch; and then, rift in the earth. It is the rift as incongruence.

The static, representational level of the schema already allows thought to pass through to a space that is non-representational. In this sense, 'thinking gets through, persists through, the distance' from circumspective space to location.[99] Philosophy, if it is taken in its representation in language, is spatial because for Heidegger, language is spatial: '[B]oth the self-interpretation of Da-sein and the content of significance of language are to a large extent dominated by "spatial representations" in general.'[100] The mechanism collapsing the distance in the spatial schema also collapses the distance between the representation of philosophy and philosophy itself. But the articulation of *Dasein* is not dependent on space; Heidegger makes sure to deflate the importance of space as the representation of philosophy: 'This priority of the spatial in the articulation of significations and concepts has its ground, not in some specific power of space, but rather in the kind of being of Da-sein.'[101] Because *Dasein* takes space in, this spatial representation is diagrammatical; a temporal sketch captures the non-representational. The image of a concept cannot be represented but can be articulated through a series of suggestive sketches that are framed and slowed down in time. Space and time become the condition of representation in philosophy; but even more, it is the diagrammatical dynamic that animates them both as non-representational forms and allows for an adequate sketch of thought.

In its second manifestation, the notion of rift as sketch progresses towards a rift in the earth. The sketch, or outline, is defined by Heidegger in a very particular context: the earth itself is the foundation of art. This art that is grounded upon the earth constitutes a realm of art whose core is the rift, itself grounded in the earth. Heidegger takes us from the earth as location

Gilles Deleuze's Diagram

to the imagination. The imagination is central to the mechanism of the schema for Kant as well as Heidegger:

> Earth, bearing and jutting, strives to keep itself closed and to entrust everything to its law. The conflict is not a rift (*Riß*), as a mere cleft is ripped open; rather, it is the intimacy with which opponents belong to each other. This rift carries the opponents into the source of their unity by virtue of their common ground.[102]

Let us not forget that in the *traits diagrammatiques*, which are the orientational, directional movements of the plane of immanence, trait can also mean 'to pull' in the Middle French, which is not only about action of extraction (from the earth and from the skin) but can be taken to mean 'to rend apart', 'to draw and tear apart', which is particularly fitting in this Heideggerean context. But to bring it even closer to Deleuze and Guattari's definition of the plane of immanence, which is the instauration of the concept (the beginning of philosophy): 'The plane is clearly not a program, design, end, or means: it is a plane of immanence that constitutes the absolute ground of philosophy, its earth or deterritorialization, the foundation on which it creates its concept.'[103]

Having grounded the rift on the earth, Heidegger defines it more concretely in terms of sketch than we have understood it until now. Playing with the dual meaning of *Riß*,[104] Heidegger is able – after he has discussed rift as a fissure in the earth that nevertheless brings two opponents together – to describe the rift as an outline:

> It is a basic design, an outline sketch, that draws the basic features of the rise of the lighting of beings. This rift does not let the opponents break apart; it brings the opposition of measure and boundary into their common outline.[105]

Yet, in this context the rift does not merely tear apart but brings together through the incision. We see the contraction of two concepts: equally grounded on the earth, equally constructed as a building might be. The space the rift opens or closes is present as a space marking the contraction. It can be read through Heidegger's notions of space in 'Building, Dwelling, Thinking' and the notion of circumspective space elaborated in *Being and Time*. The rift is not a mere sketch, but a space that opens up in the collapse of a distance. It is also open to the dynamism the Kantian schema carries in its temporal facet.

Time is what accounts for the dynamics of the spatial representation and gives a schema its movement. We have to go back to Kant to see how space and time constitute the schema: on the outside, space; on the inside, time. Thus Kant, in his Transcendental Aesthetic, states: 'Time can no more be intuited externally than space as something in us.'[106] In the section on the Schema, Kant explains:

> [The image] is a product of the empirical faculty of productive imagination, the **schema** of sensible concepts (such as figures in space) is a product and as it were a monogram of pure *a priori* imagination, through which and in accordance with which the images first become possible.[107]

The image, in a first step, must then be attached to its concept. It can only be so through the schema. And the schema, at the same time that it connects the image to its concept, opens a gulf between the two that is never fully closed: an incongruence must exist. The schema opens the rift by drawing attention to it. The gulf is already there. It is part of one matter, which is why it opens and closes at the same time: it is a contraction folding and unfolding instead of cutting and dividing. The schema simply outlines this process. The schema, then, cannot be converted into an image and remains unrepresentable. This unrepresentable state, however, has a shape. It is not the shape of an amalgam of many fragments of a house brought into a totality. The possible shape, if we can imagine, is the shape the synthesis would take if it could be perceived, as it brings the many fragments together.

> The schema of a pure concept of the understanding, on the contrary, is something that can never be brought to an image at all, but is rather only the pure synthesis, in accord with a rule of unity according to concepts in general, which the category expresses, and is a transcendental product of the imagination, which concerns the determination of the inner sense in general, in accordance with conditions of its form (time) in regard to all representations, insofar as these are to be connected together *a priori* in one concept in accord with the unity of apperception.[108]

In a metaphorical flourish, we can describe the schema as something that, in order to function to represent the unrepresentable, goes inside of itself through time and leaves its outside spatial shell to collapse. The schema is therefore non-figurative and produces the link between the image and the concept, which makes the figure appear as a rift.

This house is located somewhere between the graphic representation of its structure and its actual structure. But as representation, it dissolves between both. This fluid terrain the schema occupies is of an image, not as *logos* or *analogon*, but rather as a graphic sketch. Two elements come into the construction of the schema: space, which outlines the schema's empirical image; and time, its inner, dynamic aspect as image of understanding. The graphic aspect of the schema must be approached at the diagrammatical juncture between both space and time. The point of focus is the movement of the schema between both on the terrain that can be represented spatially. It is the closest we can hope to get to an outer representation of the schematic process.

Time as schema is central to the process: 'Although it is formative in this first sense, it is so in yet a second sense as well, namely, in the sense that in general it provides for something like an "image" [*Bild*].'[109] This schematic building, through the imagination (an integral component of the mechanism of the Kantian schema), if already visual and spatial, requires a crucial element in order to achieve the 'second sense' of image that Heidegger mentions: time. The house, as in a Cubist painting, shows more facets of the objects represented than it would through a classical perspective.

How can time be brought into Deleuze's vastly spatialized diagram? For this, we would have to go back to the geography constituting the concept inhabiting the plane of immanence. There, the concept is surveyed at infinite speeds. Perhaps time enters the diagram through another facet than the one explored here: a facet closer to the poetic formulas with which Deleuze captures Kant's notion of time.

Kant Makes a Map

Kant spent 40 years teaching a geography course. Clocking the subject just under the amount of time he taught logic and metaphysics, it is worth noting, from the perspective of geophilosophy, that he was among the first to introduce it to the university.[110] It is little wonder that Kant resorts to geographic metaphors to represent his architectonic in *The Critique of Pure Reason*.[111] These metaphors are instrumental in the self-reflexive process of the philosophical system. They gather weight in their function as a commentary on systematicity in their capacity as images: they add a spatial articulation to the process of imagining the system. And, more precisely, they reflect on system from the vantage point of the system's boundary. To reflect on the system, one must be part of it, but enough on the sidelines to see it from the broadest angle – in a similar way to standing against a wall to see most of the room. The following passage displays such geographical and spatial imagination – it should be read as a map:

> We have now not only **traveled** through the land of pure understanding, and carefully inspected each part of it, but we have also **surveyed** it, and determined the **place** for each thing in it. This **land**, however, is an **island**, and enclosed in unalterable **boundaries** by nature itself. It is the **land** of truth (a charming name), **surrounded** by a broad and stormy **ocean**, the true seat of illusion, where many a **fog bank** and rapidly melting **iceberg** pretend to be **new lands** and, ceaselessly deceiving with empty hopes the **voyager** looking around for new **discoveries**, entwine him in adventures from which he can never escape and yet also never bring to an end.[112]

A geographical system organizes the totality of the earth in a textual form. More precisely, geography, as a representation of the physical earth, serves to *schematize* the earth so that it can be grasped systematically in its totality. Therefore, it offers an image of an object that can be surveyed in its totality in a representational form. *Surveyed* here emphasizes the function of the image both in a visual and in a spatial sense. While describing the geographic traits of their image of thought, especially in the way that concepts on the plane of immanence constitute an archipelago, Deleuze and Guattari invest into the word survey: 'The concept is in a state of *survey* [*survol*] in relation to its components endlessly traversing them according to an order without distance.'[113] It is a bird's eye view or an immanent aerial perspective of the concept conducted at infinite speed.

Geographical images as a way of reflecting on the architectonic are not simply metaphors of a philosophical system but of the constitution of a system proper. Richard Hartshorne restricts the field of vision to a geographical perspective, showing how in the eighteenth-century theories were developed for the purpose of inserting the human being into a system of nature. In this context, however, they were part of the geographical setting; humans, in Kant's period, are part of the landscape:

> For Butte the individual lands and districts were 'organisms' which like any organism included a physical side – inanimate nature, and a psychical side – animate nature including man. 'The unit areas (*Räume*) assimilate their inhabitants' and 'the inhabitants strive no less constantly to assimilate their areas.'[114]

Geography was organized in such a way as to become an organism, with the human being as a vital component of the structure. And, as this image strikingly conveys, the struggle between area and inhabitant, each trying to make the other assimilate, constitutes the organism. The process is akin to sinking in a bog: the more one struggles the more one sinks. The notion that the inhabitant is dependent on nature and the surrounding environment is inescapable in Kant's time: 'Thus Kant not only included man as one of the features, "encompassed in the earth surface (*Erboden*)", but also considered man as one of the five principal agents affecting changes on the earth.'[115] The space the inhabitants occupy on the physical ground, insofar as they are part of the system of nature, indicates the importance of the spatial location of the human being as part of existence and, by extension, as a ground for politics. The political concept of cosmopolitanism, for example, functions teleologically, enfolded within the overall system of nature: 'Yet it may be assumed that nature does not work without a plan and purposeful end, even amidst the arbitrary play of human freedom, this idea might nevertheless prove useful.'[116] On a larger scale, however, a systematic organization is crucial to the understanding of this view of the world. Nature, in its systematicity, provides a model for the organization of thought to be emulated. Cosmopolitanism is a product of such a systematic organization of the world:

> And although we are too short-sighted to perceive the hidden mechanism of nature's scheme, this idea may yet serve as a guide to us in representing an otherwise planless *aggregate* of human actions as conforming, at least when considered as a whole, to a *system*.[117]

The scale of organization of human action is not determined by a history, but by the spatial arrangement of nature's system.

For Kant, the geographical model represents this organization. It switches from the local to the general scale of existence. The spatial organization of geography illustrates the world of experience within a spatially organized system.

> Furthermore, we also have to learn to know the *totality* of the objects of our experience, so that our knowledge does not form an *aggregate* but a *system*; because in a system the whole precedes the parts whereas, on the contrary, in an aggregate, it is the parts that precede the whole.[118]

The movement between aggregate and system, between the local and the universal, is a representation in thought of the organization of the system of nature.

The problem of a geographical symbolism is not lost on Paul de Man,[119] who in his deconstructive treatment of Kant's concept of the sublime in the *Third Critique*, refers to another geographical image of Kant's. Kant argues that to see the world as sublime, we must look at it the way poets do and see the sky in terms of a vault and the ocean as a mirror.

> If, then, we call the sight of the starry heaven *sublime*, we must not place at the foundation of judgment concepts of worlds inhabited by rational beings and regard the bright points, with which we see the space above us filled, as their suns moving in circles purposively fixed with reference to them; but we must regard it, just as we see it [*wie man ihn sieht*], as a distant, all-embracing vault [*ein weites Gewölbe*] . . . To find the ocean nevertheless sublime we must regard it as poets do [*wie die Dichter es tun*], merely by what the eye reveals [*was der Augenschein zeigt*] – if it is at rest, as a clear mirror of water only bounded by the heavens; if it is stormy, as an abyss threatening to overwhelm everything.[120]

According to de Man, this is Kant's purest representation of his architectonic. However, de Man cautions the overly enthusiastic reader who might fall into the trap of interpreting the passage from a symbolist point of view and be swept away by Kant's poetics:

> [A] misguided imagination, distorted by a conception of romantic imagery, runs the risk of setting the passage awry. It may appear to be about nature in its most all-encompassing magnitude but, in fact, it does not see nature as nature at all, but as a construction, as a house.[121]

The way the poet sees the world then, according to Kant, is not symbolic, but through a formal, shallow and depthless vision.[122]

De Man explores Kant's discussion of the schema and the symbol in *The Critique of Judgement*, and by focusing on the figure of the hypotyposis,[123] he demonstrates the paradoxes that issue from the crux of philosophy and language, particularly from a philosophical language: 'Hypotyposis makes present to the senses something which is not within their reach, not just because it does not happen to be there but because it consists, in whole or in part, of elements too abstract for sensory representation.'[124] Giving a face to what is devoid of it can be split into two cases: the schemata, on the one hand, and the symbol, on the other:

> Things are different in the case of genuine hypotyposis. A relationship exists but it can differ in kind. In the case of schemata, which are objects of the mind (*Verstand*), the corresponding apperception is a priori, as would be the case, presumably, for a triangle or any other geometrical shape. In the case of symbols, which are objects of reason (*Vernunft*) comparable to Condillac's abstractions, no sensory representation would be appropriate . . . but such a similarity is 'understood' to exist by analogy.[125]

But the difference between schemata and symbol is not clearly defined: de Man reveals the word 'perhaps' infiltrating Kant's text, and shows that on this word is hinged the uncertainty of language and the impossibility of systematizing it through philosophy. Yet the dimension at which this paradox can be accessed is on the surface level of language, a surface pierced through in the nineteenth century:

> He who takes it [language] and gives it the attributes of predictability and transcendental authority that pertain to the objective reality of entities unmediated by language is guilty of reification . . . and he who thinks that the symbolic can be considered a stable property of language, that language, in other words, is purely symbolic and nothing else, is guilty of aestheticism – 'whereby nothing is seen as it is, not in practice either'.[126]

De Man demonstrates how Kant's concept of the schema unravels the text that it is supposed to hold up, since symbol and schema, according to de Man, do not adequately cover the field of language in a systematic way. The schema for de Man is a device that makes Kant's architectonic cohere, but at the same time, the schema is a loose thread that, if pulled ever so slightly, will make the text unravel. It is a delicate operation since Kant himself is aware of its weakness, calling it a true secret, a hidden art. The schema's strength lies in this concealment. The device cannot be something rigid. Rather, it must allow the movement between language and thought, text and philosophy like giant high-rise buildings swaying in the wind. Without the structural play, a building that is too rigid will crack and fall, but the curvature of a high-rise is an illusion: the dome of the eyeball curving the straight line. De Man is able to pull at the schema to make language topple because he makes it rigid, as evidenced in his description of 'the infinite . . . frozen into the materiality of stone'.[127] This is for de Man the material teleology of the sublime dynamic, when the formal aspect of language shows itself in a frozen, rigid moment.

This world perspective in Kant is concretely, if insufficiently, manifested in his *Physische Geographie*: an attempt at the systematic representation of the earth and, at the same time, a reflection of Kant's desire to restructure the science of geography through an organization of the geographical categories and the terrain that geography, as science, is destined to cover. Kant was forced to publish his *Geography* towards the end of his life (1804) in order to put his name to an official edition after enthusiastic students published a pirated version of his lectures on geography.[128] The end product of his 40 years teaching geography, *Physical Geography* is Kant's attempt at a systematic model of the surface of the earth and it reads like a pleasure trip to a dream world. The theme of travel is addressed in the opening pages of the *Geography*, putting into question the issue of movement, not only the physical movement on the surface of the earth, but also the intellectual movement required to have an image of the world:

> We anticipate our future experience, the one that we will later have in the world, thanks to an instruction and general survey of the kind that provides us with a preliminary concept of all things. Of one who has made many trips, we say that he has seen the world. But he who wants to gain a profit from his voyage must already have sketched a plan in advance and not be satisfied with looking at the world as an object of the eternal sense.[129]

The schema is invoked in this context of travel by the words 'sketch' and 'plan'. Kant, of course, is not describing the philosophical concept here, but we can take these words at their shallow meanings and infer some inchoate depth that reveals the philosophical concept. The main difference between the sketch and the concept of the schema lies in Kant's use of the sketch to literally mean image or representation. The sketch here is closer to the 'graphic' component of geo*graphy*, in the sense of a representative or descriptive rendition of an object – in this case, the earth – through writing or drawing.[130] As an image of the world, the *Geography* behaves like a map that allows the readers to orient themselves in the world. But of course the concept of the schema has to intrude if we are to use a sketch as a representation of the world. The concept of the schema is not actually an image, not even in the sense of an image in the mind. Kant seems, in a first instance, to reject practical experience, stating that it is said of the one who has travelled extensively that he has seen the world. The traveller has experienced the world but has not drawn any profit from this experience since he has not started from a general overview that would have given him a preliminary concept of all things. In order to profit from the trip that one undertakes in experience, one has to first sketch out a plan (i.e. to create a general concept of the object) or abandon the possibility of penetrating deeper than the surface of the object. Objects of practical experience have to be transformed into general concepts to reap profit from them in the form of understanding. Therefore, the *Geography* serves as a sketch of the empirical that permits the formation of general concepts that, in turn, will guide the reader in his future travels. Within the context of geography as a middle term between theory and practice, orientation is a concept that allows us to devise a path from the practical to the theoretical.

While tracing a possible origin of the diagram within the Kantian schema, the spatial aspect, with all of its dimensions, comes to light. The schema, viewed through a spatial perspective and read in its temporal dimension, exhibits elements of a device that is productive, instrumental and active in the systematic organization of thought. The movement from the real to the systematic is one that drags – to use a word associated with Heidegger's conceptualization of space – time and space with it. The diagram, as a concept of Deleuze, is not a path that is to be taken. It is a dimension that is productive. It functions through constraint and it breathes. It folds and unfolds like lungs.

Conclusion

The fog of the north might have wafted a geographical imagination to Deleuze and Guattari's own configuration of the inner workings of philosophy. The landscape representing their image of thought is not the terrain fraught with danger Kant perceives, but an archipelago inhabited by birds with two wings and fish with two fins. 'Mental landscapes do not change haphazardly through the ages: a mountain had to rise here or a river to flow by there again recently for the ground, now dry and flat, to have a particular appearance and texture.'[131] Deleuze and Guattari have followed the map drawn by Kant. The diagram – as a critical mode of representation of an image that is not quite an image or, more precisely, the terrain between the visible and the articulable – steers the traveller clear away from the illusions forewarned by Kant floating between the icebergs and islands. The diagram is the mechanism to get us out of the 'internal arctic zone where the needle of every compass goes mad'.[132] And applied to Kant's map, the diagram is our navigational tool to manoeuvre away from the 'Nordic fogs that cover everything'.[133] The diagram disperses the fog to reveal an extraordinary architecture.

In the following section, the geographic element will be explored, but with an anatomical addition. These two aesthetic threads will yield a blueprint of the conceptual becoming material.

Chapter 4

The Extraordinary Contraction

The extraordinary contraction refers to François Dagognet's assessment of a mechanism of imaginative folding between incongruent elements. Anne Sauvagnargues isolates this expression in order to describe the non-metaphorical analogical process of Étienne Geoffroy Saint-Hilaire in Dagognet's book, *Le catalogue de la vie: études méthodologiques sur la taxonomie*. Geoffroy Saint-Hilaire is a nineteenth-century French biologist who theorized a classificatory method based on inchoate functions of animals and therefore found fantastic and controversial connections across species' lines. Most strikingly, Geoffroy Saint-Hilaire theorizes the topological passage from a quadruped, like a dog, to a cephalopod, like a squid. For Geoffroy Saint-Hilaire, analogy is not a mere metaphorical suspect or confused resemblance. It is rather, according to Dagognet, an extraordinary contraction that accommodates monism within animal diversity. Geoffroy Saint-Hilaire establishes a structural morphology and breaks with past classificatory models. He is not interested in the exterior forms of organisms, unlike his main rival Georges Cuvier. Instead, he focuses only on the constituting matter of animals. This is because Geoffroy Saint-Hilaire believes that nature constantly reuses the same materials and only varies the forms they take.[1] Dagognet explains:

> This sort of unitary topological reading would immediately sanction the erasure of the separation – and correlatively found the difference – between invertebrate and vertebrate; it would transform completely the system, and bring it what it dreamed of: an extraordinary contraction; but one that is no longer the ancient or suspect assimilation nor an illusory confusion (in the continuity of beings, all are built on the same basis).[2]

The extraordinary contraction is the diagrammatic concept that allows the conjunction of two incongruous elements and the passage of an abstract function from one system to the next. Deleuze often refers to Geoffroy Saint-Hilaire in his writings, praising his notion of abstraction – a notion that skips over hard and fast categories and thus allows a possible passage between elements in a heterogeneity. And even though Deleuze does not refer to Geoffroy Saint-Hilaire directly in the context of the diagram or mention the extraordinary contraction as coined by Dagognet, it seems to be an apt image of the contracting function of the diagram. Before I explain the extraordinary contraction in detail, I will illustrate the various connections and contractions Deleuze performs throughout his corpus. First, I will focus on the images surrounding the archipelago and then I will focus on the squid that dwells within its waters.

In the first section of the chapter, I look at Deleuze's use of the image of the island to describe the plane of immanence. The plane of immanence is a variation on the diagram. The section ends with the fusion between the geographical image and the anatomical image – a fusion through which the traits of the landscape come to populate the body in a diagrammatical movement from one system to the next. The second section continues with the anatomical image that ends the first section. The anatomical system becomes the site of the extraordinary contraction: an ontological device that allows the transposition from one incongruent element to another. In effect, it shows a diagrammatic function in an assemblage. The third section shows how this contraction, through plicature, is involved in a literary context in content and form and how it ties into cinematic dynamism in the form of the egg. Here, I am describing the potential of folding within the egg that explains the Body without Organs (BwO). This section then introduces the final chapter, which will deal with foldings, topology and the skin in art.

Islands and Bones

What follows is not a discussion of landscape and the body but, more specifically, of geography and anatomy. The double episteme of geography and anatomy is crucial for Deleuze and Guattari because it serves to portray the image of their philosophy. *What Is Philosophy?* explains how the philosophical discipline of thought functions. In the process, a whole landscape emerges that makes the components of thought appear like so many geographic formations: immanence is a plane upon which concepts emerge like islands where they can be surveyed.

The object of anatomy provides a route for the exploration of the classification of knowledge, of the construction of ideas and the flexibility of epistemological models. It is the 'extraordinary contraction', the action of the body and thought at the same time. What fuses thought to the bone; what makes the swimmer that does not swim take the plunge? The geography is part of the ontology of the physical, thinking being. It combines with the landscape of the mind, which is geographical and physical instead of transcendental and ideal. It is the transcendental empiricist surface into which the swimmer plunges. 'Geography is not confined to providing historical form with a substance and variable places. It is not merely physical and human but mental, like the landscape.'[3]

The anatomical and geographical instances in Deleuze and Guattari's philosophy are wonderful images that think themselves, create their own concepts and organize their own system. Through them, Deleuze provides a guide to his corpus. From the point of view of aesthetics, I will follow the dual path with the aid of the concept of the diagram; as I am tracing the instances and the context of the diagram within the philosophical system, it will open up and shed light on the very mechanism of the system that holds the device of the diagram in its midst. The diagram will help us navigate the ocean's smooth surface and map out islands when and where they come forth, surging from the depths. Where nothing yet exists on the map – in the blank, smooth spots in the middle of the not-yet-crossed oceans, in the unexplored countries – it will trace monsters and skulls and bones.

There is the figure of a swimmer in Deleuze and Guattari's writing. In *What Is Philosophy?* artists[4] come back from the depths with their eyes red and their eardrums perforated; they cannot articulate what they have seen or heard. They have taken a dip into the deep end and, upon their return to the surface, suffer from the bends. The philosopher who stands on the firm ground is not always privy to the exploration of the unknown in philosophy. The diver or the artist has to be enlisted to leave the terra firma.

This exploration of the depth of the surface of the system of philosophy is the sport of a swimmer that cannot swim. In Proust, 'lifeguards are prudent, rarely knowing how to swim'.[5] Deleuze and Guattari recuperate a swimmer from Kafka, who famously noted in his diary on the day the war was declared that he went for a swim.[6] Also, an aphorism by Kafka reads:

> I can swim like the others only I have a better memory than the others, I have not forgotten my former inability to swim. But since I have not forgotten it my ability to swim is of no avail and I cannot swim after all.[7]

The action of swimming is also vital for Henri Bergson, who exercised a powerful influence on Deleuze. 'Action breaks the circle', announces

Bergson in *L'évolution créatrice*.[8] The circular argument Bergson writes against is illustrated by the idea of swimming. If you have never seen a man swimming, he writes, how could you even consider it a possibility? In order to swim, the swimmer would need to hold himself up on water and thus would already be able to swim. The action of reason consists in launching oneself from the solid land and throwing oneself into the water. Being used to the solidity of the land, the novice swimmer who does not yet know how to swim will try to hold on to the fluid water. The swimmer, Bergson writes, finally gets used to the inconsistency of the liquid. It is the same for our thought, he concludes, when it decides to take the plunge.[9]

Swimming is an essential skill when exploring Deleuze and Guattari's philosophical archipelago. In this section I will survey the open system that Deleuze and Guattari set up through their philosophy. 'Set up through', because their system is not dialectical, nor is it teleological. A system is given in detached parts, as a diagram. Instructions, which are given in the corpus, have to be followed. But they themselves have to be constructed. So readers can create their own instructions to follow a path of their liking in order to construct a system that is the very outcome of the instruction they have chosen to follow. For example, the premise could be that the image of islands that Deleuze invokes as early as the 1950s is used differently[10] than the image of islands that Deleuze and Guattari use in *What Is Philosophy?* A path can be burrowed through the system by tracking a duality that consists of, on the one hand, Deleuze's involvement with anatomy and the idea of biology following the call to arms he borrows from Spinoza, '[W]e do not yet know what the body can do',[11] and, on the other, a geography that starts off from a material survey of the earth as the ground for thought, but becomes a geography of the mind, the thought as landscape. Both anatomy and geography serve as aesthetic objects that Deleuze sometimes uses as examples to illustrate his philosophical theories, sometimes in their capacity as illustrations of concepts, and sometimes as concepts in themselves, ready-mades. I have chosen these two objects because they are present throughout the corpus and also because they are evocative and hard to miss.

Swimmers turn to Micronesian navigators, who can expertly figure out their place on the ocean because their bodies fuse with the landscape. They are not only looking at stars in the night, but are able to notice the difference in the water sprayed into the boat from the waves that change direction according to the current. In fact, Edward Casey relates the story of one such navigator who was better able to guide his boat by not looking at the ocean at all: he would retire into the cabin, lie down, and close his eyes and in that way he was able to feel the waves hitting the hull of the boat with more sensitivity and figure out his place in what was otherwise a smooth, unmarked space to Western eyes.[12] The island of their destination was always in movement but always present as a goal.

In *Getting Back into Place*, Casey considers the notion of space in relation to two phenomena, the body and the landscape: 'Pondering both curiosities, I am led to ask: are these two non-named – but intensely present – phenomena, landscape and body, somehow covertly connected when it comes to matters of place?'[13] Lyotard agrees with this conjunction: 'There would appear to be a landscape whenever the mind is transported from one sensible matter to another, but retains the sensorial organization appropriate to the first, or at least a memory of it.'[14] What is important to us here is the way that Lyotard describes the space of the landscape as the movement between two structures. This is the functional aspect of a vision of geography that organizes what is seen and thought of in terms of a structure. The movement, in diagrammatic traits, is itself analogical with the movement of the body in space. We can imagine space as a landscape in which the movement is twofold: the movement of one's body in the landscape or the movement of one's eyes over the landscape. Both these movements articulate space.

Lyotard formulates the duality between the landscape and the mind through the geographical image he creates of Kant's critiques. As in the passage above, Lyotard is interested in the passage from one state to the next, from one matter to the next. He uses certain rhetorical elements in Kant's introduction to the Third Critique to spatialize the notion of judgement and then draw a geographical model out of the spacing of the categories:

> What object could correspond to the Idea of this gearing of the faculties, which are understood as capacities for cognition in the broad sense, that is, as capacities to have objects (sometimes as realms, sometimes as territories, sometimes as fields) (*KUK*: 10)? This object could only be a symbol. Let's say, an archipelago. Each genre of discourse would be like an island; the faculty of judgment would be, at least in part, like an admiral or a provisioner of ships who would launch expeditions from one island to the next, intended to present to one island what was found (or invented, in the archaic sense of the word) in the other, and which might serve the former as an 'as-if intuition' with which to validate it. Whether war or commerce this interventionist force has no object, and does not have its own island, but it requires a milieu – this would be the sea – the *Archepelagos* or primary sea as the Aegean was once called.[15]

In order to get at an image of Kant's system, and particularly the image of the place of the Third Critique – or more precisely, the function of judgement within Kant's architectonic – Lyotard searches the spatial or topographical clues that Kant leaves at the beginning of the *Critique of Judgement* (*domaine, territoire, champ*): 'In the Introduction to the third *Critique*, the dispersion of the genres of discourse is not just recognized, it is dramatized to the point that the problem posed is that of finding "passages" (*Uebergänge*) between these heterogeneous genres.'[16] Assessing that an object representing the spatial arrangement of the architectonic can only be a symbol, Lyotard settles for the archipelago, a geographical image that spatializes concretely and designates the place of the object that he has in mind.

It would be useful here to remember Deleuze and his description of the virtual as a non-fictional symbol:

> The virtual is opposed not to the real but to the actual. *The virtual is fully real in so far as it is virtual*. Exactly what Proust said of states of resonance must be said of the virtual: 'Real without being actual, ideal without being abstract'; and symbolic without being fictional. Indeed, the virtual must be defined as strictly a part of the real object – as though the object had one part of itself in the virtual into which it plunged as though into an objective dimension.[17]

This is pertinent when we consider that Lyotard's use of the symbol comes directly from Kant's differentiation between the schema and the symbol in the Third Critique:

> All intuitions which we supply to concepts *a priori* are therefore either *schemata* or *symbols*, of which the former contain direct, the latter indirect, presentation of the concept. The former do this demonstratively; the latter by means of an analogy (for which we avail ourselves even of empirical intuitions) in which the judgment exercises a double function, first applying the concept to the object of a sensible intuition, and then applying the mere rule of the reflection made upon that intuition to a quite different object of which the first is only the symbol.[18]

For Lyotard, this symbol indicates the notion of the passage: 'All of these faculties find their object in this field, some delimiting a territory there, others a realm, but the faculty of judgment finds neither one nor the other, it ensures the passages between the others.'[19] This passage between

The Extraordinary Contraction

the abstract and the concrete is traced on the schematic function that Kant explicates in the Third Critique. Lyotard is in effect using Kant's own material to represent this very matter. Thus, Lyotard summons the archipelago as the possible symbol that will represent the place of the Third Critique in the architectonic and deconstructs it in a concise fashion.

After Lyotard has idiosyncratically restructured the categories delimited by Kant into discursive genres, which he now incarnates as islands, he argues that the faculty of judgement will be the admiral who launches expeditions between shores. Yet the faculty so described does not have an object: Lyotard liquefies his figure into the shapeless in-between of the islands, the sea. Here, this figure takes the shape of the *Archepelagos* or the main sea: the archipelago dissolves itself, flowing out into the ocean. The object, captured briefly in an image, turns out to be the image itself, the imageless image, the mechanism of which dissipates.

Perhaps this shapeless figure is the fog Deleuze complains about and which suffocates him.[20] On the same terrain of this image of the archipelago, what is made clearer is that the representation cannot be fictional, and hence the image of the archipelago is virtual, something real that does not dissolve. The space of passage that Lyotard dissolves, the sea that separates the islands of the archipelago, for Deleuze becomes a space with clear parameters that can be populated with a functional mechanism instead of being vaporized into a non-place. Since there are no representations, the islands do not stand for something and the ocean for something else; they are a process, a method, an Idea.

Another image of an island comes from the pages of *Cinema 2*. Deleuze describes the island of Stromboli, not from 'real life' but from the 1950 Rossellini film *Stromboli* starring Ingrid Bergman. The film's frames of representations are multiple and unstable. Deleuze's account of the island, as he describes a scene from the movie, is enough to be called an island on the page. It is Deleuze's paper-island in the shape of Rossellini's film. Rossellini's *Stromboli* is a film-island: an island made up of film stock. Furthermore, coming back to this paper-island, the description is not fully faithful to the film-island, which in turn is not fully faithful to the actual island; Deleuze's paper-island is also distorted in order to take on the shape of his philosophy. As Massumi explains, the diagram is false and true at the same time – false because it subsumes heterogeneities under its homogeneous unity and true since it underscores the artificiality of bringing together heterogeneous elements together.[21] Each of these islands is a representation of islands and is an island in itself. They are actual island concepts. Deleuze's paper-island carries all of these different layers of diagrams while at the same distancing itself from them:

> Thus, in Rossellini, the island of *Stromboli* passes through ever deeper descriptions, the approaches, the fishing, the storm, the eruption, at the same time as the foreign woman climbs higher and higher on the island, until description is engulfed in depth and the spirit is shattered by a tension which is too strong. From the slopes of the unleashed volcano, the village is seen far below, sparkling above the black waves, while the spirit whispers: 'I am finished, I am afraid, what mystery, what beauty, my God . . .' There are no longer sensory-motor images with their extensions, but much more complex circular links between pure optical and sound images on the one hand, and on the other hand images from time and thought, on planes which all coexist by right, constituting the soul and body of island.[22]

The *Stromboli* island, as described by Deleuze, does not illustrate an idea analogically. The dual geographical and anatomical elements are inchoate in this image of the island: Deleuze writes of the body and soul of the island as if it were more than just a geographical place. These anatomical and geographical elements make for a strange mix. In Rossellini's film this is captured, as Deleuze writes, by the descriptive elements being 'engulfed in depth' – as Bergman's character, in an attempt to flee from her stifling life with a fisherman, runs towards the mouth of the volcano. She is attempting to cross the island to a village on the opposite shore, a village with motorboats. The volcano that stands in her way could easily be crossed in the idea of the island if a line were drawn from one village to the next through the centre of the island. But as Bergman's character physically experiences the mouth of the volcano, the altitude and the sulphuric fumes, the idea of the linear trajectory is shattered – in the same way that the linear film is shattered, according to Deleuze, 'by a tension which is too strong'. The descriptive film narrative is now parcelled into close-up shots cut with images of the volcano, the night sky and the island from a distance. The representational image of the island is discarded and the possibilities of multiple, diagrammatic dimensions of the island are in turn presented.

Seen diagrammatically, another component this film-island encompasses is the cluster of various conceptual elements that make up the material Deleuze uses to construct his philosophical system. Islands are representations of planes, but they are also planes that can be sites in the philosophy according to which organization of the system is possible – as Deleuze explains in the block quote above, 'images from time and thought, on planes which all coexist by right, constituting the soul and body of the island'.[23] While the planes constituting the island represent a way of seeing thought in terms of archipelagos – discreet elements within a system – thought functions through subsystems of islands, images and various other elements. These elements function on their own terms and as the frame is opened to reveal another frame within it, the collapse of representation is complete and the idea that is represented by the image of the island is that very island itself. It is that idea immanent to itself.

Writing about the work of Serge Daney, a prominent French critic of cinema, Deleuze observes:

> The first period of cinema is characterized by the art of *Montage* – culminating in great triptychs and corresponding to the beautification of Nature or the encyclopedia of the World – but also by a depth ascribed to the image taken as a harmony or consonance, by a network of obstacles and resolutions in this depth . . . the role of always furthering a supplementary vision, a 'seeing more'.[24]

What we are doing here – putting into relation images of swimmers, navigators, oceans, islands – is in effect creating a montage of images, an aesthetic assemblage. In this discussion of Daney's critical work, Deleuze isolates the image used by the film critic with regard to the work of Eisenstein, the Russian filmmaker renowned for his pioneering montage technique. Furthermore, Deleuze calls 'the Cabinet of Doctor Eisenstein . . . a symbol of this great encyclopaedia'.[25] It is a figure of a film as an encyclopedia: the encyclopedia based on a timely arrangement of images and set in motion. This view of the system as an encyclopedia, as an aggregate of knowledge, is subtly discussed by Deleuze as pedagogy, the etymology of encyclopedia.

> Finally, this new age of cinema, this new function of the image, was a *pedagogy of perception*, taking the place of an *encyclopaedia of the world* that had fallen apart: a visionary cinema that no longer sets out in any sense to beautify nature but *spiritualizes* it in the most intense way.[26]

This constellation of cinematic motion, encyclopedia dispensing pedagogy, and images arranged in a *montage* is a good place from which to start a discussion of open systems – systems in motion, made of assemblages – before comparing them to the encyclopedia, that is, an encyclopedia filtered through cinema. Kinema, or movement, of the images in Deleuze's corpus articulates thought.

The idea of the island, writes Deleuze in *Difference and Repetition* – which in French, as *l'Idée d'île*, is a rather approximate anagram – is one such occurrence. The imprecision of the transposition of the letters from one word to the next, which detracts from the sharpness of this play on words, is complementary to Deleuze's overall view of the formation of concepts and the image of thought, which, according to him, have ripped and uneven edges. However, such a textual analysis should not be pursued any further if we are to get at what Deleuze is really writing about; instead, a juxtaposition of the island imagery he conjugates through his writings yields the complexity of the method as its evolution is observed.

In the pivotal passage, Deleuze considers the formation of islands as a model for the emergence of thought:

Take the Idea of an Island: geographical dramatisation differenciates it or divides the concepts into two types, the original oceanic type which signals an eruption or raising above the sea, and the continental drift type which results from a disarticulation or fracture.[27]

Deleuze treats the difference between the two types of islands in a recently published text that was written in the 1950s: the continental islands are described in 'Desert Island', the translated title of 'Causes et raisons des îles désertes', in more detail as 'accidental, derived islands. They are separated from a continent, born of a disarticulation, erosion, fracture; they survive the absorption of what once contained them.'[28] The oceanic type, however, has the element of organism incorporated into this more detailed definition: '*Oceanic islands* are originary, essential islands. Some are formed from coral reefs and display a genuine organism. Others emerge from underwater eruptions, bringing to the light of day a movement from the lowest depths.'[29] And to the definition of the oceanic island in *Difference and Repetition*, in the older version of the text, Deleuze adds an explicitly temporal element: 'Some rise slowly; some disappear and then return, leaving us no time to annex them.'[30] Finally, these islands about which Deleuze is writing do not remain static geographical organizations. The image implies a necessary dynamism: 'The Island dreamer, however, rediscovers this double dynamism because he dreams of becoming infinitely cut off, at the end of a long drift, but also of an absolute beginning by means of a radical foundation.'[31] The literary manifestations of the island bear witness to new depths in the context, especially the hybrid image of geographical and anatomical features.

Robert Smithson, the artist famous for Earth-Art and pieces such as *Spiral Jetty*, a spiral rock formation in a lake best appreciated from an airplane, describes his concept of 'abstract geology', the artistic depiction of a geography of the mind:

> One's mind and the earth are in a constant state of erosion, mental rivers wear away abstract banks, brain waves undermine cliffs of thought, ideas decompose into stones of unknowing, and conceptual crystallizations break apart into deposits of gritty reason. Vast moving faculties occur in this geological miasma, and they move in the most physical way. This movement seems motionless, yet it crushes the landscape of logic under glacial reveries. This slow flowage makes one conscious of the turbidity of thinking. Slump, debris slides, avalanches all take place within the cracking limits of the brain.[32]

It is this interconnection between mind and earth – between a geographical and spatial representation of the mind – that makes way for another epistemic coupling: as Smithson announces, the spatial representation of the mind comes into contact with a geography. This geography, it must be noted, is itself connected with the exteriority of the body. It constitutes a bridge of sorts:

> The entire body is pulled into the cerebral sediment, where particles and fragments make themselves known as solid consciousness. A bleached and fractured world surrounds the artist. To organize this mess of corrosion into patterns, grids, and subdivisions is an esthetic process that has scarcely been touched.[33]

This passage from Smithson illustrates where the notions of graphics, geography, and thought are to be taken: in the epistemic coupling of geography and anatomy placed upon diagrammatic elements – patterns, grids and matrices.

Deleuze and Guattari show that there is constant movement and change in the geography of the mind: 'Mental landscapes do not change haphazardly through the ages: a mountain had to rise here or a river to flow by there again recently for the ground, now dry and flat, to have a particular appearance and texture.'[34] The mental landscape is not a static image but a representation of the movement and dynamism that allows the transformation from one plane to the next. This is similar to what, in Claire Parnet and Deleuze's analysis, represents yet another configuration in which to imagine the mind – more specifically, the Unconscious.

> The analysis of the unconscious should be a geography rather than a history. Which lines appear blocked, moribund, closed in, dead-ended, falling into a black hole or exhausted, which others are active or lively, which allow something to escape and draw us along?[35]

An active image of a dynamic landscape of the mind appears on the page:

> Deleuze explores the epistemology of life sciences and privileges the pre-Darwinian variation of Geoffroy Saint-Hilaire, who is less evolutionist and historical than geographical and topological. It allows the exploration of the organic strata, by thinking the organic individuation as a cinematics of forces.[36]

The spatial element suffuses all other considerations within the discussion of knowledge and thought. But the movement of space, connoted by the suffusion, implies a temporal dynamism. In the process, what is important is the dynamic aspect; it is only then that space matters.

A passage from Combes reverses the relationship between metaphors as Smithson presented them. The mind's landscape transforms into a geography. She describes thoughts as environmental, geological, geographical objects. Furthermore, she shows how far Deleuze is situated from Plato's idealism by insisting that thoughts are not stars in the sky:

> Like every *real* being, like every fragment of the real that individuates itself, a thought takes root in a *milieu*, which constitutes its historical dimension; thoughts are not ahistorical, like stars in the sky of ideas. They emerge from a theoretical environment from where they get the seeds (*germes*) of their development, with the understanding that everything does not provide a seed for a thought and that every thought operates, in the theoretical *milieu* of the epoch where they are submerged (*baignent*), a selection. From this selective inscription within the epoch, thought structures itself, resolves little by little its problems and, in doing so, autojustifies itself.[37]

This passage can be considered as a gnome for what follows, a sort of small map or point of reference. Thoughts are individuating beings that are part of an environment that is not physical but theoretical. They emerge as islands do in the ocean, rather than being stars in the sky. Thoughts are already a thing present and eternal that have to be explored and exposed.

In order to describe the plane of immanence, Deleuze and Guattari must simultaneously describe the concept. The plane of immanence and the concept mutually define each other. The plane of immanence is an invisible mental landscape that can only be seen through the concepts occupying it. This place becomes noticeable through the objects occupying this space. It is like cities that appear to an airplane flying over dark continents when, after night has fallen, the lights come on. From the height of this plane, we can map out the geography of the plane of immanence because geography 'is not merely physical and human but mental, like a landscape'.[38] From geography to landscape, a conceptual movement must take place – from the flatness of geography to the verticality of the landscape as something mentally, aesthetically hierarchized, framed, hung on a wall.

There is another movement between geography as mental and the plane of immanence as thought in terms of geography: 'The plane of immanence is not a concept that is or can be thought but rather the image thought gives itself of what it means to think, to make use of thought, to find one's bearings in thought.'[39] The previous movement, from geography to a mental landscape, is conceptual, aesthetically ordering; it frames. The concepts are what frame the plane, in much the same way that a landscape is always framed by the limits of the canvas, the edge of a picture, the frame of the camera or the viewer's own field of vision. But it is an inverted frame, a frame that does the job from the inside, in-between. A frame of thought does not delimit: it surrounds and flows through, so it is more like a landscape described with words, discriminating from the geographical elements in order to construct something limited and coherent. This coherence is as aesthetic and artificial as it is external and regulated.

The plane of immanence is an archipelago where concepts are positioned like islands surrounded by the sea. The plane cannot simply be the sea on which concepts/islands float; it is not the empty sea waiting to be populated through underwater volcanic eruptions. It is an archipelago only because there are islands surrounded by water. It is not an open sea and it is not just islands, but the combination of both. It is not the infinite stretches of water but the occurrence of a cluster of islands that frame the sea from the inside to create the archipelago/plane of immanence: 'Concepts are the archipelago or skeletal frame, a spinal column rather than a skull, whereas the plane is the breath that suffuses the separate parts.'[40] Following this line of thought, Deleuze and Guattari later identify the elements of the plane as diagrammatic features and concepts as intensive features.[41]

To see the plane in terms of a map entails seeing it diagrammatically, as a plan of the direction one is to take in thought sketched out in order to situate oneself. Not exactly a place, the diagram of the plane is a space in words and hence a sketch of the actual place. Diagrammatic, the plane maps out thought, traces its features so as to allow us to find our bearings in thought.

The plane as breath suffuses the concepts that delimit the archipelago; this action is also demonstrated on the level of the paper through the etymology of *dia* in diagrammatic, which demonstrates the multiple dimensions of the directions in this diagram of thought: the prefix *dia* as in (a) through, (b) apart and (c) across. So the plane of immanence as a diagram of thought is much more dynamic than a preliminary sketch of an object. If these are the multiple directions of the plane as diagram that, like breath, suffuse the concepts – spread from within, around and over them – we can see that geographically, this archipelago is not a flat ensemble of islands with water between them; as flat as a map of an archipelago, it is a three-dimensional, underwater archipelago.

There is movement in this archipelago. The islands as regions are constantly remapping the diagram of the plane of immanence, since it is only visible through the concepts that frame it from within: 'The plane has no other regions than the tribes populating and moving around on it: it is the plane that secures the populating of the plane on an always renewed and variable curve.'[42] The archipelago is buzzing and vibrating with life: 'Philosophy is at once concept creation and instituting of the plane', according to Deleuze and Guattari, for philosophy needs both 'like two wings or fins'.[43] For this reason, the plane of immanence must be described simultaneously with its concepts, which are like the birds that fly from one island to the next but remain for millennia and let geography transform them. The Galapagos archipelago demonstrates this: the same species of birds can be found on many of the islands, but with different characteristics depending on the ecosystem of the particular islands they inhabit. The ecosystem, for example, changes the beaks of the birds. There is a block of becoming between the beak and the nut. In our underwater archipelago, it is not a question of beaks and nuts or wings and fins, but both; for the migrating flying fish, we see a synthesis of two animals.

If the concept is the island on the plane of water, on the plane as earth, the concept is also a bird: 'The concept of a bird is found not in its genus or species but in the composition of its posture, colours, and songs:

something indiscernible that is not so much synesthetic as syneidetic.'[44] It is the becoming-animal of a concept.[45] The concept of the bird is then found in the diagrammatical layers that make up the bird. The bird as concept is in constant flight within itself and on the plane of immanence: 'The concept is in a state of survey [*survol*] in relation to its components, endlessly traversing them according to an order without distance.'[46] The bird is a concept flying in an imaginary landscape where there is no distance. The image of thought is flown over at infinite speed. The concepts inhabit a diagrammatic mental landscape or an imagined mental geography; the birds make their territory: '[I]t is a plane of immanence that constitutes the absolute ground of philosophy, its earth or deterritorialization, the foundation on which it creates its concepts.'[47]

The plane is constantly shifting with the concepts flying over and within themselves, creating the regions of the plane as they populate it. Just as space that is always in the process of negotiating its territory as it is being created, it is a space without distances, something in the dark about to be turned on.

Throughout his corpus Deleuze posits that it is necessary to reconstitute the disparate parts of a concept or an image, not so as to reconstruct a system, but in order to demonstrate the process that he himself theorizes. A geographic and anatomical episteme can unfold multidimensionally. Geography and anatomy can be taken separately. Geography is for Deleuze the ground, the foundation, the base. Our two feet are planted on the ground and this ground is the planet spinning; geography traces the globe and the planet as striated and smooth space, as deterritorializations and reterritorializations. Or they can be taken together: on the anatomical side, the body is also a geographical site. It points towards the BwO because everything in the body is hierarchized.

It is no surprise then, that these instances of islands would emerge in conjunction with English-language literature: Deleuze did after all call the English their own island. As 'On the Superiority of Anglo-Saxon Literature' in *Dialogues* demonstrates, Deleuze had a fondness for American literature. He transposes a whole liberating geography onto English and reads American literature through rather nautical landscapes. If in 'Bartleby; or, the Formula' Deleuze was exploring zones of indifferentiation within language – a space in language where another foreign language resounds – he was able to transpose these zones found in language onto a larger worldview that, according to him, was designed and mapped out by Herman Melville. This is the principle of the *dérive*. And what will be soon washed ashore of the archipelago is a squid. We will get to that in the following section.

Traits are what abstracted from one structure (a portrait, in Melville's case) and another (the image of a squid). Thus the traits that Melville draws and extends affirm a process that Deleuze associates with the archipelago:

> It is first of all the affirmation of a world in *process*, an *archipelago*. Not even a puzzle, whose pieces when fitted together would constitute a whole, but rather a wall of loose, uncemented stones, where every element has a value in itself but also in relation to others: isolated and floating relations, islands and straits, immobile points and sinuous lines – for Truth always has 'jagged edges'. Not a skull but the vertebral column, a spinal cord.[48]

We can look to Guattari for a definition of process.

> [It is a] continuous series of facts or operations that can lead to other series of facts and operations. A process implies the idea of a permanent rupture in established equilibria. This term is not used in the sense of schizophrenic processes in classical psychiatry, which always implies an arrival to a terminal state. Rather, it [resembles] 'dissipative processes'.[49]

The process follows the lines of the diagram as it was defined at the beginning of the book. The archipelago is not only an image that represents multiplicities, differences and dynamism, but here it is also equated with the procedure. If the archipelago becomes a method, not just an image, then let us call it a schema in motion, a diagram. This worldview is determined not so much by the definite factual material elements as by the wind that blows through the fissures and the fractures in-between. What surfaces here is the inclusion of anatomical elements in close proximity to geographical ones. In his discussion of the process, Deleuze utilizes the image of islands and archipelagos in the same passage in which he deploys images of craniums, spinal cords and bone marrow.

Finally, in *What Is Philosophy?* Deleuze and Guattari directly juxtapose the archipelago and the vertebrae. Separated only by an 'or', archipelago and the skeletal frame resound visually in the space that these two elements occupy on the page:[50]

> Concepts are the **archipelago** or **skeletal** frame, a **spinal column** rather than a **skull**, whereas the plane is the breath that suffuses the separate parts. Concepts are absolute surfaces or volumes, formless and fragmentary, whereas the plane is the formless, unlimited absolute, neither

surface nor volume but always fractal. Concepts are concrete assemblages, like the configurations of a machine, but the plane is the abstract machine of which these assemblages are the working parts.[51]

Deleuze and Guattari, on many occasions, compare the images of thought, such as the process or the concept, to archipelagos, which they in turn compare to anatomical structures. Here, however, the archipelago and the spinal column heal together, one over the other. They become the image of the concept. It is quite a reversal from Deleuze's original use of the image of the archipelago. If in *Difference and Repetition* in 1968 we saw a juxtaposition between the archipelago and the manner in which bones evolve, this image has hardened around the bone – it has become the bones themselves. The archipelago, as an idea for an idea, has turned into a concept.

It may appear that it took close to 20 years for the idea of islands to harden into an image of a concept, yet this illusion only shimmers when we keep in view Deleuze's early renunciation of dynamism in the mechanism of the concept: 'A concept alone is completely incapable of specifying or dividing itself; the agents of differenciation are the spatio-temporal dynamisms which act within or beneath it, like a hidden art.'[52] These spatio-temporal dynamisms, as we have seen, are what for Deleuze constitute the skeleton of the Kantian schema. Acknowledging it as an immense force, the schema is what divides the concept: 'Schematism possesses an immense power: it can divide a concept and specify it according to a typology.'[53] Deleuze locates the schema spatially vis-à-vis the concept: placed under the concept, the schema is the concept's engine. But the schema has a shortcoming; it is not able to account for the vigour with which it acts. The dynamic element is then filtered out of the schema: 'Dynamism thus comprises its own power of determining space and time, since it immediately incarnates the differential relations, the singularities and the progressivities immanent in the Idea.'[54] Filtered out and abstracted through constraint from the Idea, dynamism becomes for Deleuze the unit at the base of systematic formation. It can then be transposed from image to idea to concept as these notions are interspersed throughout Deleuze's corpus.

What happened was not a shift in his definition of the idea, but rather a newfound flexibility in the concept. The concept, once as hard as bone, is restructured and made supple and pliable, like the spine, central without being hierarchically superior. Here, the archipelago has become the manifestation of a multitude of other charged Deleuzean concepts: assemblages, machines, abstract machines.

Deleuze designs his philosophical system as a geophilosophy so that the territory is constantly deterritorialized: one cannot trace his system, but one can map it. And if mapping means writing for Deleuze, then one must write diagrammatically so as to sketch out the ideas and, in the process, turn them into concepts. Writing about Deleuze is to structure, to sketch out an organism, to map out a dynamic geography.

The Contraction of Geoffroy Saint-Hilaire

The series of concept/images, comprised until now of the orchid/wasp assemblage and the archipelago/spinal column diagram, is extended with yet another striking duality: the cephalopod[55]/quadruped contraction. These two categories of animals, side by side, form an uncommon dyad; any premise that would involve a comparison between a squid and, for example, a dog, must be uncanny to begin with. But the reason for their conceptual coupling is decidedly spectacular precisely because it does not simply involve their comparison but the anatomical reassemblage of such different animals. The passage of one animal into the next, its forced plicature, makes one cringe if only the bones are considered when the organs of a quadruped are brought onto the same plane as that of a cephalopod. The image arises in *Difference and Repetition* and *A Thousand Plateaus*. Deleuze and Guattari discuss this dyad in the context of the nineteenth-century debate (1830) between two French anatomists: Cuvier and Geoffroy Saint-Hilaire. The image this dyad evokes is further surprising when its use becomes clear: it is employed by the philosophers to demonstrate a leap in thought, an extraordinary contraction. The wonder does not cease yet: what is of epistemic interest is the fact that thought is described by an anatomical leap. And this leap in the classification of anatomy is what is spurred by thought, that which allows for a complication of this sort. In order for such a passage to occur, the categories of animals must be diagrammatized, abstracted as a BwO.

Why was Geoffroy Saint-Hilaire able to make the cephalopod/quadruped claim, a claim that when read diagrammatically, constitutes the extraordinary contraction? Sauvagnargues summarizes the debate as follows:

> Geoffroy's transformism unifies Cuvier's fixism well, contains a refutation of his classification, and even, we should add, in relation to his interest in teratology, a refutation of all classification. **It is a logical contraction of the fixist position.** Better yet, it is the introduction of a new conception of form, as a modal variation and a composition of identical

material elements for all animals that transforms classification into a temporary snapshot.[56]

The passage of the real into a representation of a cephalopod and a quadruped – such as, for example, a squid or a cuttlefish twisted into a horse or a cat: two groups of animals that have not much in common – can only be achieved through a contraction not of structure but of function. At the abstracted level of their organs, independent of the hierarchy of the body – the concept of the BwO can be taken as a model – can we *imagine* a passage across the categories of animals? Such a contraction in function depends on an abstraction of the line, clearly drawn, exuding authority in its scientific style, augmented through a lens: Can a cephalopod look convincingly similar to a horse if they both are represented as being of the same size? Foucault addresses this question of scale through the view of a microscope: 'A change of scale in the visual sphere must have more value than the correlations between the various kinds of evidence that may be provided by one's impressions, one's reading, or learned compilations.'[57] And then a diagram can make the leap: obviously the organs of one animal and another are categorically different but the drawing, once it has put them on the same scale, also removes their feel, their smells, textures, and so on. Then the foldings can be made in the way that Kwinter explains through *complication/explication*.

Cuvier is there, with reason, to say that this cannot be done. He is the naysayer. But he misses the point of the operation if he denies it: this illustrates the leap of knowledge that is the extraordinary contraction. What is at stake is not whether a cephalopod and a quadruped can in fact be brought onto the same plane. Foucault, in this context, is not describing the hardware of consciousness, but an epistemological shift in vision that we choose to decontextualize and apply to Geoffroy Saint-Hilaire's operation. The French naturalist's resultant conclusion shows the power of the mechanism of thought as it leaps across categories. And in this spirit, the epistemological bounds set up by Foucault in his discussion of classification are crossed so that a description of the tabulation of knowledge can be remanufactured into an ontological device made of bits of bones and ideas.

Deleuze explains this transformation that takes place following a line of flight. Describing Melville's writing diagrammatically, Deleuze focuses on the intermediary stage of plicature before the image of the father turns into a cephalopod:

Everything starts off as an English novel, in Dickens' London. But in each case, something strange happens, something that blurs the image, marks it with an essential uncertainty, keeps the form from 'taking', but also undoes the subject, sets adrift and abolishes any paternal function. It is only here that things begin to get interesting. The statue of the father gives way to his much more ambiguous portrait, and then to yet another portrait that could be of anybody or nobody. All referents are lost, and the formation [*formation*] of man gives way to a new, unknown element, to the mystery of a formless, non human life, a *Squid*.[58]

This squid is the manifestation of a topological deterritorialization. Deleuze explains this zone as the passage from the old world neurotic to the new world schizophrenic:

In the first place, the formless trait of expression is opposed to the image or to the expressed form. In the second place, there is no longer a subject that tries to conform to the image, and either succeeds or fails. Rather, a zone of indistinction, of indiscernibility, or of ambiguity seems to be established between two terms, as if they had reached the point immediately preceding their respective differentiation: not a similitude, but a slippage, an extreme proximity, an absolute contiguity, not a natural filiation, but an unnatural alliance. It is a 'hypperborean', 'artic' zone. It is no longer a question of Mimesis, but of becoming.[59]

This zone of indiscernibility is what captures the artistic diagram. But how do we get to this zone, through which mechanism? The answer is the technique of plicature, as Deleuze will show.

The historical debate between Geoffroy Saint-Hilaire and Cuvier is the forum for this epistemological/ontological leap. Toby Appel's book, *The Cuvier-Geoffroy Debate: French Biology in the Decades Before Darwin*, chronicles the ideologically polarized relationship between the nineteenth-century biologists and ascends, for a reader of Deleuze, to the cephalopod disagreement. This disagreement is used by Deleuze in his philosophy to demonstrate the emergence of the Idea in *Difference and Repetition*. And even if in *A Thousand Plateaus*, Cuvier and Geoffroy are turned into philosophical personas who seem to be more than expressive; it leads one to wonder if in fact this dyad of thinkers was not artificially coloured by Deleuze and Guattari in order to vividly illustrate a pair with clashing traits, as paradoxically complementary to each other as the tracing and the map resulting in a diagram described a couple of plateaus prior to this:

Thanks in large part to the hindsight gained from the work of Geoffroy and his followers, Cuvier's framework for zoology was considerably broadened by the next generation of naturalists. Philosophical anatomy, divested of its more speculative and rigid trappings, entered the mainstream of natural history and comparative anatomy as an indispensable tool for clarifying the natural system of classification.[60]

In fact, the same themes are taken up in these two personas. Cuvier acts as the tracing, monotonously and stubbornly capturing what is already out there and classifying it without any bending of the rules. Geoffroy Saint-Hilaire is the map persona. He yearns for undiscovered countries. He even embarks on a long mission to Egypt with Napoleon. The Egyptian trip results in a career self-sabotage; Cuvier was left to tend to the *Muséum*, where he was able to expand his influence, while Geoffroy was lost in the desert. While Cuvier remains firmly entrenched within the lines of the four *embranchements*[61] of his classificatory model, Geoffroy desires to take a line of flight over them all with his *philosophie anatomique*. The story of Cuvier and Geoffroy is relevant because they are archetypal opposites; it is a tale of structure versus function, of classification versus system, of description versus philosophy.

Back to the cephalopod. After years of Cuvier asserting his superiority both in terms of knowledge and power at the *Muséum*, Geoffroy was slipping in popularity because his work was not considered as serious as his rival's. An opportunity arrived for Geoffroy to publicly demonstrate his theories while refuting Cuvier on his own ground – that is, the category of cephalopods on which Cuvier had worked in depth. This opportunity took the form of Meyraux and Laurencet, two naturalists who came to Paris from the south of France to present a paper on a novel theory:

> Working with the cuttlefish, a cephalopod, as a representative mollusk, they attempted to show that if a vertebrate was bent backwards so that the nape of the neck was attached to the buttocks, then the internal organs would be arranged in a manner similar to that of molluscs.[62]

Hervé Le Guyader, in his book on Geoffroy Saint-Hilaire, attests to the scientist's exuberance when Laurencet and Meyraux's memoir came in. A comparison that was pushed 'far, too far', according to Le Guyader, was made even more explicit by Geoffroy Saint-Hilaire, who decided to read their thesis in support of the unity of plan theory between mollusks and vertebrates.[63] Geoffroy Saint-Hilaire's enthusiasm was such that it made Laurencet and Meyraux distance themselves from him, as he was writing their defence in a nervous letter to Cuvier.[64] This theoretical conclusion concerned the 'unity of organic composition', which proposed that since the cephalopod had so many organs in common with vertebrates, it could not be built on a different plan: 'Geoffroy contended that if the organs of a mollusk were in harmony with each other, that must be because they retained the same arrangement of parts as in the vertebrates.'[65]

Geoffroy took the presentation as an opportunity to discredit Cuvier's work on the cephalopod, even though Geoffroy, as compared to Cuvier, 'knew very little about the anatomy of these animals'.[66] Cuvier, defending himself against Geoffroy, dismantled piece by piece the work of Meyraux and Laurencet. He even brought in visual aids to make sure he made his point clear: 'With him he brought two large and impressive multicolored diagrams drawn by Laurillard from sketches he had provided. One showed an octopus (a cephalopod) and the other a duck-shaped mammal bent over backwards.'[67] With the diagrams, he was able to show that the cephalopod and the vertebrate were not made on the same plan even if they did share organs in common. To begin with, some of the organs of the cephalopod did not make it into vertebrates and vice versa. Some extensive mental acrobatics, it seemed, were necessary to make the theory hold.

'Geoffroy was depicted by some of these critics as a philosopher dedicated to unravelling the mysteries of nature of the common man.'[68] Cuvier was his antithesis; not only did he have a religious bent, but he was also a 'manipulator of patronage'.[69] Both religious orthodoxy and politicking led Cuvier to stand against Philosophical Anatomy, which he considered suspect from a religious perspective.[70] Philosophical Anatomy came to France from Germany, and that is why Goethe was a proponent of Geoffroy while Cuvier's theories found an agreeable response on the other side of the Channel, with the English and their religiously based science.

Geoffroy did not want to restrict himself to a 'natural system of classification'.[71] He was also not keen on publishing great treatises in a particular field of study. Rather, his interest lay in 'the enterprise of reducing nature to universal laws primarily through the use of reason rather than by the painstaking collection of data'.[72] The painstaking collection of data was more Cuvier's style, exploring the empirical evidence and fitting it into his four *embranchements*. Geoffroy, like Deleuze and Guattari's professor Challenger in *A Thousand Plateaus* – who is neither a geologist nor a biologist, neither an ethnologist nor a linguist – was a multidisciplinary thinker. Of course, Deleuze and Guattari describe themselves in *A Thousand Plateaus* and foresee the kind of criticism that they can expect from their detractors. But Geoffroy, on a lesser level, was a proponent of a multidisciplinary stance on biology and science in general. He pronounced himself against the fact that sciences specialized themselves into individually insular parcels. Quoting from Balzac, who wrote, 'Science is one and you have divided it', Geoffroy added that specialists who divide science into tiny terrains are sheltering themselves to the point of living at the bottom of a well.[73] Geoffroy asks:

> Would it be rational . . . if from a purely zoological proposition, consequences unfold which invade the domain of sciences that are considered distinct, as, for example physics proper, to refuse to deduce them, to expect him to limit himself to zoology . . . would be to require him to impose limits on logic itself.[74]

It has to be conceded that Cuvier was working at the crux of a few distinct sciences himself, producing what Appel calls a 'synthesis of paleontology, taxonomy, and comparative anatomy'.[75] From Deleuze's perspective and especially the imaginative coming to be of an Idea in *Difference and Repetition*, this synthesis 'was based on a teleological approach to nature, one that gave primacy to functional purpose over structural affinity'.[76] It is this teleological doxa that Deleuze writes against in describing the ideal asymmetrical synthesis of ideas. This teleologically based synthesis works by having God create an environment and then provide the living beings with what is necessary for them to function. Not that Geoffroy was not meticulous: 'He was one of the first to analyze osseous structures in different animals into individual bones, even parts of bones, and to seek bone by bone correspondences among mammals, birds, reptiles, and fishes.'[77] He then linked these elements through an analogical method, one that he wanted to push to a limit, which became a theory during the cephalopod debate.

> The skeletal system was the focus of his efforts, for it was not only the easiest system to analyze, but also (as it appeared to Geoffroy) the framework for all the other systems of organs. For the first time, osseous structures in fishes were systematically analyzed into individual bones and compared bone for bone to structures in other vertebrates. Instead of function determining structure, Geoffroy brought to light the disquieting possibility that homologous bones in different animals could be modified to perform entirely disparate functions. Bones could henceforth be perceived in abstraction as 'materials of organization' that in different animals could be developed, atrophied, modified, sutured together, or even annihilated.[78]

This is the key difference in the approaches to anatomy of these two men. Cuvier's primary focus, contrary to Geoffroy's, was function. If Cuvier discovered which part was responsible for which function, his analysis would compartmentalize the part with the function: 'Cuvier's aim was rather to exhibit the *different* structural means by which animals performed the same function. Thus his volumes were organized by functional systems, such as respiration, circulation, digestion, and movement.'[79] Once the part fit into the classificatory structure, there was no need to look in further detail:

> In his treatment of the skeleton of fishes, Cuvier relegated the pectoral fin to a separate section from the anterior extremities of other vertebrates, and made no effort to describe the bones in detail or to compare them to bones in other vertebrates.[80]

Even though homologies could be discerned, they were not pursued if the function or even the shape of the part also changed. Geoffroy lamented this and the method used by Cuvier, saying that 'the thread of Ariadne escapes from their hands'.[81] It seems that for Geoffroy, the problem resided in the fact that the classificatory system did not allow different categories to be crossed. The gulf that separated them was unbridgeable and did not allow for anything to fit in-between them: '[T]he method of comparative anatomy . . . required the existence of intermediary forms so that a structure could be traced from one extreme to the other.'[82] Because there are no intermediary forms between 'the pectoral fin of a fish and the arm of a man . . . the comparison stalled in its tracks'.[83] Geoffroy Saint-Hilaire's contribution to the solution to this problem of classification was to organize the process of the development of organs, homologies or analogies in increments, so as to allow for a jump between the categories in the classificatory grid. According to Geoffroy Saint-Hilaire, as Appel reports:

> Strictly, it will suffice for you to consider man, a ruminant, a bird, and a bony fish. Dare to compare them directly, and you will reach in one stroke all that anatomy can furnish you of the most general and philosophical [nature].[84]

This analogical method, which was articulated according to a 'torsion' or a '*plicature*', as Le Guyader explains, in order to provide a path for the vertebrate to be broken and twisted into a cephalopod, is what is exciting for Deleuze, along with the deployment of a mechanism of folding (*pli*), refolding of terms (*re-pli-ment*) and explication of an idea (*ex-pli-cation*).[85] This functional *plicature* occurs when an idea can cover terrain without bordering itself with classificatory limits. The question here is also to see if bones can skip from one animal to the next, and what that tells us about ideas that change their form through analogy. Thoughts would be as solid as bones – which means, not that solid anymore.

Foucault, in *The Order of Things*, explains that techniques are necessary in order to chart all the similarities and dissimilarities between living entities. Without techniques, the task of tabulating the natural world would be endless, like Borges' map of the empire, which coincides point for point with the empire itself. These techniques are two: the first is the method that consists of 'total comparisons, only within empirically constituted groups in which the number of resemblances is manifestly so high that the enumeration of the differences will not take long to complete'.[86] This is a surefire method that would guarantee that everything would be caught in the net of knowledge. The other is the system that consists of 'selecting a finite and relatively limited group of characteristics, whose variations and constants may be studied in any individual entity that presents itself'.[87] In the case of the method, a structure emerges in the relation between individuals, within the scope of the actual. With the system, especially as Geoffroy Saint-Hilaire articulates it, the structure is internalized by each individual and operates at the virtual level of the individual: each individual carries the structure that is not yet actualized and therefore carries a potentiality. As Foucault explains, 'The internal link by which structures are dependent upon one another is no longer situated solely at the level of frequency; it becomes the very foundation of all correlation.'[88] This is particularly important since it is unlike the methodical classification, which creates boxes needing to be filled and does not offer any escape routes. The system here, which is manifest at the virtual strata of the individual, is not yet actualized but carries a germ of its own becoming and offers a structural flexibility of future relations.[89]

Geoffroy Saint-Hilaire becomes emblematic of this flexible way of structuring a system, not only insofar as he can be used as an example of a kind of systematization but also as its blueprint. Foucault writes, 'It is this displacement and this inversion that Geoffroy Saint-Hilaire expressed when he said: "Organic structure is becoming an abstract being . . . capable of assuming numerous forms."'[90] We are reminded of a previous discussion of Simondon's allagmatic through DeLanda's theory of epistemic function; the ontological being is not the being as it is formed, but the relation between beings, or between beings and their environment. The relation for Simondon is the real, the ontological ground. For Geoffroy Saint-Hilaire, it is not the animal or the organism in itself but rather its virtual structure that is the ontological individual, always in a process of becoming with its capacity for assuming new forms, but also of morphing into forms not yet actualized. For Foucault, there is a telling epistemological shift here in classification itself:

> The space of living beings pivots around this notion, and everything that until then had been able to make itself visible through the grid of natural history (genera, species, individual, structures, organs), everything that had been presented of view, now takes on a new mode of being.[91]

It is this excitement of a possibility of epistemic change fuelled by the diagrammatic function that is at the basis of Deleuze and Guattari's interest in the cephalopod and the quadruped.

'A "system" is then the organic ensemble formed of all the realized organs and of all of its *potentialities*.'[92] Geoffroy Saint-Hilaire urges Cuvier not to look only at what is in front of him on the dissecting table; by doing so, Cuvier will fail to see *what is not there*. The unified plan cannot be conceived of if the anatomist relies only on what is in front of him: some animals might not have the organ or bone that is needed to make a comparison, but they carry it *in potentia*. Geoffroy Saint-Hilaire assimilates embryology with the theory of evolution: '[A]n actual animal that does not exhibit the hyoid bone during the dissection possesses it *virtually*.'[93] The animal's virtual dimension is a geographical and anatomical plane that must be reconfigured and manipulated.

The constant shifting across different categories of virtual skeletal torsion – from the hyoid bone present during dissection to the one that is there only virtually, from the way that archipelagos are spinal columns and that geography is the lens through which to appreciate anatomical contortions – leads us to emblematically seal this section off with Tom Conley's transposition of these anatomical acrobatics onto the plane of aesthetics and art. He explains the gory figures in Francis Bacon's paintings:

> [A] splayed carcass reveals a dorsal column leading downward to a head with a gaping mouth whose teeth seem to be miniature vertebrae. The upper end of the body is a curved swath of lines of red and white pigment that surround an ellipse that might be a mouth above an eye.[94]

Conley talks about folding and about the breaking of bones in what seems to be a description of a plicature midway from one system to the next. The contraction moves into the function of art as the diagram is exposed within the material of figural representation in painting. The question remains of how to capture a portrait of this process. I will consider this question through Francis Bacon, or more specifically, through Deleuze's reformulation of the diagram through the painter's art. We must first explore the basis of the diagrammatic dimension of the body within the dynamic of the abstract body. We must trace the cinematics of the function.

Egg Cinematics

Conley, who is an expert at describing the visual aspect of Deleuze and Guattari's writing, captures the dynamic and vibrant optics of their style. He reveals active currents and moving networks within the prose that must be read as an extra dimension to the content of the works:

> The polemical style of *Mille plateaux*, like that of *L'Anti-Oedipe*, owes much to the divided structure of its writing. Its camera-stylo prose constantly splinters into different 'tracks' that recombine, bend, and bifurcate, looping back, unwinding, and knotting together. Deleuze's more strictly philosophical works have a relatively controlled quality, but are nonetheless informed by the same creative disposition. Reduction or extrapolation of their content from this process is almost impossible, while the art of a book like *Le pli* comes from a design based on this process and can be grasped simultaneously from several perspectives. The implied shape of *Le pli* suggests a point of view that originates in multiplicity and is read through Leibniz's philosophy of space. An operative concept that bifurcates and loops ahead and back through images and language, point of view becomes an active and mobile element in the very architecture of *Le pli*, that is, in the textual space it creates from the disposition and strategic placement of its arguments. Also vital to this textual architecture is the book's emblematic design.[95]

Conley describes how the work must be grasped from simultaneous perspectives: a whole new space of the philosophy is opened because of the very material organization of the book.

And how does this amphibian device, the diagram, a hybrid machine of flesh and ideas, of paper and bones, have the power to break a quadruped into a squid? Burroughs's technique of the fold-in gives rise to the new dimension described within the diagram. In *A Thousand Plateaus*, Deleuze and Guattari write of the supplementary dimension that comes about with the folding of the text:

> Take William Burroughs's cut-up method: the folding of one text onto another, which constitutes multiple and even adventitious roots (like a cutting), implies a supplementary dimension to that of the texts under consideration. In this supplementary dimension of folding, unity continues its spiritual labor.[96]

This is yet another call for a dimension that comes out of a process – here, the material technique of folding a text with another – which also frees a function that continues independently of the object of the text. This book as flesh, this soft machine that necessitates the duality of a geography and an anatomy, is discussed by Kathryn Hume in an article that enumerates the geographical places in Burroughs's novels – the desert, the jungle and the city – through roaming, anarchic, unlikely utopias, organic, swampy vegetal life pools and the constraining space of oppressive powers. Hume shows how each of these spaces affirms an endless potential of lost possibilities and a dedicated resistance to all forms of conformity. She also notes in Deleuzean terms the shape of Burroughs's corpus: 'Given Burroughs's view that his every novel (and every draft) are but parts of a single, continuous book . . . one might label his product a rhizome that branches out from and is held together by these repetition- nodes.'[97] She tabulates the way that Burroughs's work has evolved and was honed from a rhizomatic model to an arborescent structure: 'Burroughs's project may have been nomadic and its form rhizomatic at first, but this final setting directs us toward that quintessence of antirhizomatic "arborescence", a tree. Landscapes signal the major shift that took place in Burroughs's fiction in the last trilogy.'[98] Whether this shift is an accurate trajectory in Burroughs's corpus may seem plausible if only in the more 'traditional' narrative style that he adopts in his later works. What is important in Hume's assessment of Burroughs's work is the dichotomy that she fits into the extremities of his creative life. The organic, vegetal model holds not only in the overall spread of his books but also in the images with which he fills his narratives. Yet, by looking at the structure of the texts that carry these images, we can observe another dimension of organicity that Burroughs manipulates. It is one that is akin to Deleuze and Guattari's programme of dehierarchizing the organism and thereby disorienting the sense of organization itself.

Hume adroitly pre-empts this point by mingling the geographic aspect of Burroughs's settings with his exaggerated and distorted anatomical mechanisms. Where geographical situations are made fantastic by overloading the senses with an accumulation of vegetal and biological details, anatomy is contorted, cut-up and sewn back senselessly into the geographical setting. The geographical and the anatomical mix together, exploding and imploding with one another.

To focus on the marshy vegetal place of the jungle that Hume tabulates in Burroughs's corpus is to yield images of monstrous births and sexual manifestations in bizarre copulations and appendages. The heavy-handed biological functions that Burroughs uses to draw glistening creatures and viscous processes make for sweltering and dripping passages of sex between boys and amphibians. Hume pulls out of these gelatinous semantic fields incarnations of a desire to demonstrate the body as fluid with its environment. One of the examples she uses comes from *The Ticket That Exploded*, in which a young man takes an embryo in a jar to a Chinese shopkeeper. The young man, waiting for the embryo to develop in the sewers under the city, has jelly rubbed into his anus and spawns fish-like eggs that flow out into the water. This example is evocative of a damp sexuality, something that crosses species and lines of biological classification, an extra-species transgression, to say the least. It echoes images of the BwO, surpassing its dehierarchized limits.

But the structure of the text has also to be taken into consideration. The passage that recounts the boy's actions with the embryo in a jar, the shopkeeper and the orgasmic spawning of eggs in the sewer is repeated three times. The second time, the story is told from the beginning to the end but in a shorter space. The space of the text is contracted and the function of thought, which still constructs an image of the passage, is laid bare. Words are taken out randomly and the syntactic sense is sacrificed in the folding. The third time the story is recounted, it is a short paragraph in length, but the words have been so drastically cut down that the narrative does not make any sense at all, except that the reader, who has first read the integral part of the story the first time, can fill in the blanks. The effect on the reader is uncanny: to read something that makes no sense whatsoever yet that can be understood. The text on the page is folded just as Geoffroy Saint-Hilaire folds a mollusk into a quadruped. Folded in, parts disappear, features are erased, but what remains is something that still resembles what it once was, only because of the process of folding. In this light, Burroughs's term 'soft machine' attains more depth. It is certainly more than what could be read as a simple machine–body interweaving.[99] The soft machine is interweaving only if the original sense of weaving is eked out of the term 'text'. The soft machine is the book; it is the rhizome or the root-book, but the book on which, in graphic terms, this kind of folding can take place. It is at a graphic level that the machine of the body is given the depth to be manipulated, and it is the text of the book that allows for the necessary dimension, the diagrammatic space, to perform the acrobatics on a structure.

This kind of folding in content and in form can be described through the unfolding mechanism of the structure of an egg, as a conceptual image. In his book on the baroque, Deleuze writes about Leibniz's natural history theory and how it is based on a fold. On going back and forth between Leibniz and Geoffroy Saint-Hilaire, he writes:

> The meaning of development or evolution has turned topsy-turvy since it now designates *epigenesis* – the appearance of organs and organisms neither preformed nor closed one within the other, but formed from something else that does not resemble them: the organ does not arch back to a pre-existing organ, but to a much more general and less differentiated design.[100]

This translation of *The Fold* has to be minimally rectified: the last word of the paragraph, 'design', adequately describes the activity of creating and the machinic aspect of the end product that Deleuze has in mind; but the French original, *ébauche*, also means sketching.[101]

Here, Deleuze repeats the argument that he used in *Difference and Repetition*,[102] and goes back to the object of the egg that he takes from Albert Dalcq and his *L'oeuf et son dynamisme organisateur*.[103] The virtual state of composition that prefigures the actualized being is described as a sketch, putting the onus on a term that seems trivial and unformed as a sketch might, but that for Deleuze, gathers importance precisely in its potentiality. But this sketch is the starting point: the sketch instead of the fold, or rather the sketch that contains the fold. How is it going to lead to thought? The answer is by following an ontogenesis of thought designated by the path traced by geographic and anatomical epistemes sown across Deleuze's corpus.

With such a heavy task relying on this word, which itself designates a rather flimsy process, it is important to explore the semantic field of *ébauche*. Its semantic field consists of 'beginning', 'sketch' and 'decoy', Stretching the field of synonyms, we get to the word *épure*, which means 'sketch', 'beginning', but also 'carcass', 'skeleton' and 'structure'. With the embryonic development, something that Deleuze will qualify as the virtual, we are reminded also of his statement that the skeleton of the virtual is structure. We will follow the thread tied to *ébauche* in the following section through the figure of Geoffroy Saint-Hilaire and his anatomical foldings. This will lead us to a materiality of thought, starting with the sketch of the virtual – a sketch of the virtual as a diagram. It is a virtual whose skeleton is structure, a sketch in the virtual that folds out into an embryo, an organism, a body. The sketch or diagram, through the movement of the idea towards concept and system, incarnates, in the philosophical sense, the idea in a flesh-like, organic materiality.

In *A Thousand Plateaus*' 'The Geology of Morals', with reference to the organization of the earth model, it is specifically stated after all that 'the earth . . . is a Body without Organs',[104] and in *Difference and Repetition*, that '[t]he entire world is an egg'.[105] What animates this abstract model of earth/egg/BwO is the dynamism that activates the functional torsion from one element to another: the analogy between earth and egg is obvious at best, but the functionality with which Deleuze and Guattari endow each term and abstract it into the form of the BwO is what generates the analogical force and allows for the application of the model to such diverse terms as thought, mind, body and geography. The core of this function is located within its dynamic, temporal element, as Deleuze explains here in terms of classification: 'The introduction of the temporal factor is essential, even though Geoffroy conceives of it only in the form of stoppages – in other words, progressive stages ordered according to the realisation of a *possible* common to all animals.'[106]

The dynamism that is isolated within and made productive for the function is itself conceptualized in the frame of the actual:

> For if, from the point of view of actualisation, the dynamism of spatial directions determines a differenciation of types, then the more or less rapid times immanent to these dynamisms ground the passage from one to the other, from one differenciated type to another, either by deceleration or by acceleration. With contracted or extended times and according to the reasons for acceleration or delay, other spaces are created.[107]

The fold in the process that forms this theory turns on itself and tightens. The element of dynamism is excluded or made invisible as space and time are given prominence again: spaces emerge as temporal creations. In this passage, Deleuze provides the plan of the contraction, which he formulates succinctly: 'With contracted or extended times and according to the reasons for acceleration or delay, other spaces are created.'[108] Deleuze puts back the time that he took out of classification, and, as DeLanda explains it, into the space of the egg: 'Metaphorically, an egg may be compared to a topological space which undergoes a progressive spatial and qualitative differentiation to become the metric space represented by a fully formed organism.'[109] The space of the egg that DeLanda presents is not a static space; it is already in motion, which makes it a perfect site for the introduction of the time element.

With Geoffroy Saint-Hilaire, not only is the system pliable, but time comes back into the equation in the guise of intensities, a time that varies depending on the localized, individualized subsystems that generate their own rhythm and pace. The differentiation occurs through intensities. This resembles the Kantian schema as read through Heidegger's analysis of the concept. It does, however, follow axiomatic directions:

> Types of egg are therefore distinguished by the orientations, the axes of development, the differential speeds and rhythms which are the primary factors in the actualisation of a structure and create a space and a time peculiar to that which is actualised.[110]

A particular egg differentiates itself from others through the axes of development. These axes are the embryonic factors of the actualization of a structure.[111]

If for Deleuze the structure is the skeleton of the virtual, the embryonic axes are the skeleton of the skeleton of the virtual. Multiple layers go into the construction of a Deleuzean structure, or the strata of a structure. The taxonomy of a system is something suffusing the individual at a virtual level; its pre-individual, ontological state can already be grasped. The orientational axes, which develop at the early stages of an individuating organism, create a space and a time targeting an actual state. As DeLanda explains, a progression is made towards the actual state: 'Thus, there is a well-defined sense in which the spatial relations characterizing an egg or the still developing parts of an embryo are, indeed, an *exact yet rigorous*.'[112] But as the process continues through a series of migrations and foldings, these anexact structures yield to more exact and less flexible functions. They are being actualized: 'The finished product is a spatial structure adapted to specific functions.'[113] The example that DeLanda gives for the actualization of this intensive process within the egg at an embryonic stage can manifest itself in the architectural qualities of an organism:

> Like a building or a bridge, for example, an animal must be able to act under gravity as a *load-bearing structure*. On the other hand, the spatial

architecture of an organism is not the only factor that determines its capacity to bear loads, the *qualities* of the materials making up that architecture also matter: the qualities of muscle that allow it to bear loads in tension, for instance, or the qualities of bone that allow it to bear them in compression.[114]

We cannot pass up the connection between architectural and organic elements in this comparison. DeLanda compares an animal's body to the structural elements of a building, or a bridge and the qualities of materials that make up the structures. The anexact element present at the virtual stage persists at the level of the actual in the coupling of structure with quality.

For Deleuze, this whole process of individuation from the virtual to the actual is a dynamic movement that he qualifies as a cinematics: 'A whole kinematics of the egg appears, which implies a dynamic.'[115] Deleuze's formula is tight, and the three terms: kinematics, dynamic and implies (the French *implique* contains the word *pli*, that is, the fold) are semantically very similar. The formula describing the process of the dynamics of an egg is itself as smooth as the object it contains.

But the dynamics of the organism do not stop once the organism has reached its actual state: '[A]n organism is defined both by its spatial architecture, as well as by different materials (bone, muscle) which give that architecture its specific mechanical qualities. The intensive will then be revealed to be behind both the extensive and the qualitative.'[116] The whole point here is to reveal the intensive function of the virtual before it gets actualized. Mapping this virtuality is a diagrammatic process. In this task, what is especially important is Geoffroy Saint-Hilaire's classificatory transgression, from which Deleuze draws inspiration for his concept of the fold. Folding, which Deleuze will fully express in his philosophical assessment of Leibniz in *The Fold*, is first proposed in *Difference and Repetition*: it is originally located in the very material matter of the skeleton and its articulation. The fold is also considered here as a passage (Lyotard), a transduction (Simondon) and a topological layer in the actualized organism. The passage in question is an articulation occurring in the materiality of the organism:

> The discussion finds its poetic method and test in folding: is it possible to pass by folding from Vertebrate to Cephalopod? Can a Vertebrate be folded in such a manner that the two ends of the spine approach one another, the head moving towards the feet, the pelvis towards the neck, and the viscera arranged in the manner of Cephalopods?[117]

The idea in this passage, which will reappear in Deleuze's work (*A Thousand Plateaus*, *The Fold*), obviously enchanted him and gave great impetus to the formulation of his thought. The idea became infectious and propagated itself into the very notion of organism, which was not the same from that point on – at least not for Deleuze. The BwO of *Logic of Sense*, which appears to operate within the dualities of corporeal and incorporeal, positive and negative, is replaced by the BwO that takes on the shape of the egg as the Earth.[118]

It is in the context of the organism that Deleuze, through a flexible assessment of the idea, focuses on Geoffroy Saint-Hilaire. While Foucault in *The Order of Things* mentions Geoffroy Saint-Hilaire in connection with the organization of the organism for Cuvier, Deleuze deals exclusively with Geoffroy Saint-Hilaire's abstraction as a necessary step towards the development of the Idea of the Organism. In fact, for Deleuze, the opposition is clear between these two personas: 'Cuvier is a man of Power and terrain, and he won't let Geoffroy forget it; Geoffroy, on the other hand, prefigures the nomadic man of speed.'[119] According to Sauvagnargues, Geoffroy Saint-Hilaire shifts from an organizational plane, which she associates with Cuvier and his classical taxonomical model, onto the plane of composition. On that plane, which has to be a plane so as to have some sort of field in which a taxonomy is tabulated, a single principle rules with Spinozean implications: '[A]ccording to the principle of univocity: a single substance, a single matter is said of all the animals, who do not vary except in function of variable connections of which their parts are affected.'[120]

The dynamic element between one type and another builds a passage, bridging together different types. Furthermore, it creates a network between typological elements. Sauvagnargues argues that this dynamic playing field of intensities constitutes Deleuze's plane of consistency: '[T]he organism, the egg and the embryo constitute an intense *milieu* of unformed matter that Deleuze names the plane of consistency.'[121] This would have to be contrasted with Deleuze's aesthetic plane, the plane of composition, which brings us closer to a multidimensional diagram: a diagram that has to take into consideration a system that simultaneously moves from the virtual and the actual and is implanted in a state of affairs: 'Geoffroy Saint-Hilaire places underneath the organs a virtual plane of composition and explains the genetic difference between the animals but also between the animal and man through an intensive difference of arrangement of the same constituting.'[122]

In *Difference and Repetition*, Deleuze uses the classificatory flexing of Geoffroy Saint-Hilaire to describe analogically the notion of the Idea:

> The idea is thus defined as a structure. A structure or an Idea is a 'complex theme', an internal multiplicity – in other words, a system of multiple, non-localizable connections between differential elements which is incarnated in real relations and actual terms.[123]

It is the result of three conditions, according to Deleuze: (a) the neutrality of the elements (no sensible forms, no signification, no function); (b) the interaction and reciprocity of the elements; and (c) the contextualization (differential relation incarnated in the spatio-temporal; responding to the 'how many', the 'what', of each case of the method of dramatization). Therefore, as an Idea is spatially deployed as a structure, it forms the system. It is a virtual structure that manifests itself actually as a refutation of the Aristotelian method; it follows the same path that we have traced in the ontogenetic differentiation in the egg. The idea and the organism merge into a biological unit; the idea itself thus functions as an organism. This collapses the analogy in the same way that we have already seen in Simondon, where the analogy explaining a real occurrence moves to the structure of analogy itself and makes the analogical process 'real' in turn.

> *Second example: the organism as biological Idea.* Geoffroy Saint-Hilaire seems to be the first to have defended the consideration of elements that he called abstract, taken independently of their forms and their functions. This is why he criticised not only his predecessors but also his contemporaries (Cuvier) for not going beyond an empirical distribution of differences and resemblances. These purely anatomical and atomic elements, such as small bones, are linked by ideal relations of reciprocal determination: they thereby constitute an 'essence' which is the Animal in itself. It is these differential relations between pure anatomical elements which are incarnated in diverse animal configurations, with their diverse organs and functions.[124]

The pattern follows a gradation from the economical to the ecological, from the smallest to the largest context: first it is the social, then the biological and finally the physical. This second example is fitted between a '*first example: atomism as a physical idea*', which explains the rise of multiplicities, and the '*third example: are there social Ideas, in a Marxist sense?*', which explains how Marx abstracts labour relying on the labourer and subsequently labour on the power and social positions.[125] The biological Idea functions with the same flexibility as the ontogenetic movement from the virtual to the actual. It becomes organic. What permits this flexibility is the notion of Idea that Deleuze reconstructs from Kant through a structuralist approach. Deleuze rearticulates Kant's definition of Idea through the forms of time and space and determines its function within Kant's philosophical system as an element residing in-between the categories. He writes, 'Ideas appear in the form of a system of ideal connections – in other words, a system of differential relations between reciprocally determined genetic elements.'[126] For Deleuze, Kant's Idea functions as a mechanism, a system or network of ideal relations; it is the virtual. Deleuze then deploys in more detail the mechanism of the multiplicity of the idea, its internal circuitry: 'A multiple ideal connection, a differential relation, must be actualised in diverse spatio-temporal relationships, at the same time as its *elements* are actually incarnated in a variety of *terms* and forms.'[127]

Sauvagnargues explains finally that throughout all these multiple layers, the ideal diagram emerges based on the plane of consistency. It is formed on the virtual plane because of the flexibility of the classificatory system as imagined by Geoffroy Saint-Hilaire: '[T]he "Idea" of *Difference and Repetition* like the "problematic" of Simondon, designates the virtual plan of differentiation *in re*, the virtual diagram or the structure of singularities that animate any concrete assemblage.'[128] The classificatory plane, rearranged in terms of virtuality, is the diagram. It is not a rigid table, but the possibility of relations that suffuse the self-determining *in re* individual and at the same time relating it to an actuality, a state of affairs. The diagram is Deleuze's classification system. It is also the flexible grid that gives structure to the *assemblage*, which constitutes the relation between objects of philosophy and the arrangement of concepts within the corpus.

Conclusion

An assemblage, like archipelagos and spinal columns or quadrupeds and cephalopods, relies on the diagrammatic process of abstraction, here described as folding and unfolding, for the connection, based on function, of heterogeneous parts. Most strikingly, the image of a mammal contorting into the shape of a cephalopod drives the point home. We can image the bones cracking, the limbs twisting and the body contracting. The squid is the animal that emblematizes the diagrammatic process. But it is a squid that carries a mammal inside of it on a virtual level.

The diagram proceeds through folding. In Bacon's painting the diagram is responsible for the passage of traits from one figure to the next. But even his figures sometimes bear witness to the effects of plicature on the body. The torsions an embryo can go through are insupportable for a fully formed body. Burroughs's novels also display situations where the body is pushed to a limit and engaged in strange assemblages. But it is the fold-in technique that the author uses that creates strange literary chimeras on the level of the page. The themes explored by these two figures, Bacon and Burroughs, are close to some notions Deleuze articulates in his philosophy. And they show the manifestation of the diagram and its constraining and folding mechanism on the level of aesthetic objects. But the images Deleuze uses in his philosophical writings, the connections he makes between heterogeneous elements, are also articulated by a diagrammatic principle. Far from being simple comparisons, Deleuze shows that the diagrammatic process is an extraordinary contraction, working between forms and objects of differing matter on a virtual level.

In this chapter, I have shown the contraction that occurs between two structures. Deleuze has been juxtaposing disparate images, such as geography and the body or the landscape and the mind. Here, I have explored how, at the junction between two heterogeneous images, a new dimension opens. Like in the diagram – the function that emerges between the visual and the textual – this process of contraction is constructive, productive, creative – and also elastic. The elasticity of the diagram can be exploited within a critical, hermeneutic work of analysis. This is what I will be exploring in the next chapter.

Chapter 5

Skin, Aesthetics, Incarnation: Deleuze's Diagram of Francis Bacon – An Epilogue

The diagram is non-representational and deals with abstract matter. As we get close to it, it remains elusive. The closest to a visual representation of the diagram Gilles Deleuze provided is within the context of Francis Bacon's art. Even then, the diagram functions as an abstracting mechanism and remains out of sight. If, however, its functions could be embodied in art, we could get at a clearer representation of the concept. That is why the notion of incarnation is used in this chapter, to flesh out the diagram. Incarnation comes up sporadically throughout Deleuze's corpus and is not unfamiliar to his philosophy. But when applied to Bacon's work and his treatment of the flesh in painting, incarnation proves to be a very useful lens through which to catch a glimpse of the diagrammatic function.

Bacon's abstract strategies to represent the surface of the furies' skin in *Three Studies for Figures at the Base of a Crucifixion* (1944) and the flayed bodies of *Three Studies for a Crucifixion* (1962) can be intercepted by Deleuze's treatment of the painter's oeuvre according to notions of descent (fall) and flesh (meat) – two elements contained in his underused notion of incarnation.

Incarnation brings to mind the idea of descent (the spirit coming down) and flesh (the spiritual clothed in skin). The term is seldom used by Deleuze, a materialist philosopher, but when it comes up in his corpus, it is concerned with the virtual and the actual and, most importantly, the concept of the diagram, which has implications of systematic scale in his philosophy.

Descent implies a movement in time and flesh, a destination. Between the two, skin filters the fall into sensation. Skin is the liminal membrane that articulates the dimension of time in the concept of incarnation. Adding time to incarnation provides a fuller picture to the complexity of the concept.

Skin is not simply a receptacle but an elastic organ progressing through time, as Bacon shows with his figures shifting from one panel of his triptychs to the next, with the torsions that he puts his figures through and with the oft used circular zones endowed with arrows that illustrate movement and directionality in time. Also, Bacon's violent, sombre and horror-laden aesthetics are an apt terrain onto which to bring Deleuze's particular refinement of time through the notion of morose time. Morose time deploys a dynamic dimension in a figure teeming with potential and adds to his already rich analysis of Bacon's oeuvre.

The juxtaposition of a modern British painter and his French post-structuralist commentator opens a strange space populated by religious imagery and mythical creatures, namely crucifixions and furies. To these are added a rhinoceros' skin and incarnations into meat, cephalopods turning into quadrupeds, Bodies without Organs and masochists. There will be bones and skin and a head split in half by an ocean. Accordingly, to navigate this polymorphic crowd, the chapter will be divided into five parts. The first section is a description of Bacon's work. The second section explains incarnation through analogy, essence and the virtual/actual duality. The third section demonstrates the topological (diagrammatical) transformation of a fish into a crucified body according to the virtual mechanics of nineteenth-century biology. The fourth section shows the morose time at work on the surface of the skin between the virtual and the actual. Finally, the last section proposes a diagrammatic duality at work on the surface of the skin.

Studies of Furies

Bacon's *Three Studies for Figures at the Base of a Crucifixion* (1944) is at the centre of all this. A triptych painted towards the end of the Second World War, it is based on the three furies whose screeches torment those racked by guilt. They were referred to as 'The Kindly Ones' (Eumenides) because calling them 'The Angry Ones' (Erinyes) would lead to insanity: 'The Kindly Ones' – *Les Bienveillantes*, as in the title of Jonathan Littell's novel depicting the brutality of the Holocaust from the perspective of a Nazi SS officer. Calmly recounting his actions as a man going through the 'banality of evil', dealing with the flesh in a detached manner, he is nevertheless caught by the titular furies as Soviet and Allied troops enter Berlin. The appearance of the furies at the end of the novel coincides with Bacon's depiction of furies in the triptych at the end of war. The novel's pages scream behind the print as the soft title on the cover appeases the copy of the book. The euphemism designating the horrors of the Second World War resolutely underlines the unspeakable. What else is euphemistically designated, not by some gradation on the original term that should not be spoken, but by its absolute contrary? When the mind cannot fully grasp a concept, chimeras fly over the landscape. The monsters inhabit the regions of which the mind cannot accurately draw a map. T. S. Eliot, in his play *The Family Reunion*, exemplifies this unrepresentable vision in the speech of a man haunted by the Eumenides: 'Here and here and here – wherever I am not looking, / Always flickering at the corner of my eye, / Almost whispering just out of earshot – And inside me too, in the nightly panic / Of dreaming dissolution.'[1] The senses are not reached and therefore frustrated by something that is elusive and unlocalized. Bacon, whose avowed influence by Eliot's work manifested itself most directly in *Triptych – Inspired by T. S. Eliot's Poem 'Sweeney Agonistes'* (1967), paints these three furies from the perspective of an eye that cannot encompass their full shape. It is like an eye that wants to see the front but also the back at the same time. But these furies are not abstracted. From that point of view, they are realistically depicted, for they are imaginary creatures personifying something unrepresentable – the three screaming hags with snakes in their hair tormenting Orestes in Bourguereau's late nineteenth-century painting are far more unrealistic.

In *Three Studies for Figures at the Base of a Crucifixion* (1944), the long neck of the first figure wearing hair as a dusty mask points downwards. The dress hanging off the collapsed shoulder blades by pink strips more closely resembles a robe made of flayed pink skin. The central figure, with a blindfold above a ridiculous double row of teeth circled by red lips, exercises a quiet horror that spreads through space like a hackneyed nightmare. The naked fabric of the canvas adds to a stripped silence. These grey, pale figures seem muted against a red background. At the end of a long neck of the third figure, a wide open maw hangs open, unsupported by a head. The organ at the end of the neck is made up of dentition, with an ear at the corner of the lip: the ear is a blind and mute organ. The figure's body follows predetermined torsions, the paths of which are suggested more precisely by a white circle in the *Second Version of Triptych 1944* (1988). These act as hinges that swing in the directions of loose skin in order to achieve maximal horror.

The 1944 triptych is more subdued, but no less bone chilling, than another painted almost two decades later: *Three Studies for a Crucifixion* (1962) unwraps the horror contained in the intangible furies of 1944. The legs and feet pointing from the lower edge of the first painting are flayed. Yet, the anatomical parts they are supposed to contain cannot be determined with certainty. The ankles look like bloody pork chops and the tibia is a small spine. The calf seems to contain a thoracic cage: another species is folded within these legs. And there are two figures looking towards the presumed body of which we see only the legs. It is the figure beyond the frame. The backdrop is orange and red and black.

What is this mess on the bed in the second frame? A body so twisted on itself that it bursts at the seams? The skull is gruesomely exposed and exploded at the top, with blood splashed onto the pillow. The orange floor, the red walls and the black, drawn blinds suggest we are in the same room as in the first painting in the triptych. Has there been a change of perspective? Are we seeing what the two figures had been looking at on the first panel? Has this clutter of meat, through its brutalized skull, seen these figures and its own flayed feet, as we did? Has it been looking at this scene with us?

There is no respite. If the perspective changed again from the second to the third panel, are we looking from the vantage point of the ceiling, above the head of the bed? Or has the bed been flipped back so that it serves as an open display case for an upside down corpse? Upside down, the lower jaw protrudes with baboon fangs. There is a carcass splayed like a side of beef *à la* Soutine. Are we seeing a black dog drawn to the meat standing at the forefront of the picture plane? Or is it outside the frame, like us, with only its shadow projected onto the ground, looking very much like the black ooze trickling out of the carcass? Or is it one of the figures from the first panel, taking the triptych full circle? After all, this shadow is of a similar shape and colour as the legs of the standing figure. The floors are orange, the walls are red.

If the first triptych represents descent through the downward pointing figures and the hanging skins, then the second triptych captures the meat of the flesh so that the unrepresented crucifixion is the schema for the descent into meat underscored by the concept of incarnation.

Incarnation as Downward Movement

Bacon's paintings illustrate the mystery at the heart of the device of incarnation by hinting at an absence – the cross signalled by the crucifixion of the title is not shown. The lack of certainty on the viewer's part about what is observed on the canvases adds to the unknown. Incarnation focalizes that which, up until its fleshly manifestation, was not precisely known.

It makes, according to words Deleuze used in a different context, 'invisible forces visible'.[2] What is unintelligible is captured, trapped in the skins of representation, 'trap' being part of the etymological chain linked to 'descent'. Yet, despite its function of representing the intangible, incarnation has the advantage of tracing this aesthetic problem according to a downward trajectory.

To grasp the direction given to incarnation, an immediate comparison to the thought process of analogy should start things rolling. Analogy brings together the world of the unknown and the familiar world by translating one in terms of the other. Analogy reaches vertically into the unknown, as the etymology of the term demonstrates:

> This logos, this reason, of the ana*logy*, is at the same time an *ana*logos. Where *ana* means 'up', 'upwards', and gives the idea of a passage or a surpassing, a transcendence when it is a question of passing into a superior order. From the animal to the human, for example, from the human to the divine.[3]

However, with an etymological constraint, descent is also possible: '*Ana* means "upward", perhaps even the upward movement associated with transcendence, and so there should be, in turn, a *katalogia*, a movement downwards.'[4] This downward catalogue movement classifies, organizes and constrains. If analogy points upward towards the divine, then its contrary is the downward movement towards the flesh.

I propose to model Deleuze's incarnation on these opposing vertical paths, following the contrary euphemism of angry/kindly and the constellation grouping concepts with bodies: 'The concept is an incorporeal, even though it is incarnated in bodies.'[5] Deleuze utilizes the device of incarnation on several occasions in his writings but does not specifically elaborate on it as he does with other concepts. However, *What Is Philosophy?* addresses the issue of incarnation in the context of art and aesthetics:

> A curious Fleshism inspires this final avatar of phenomenology and plunges it into the mystery of incarnation. It is a pious and a sensual notion, a mixture of sensuality and religion, without which, perhaps, flesh could not stand up by itself (it would slide down the bones, as in Bacon's figures).[6]

It seems out of place in Deleuze's ontology as a term that usually means the materialization of something (usually spiritual or divine) in fleshly or human form. It is the skin sliding down the bones that gives us the direction to follow in this concept of incarnation.

Michael Hardt, in 'Exposure: Pasolini and the Flesh', explores this downward direction as he explains how the materiality of incarnation, even though it has its source in the transcendental, slips away from it, loses it: 'Incarnation is all about abandonment – abandonment to the flesh. Paul writes that in becoming flesh Christ abandoned the form of God; he emptied himself by taking on a limited materiality. This self-emptying is the exposure of the flesh.'[7] The contrary movement of the expected trajectory is traced from the divine to the flesh. Hardt demonstrates how Christ 'emptied the transcendental *form* and carried divinity into the material'.[8] This detachment from the transcendental does not show how the material is lesser than the typically superior dimension; rather, the full importance of the material comes into being in incarnation: 'The self-emptying or *kenosis* of Christ, the evacuation of the transcendental, is the affirmation of the plenitude of the material, the fullness of the flesh.'[9] It is precisely the materialist context of this incarnation and its falling away from the transcendental that Deleuze describes as coming into the form of meat. It is becoming meat. The furies of Bacon's 1944 triptych are pointing their necks downward; the body falling from the cross.

I wish to explore this process of incarnation through the dichotomy of the virtual and actual. The virtual is tightly encased within the play between difference and repetition, where repetition is: 'like a skin which unravels, the external husk of a kernel of difference and more complicated internal repetition'.[10] As Deleuze explains: 'Difference and repetition in the virtual ground the movement of actualisation of differenciation as creation.'[11] But in order to bring us closer to the notion of incarnation, I suggest following one aspect of the virtual, the 'essence' as explored in *Proust and Signs*. Essence is a synonym for the virtual and incarnation stands for actualization. Deleuze repeats the motto he derives from Proust that crops up in a multitude of places throughout his corpus: 'Real without being actual, ideal without being abstract'[12] to which he adjoins the explanation: 'This ideal real, this virtual, is essence.'[13] Incarnation takes part in the constellation of the virtual and the actual: 'The essence realizes itself, or incarnates itself in the involuntary memory. Here as in art, the envelopment, the coiling, remains the superior state of the essence.'[14] The point is similar to Hardt's: the mortal coil is favoured over the transcendental (in the case of Hardt) and the essential (for Deleuze), on an aesthetic platform.

But one has to be careful about the origins of essence and its incarnation. The subject does not possess an essence but is constructed by one: 'It is not the subject that explicates the essence, it is rather the essence that implicates itself, envelops itself, coils itself within the subject.'[15] This coiling or folding can be exemplified by embryology, where the foetus is the sketch of an unfolding individual, the virtuality of an individual. The development of the embryo occurs from one stage to another without design nor resemblance: 'Actual terms never resemble the singularities they incarnate.'[16] The worlds, or essences, constitute the individual, and so thought does not belong to the individual subject.[17] A force pushes thought onto us: 'Essences are coiled inside of that which forces us to think, they do not respond to our voluntary effort.'[18] We do not think out of our will: we are constrained to think. We have to think, like cells split and tectonic plates shift: 'Essence only allows us to think when we are constrained to do so.'[19] So essence, weighted down by flesh, wrapped in skin, makes us think, in effect, the virtual pushing through onto the plane of the actual.

What is the link between essences and their incarnation in the fleshly coil? It is through the process of incarnation that the incorporeal passes into the material and the concept becomes real: 'Qualities and species incarnate the varieties of actual relation; organic parts incarnate the corresponding singularities.'[20] As Hardt explains, incarnation holds the essence and existence under its banner: 'Incarnation is first of all a metaphysical thesis that the essence and existence of being are one and the same.'[21] And in this process, it is the descent into flesh through incarnation that animates essences into existence, simply because they are given flesh: 'There is no ontological essence that resides beyond the world. None of the being or God or nature remains outside existence, but rather all is fully realized, fully expressed, without remainder, in the flesh.'[22] It is the valorizing of the paradoxical depth on the surface of the skin. This is because without flesh holding together thought we cannot imagine God and therefore the transcendental is quite literally in the flesh.

The materiality takes precedence over the transcendental; Hardt even sees the transcendental as the 'empty husk' because Christ descended from it into the material. This materiality that holds the depth of existence is what is found on the meaty surface of Bacon's figures. Rather, it is at this surface that the material being dwells, in the same way the concept that captures this being is just as real: 'Transcendence, the condition of possibility of being, should not be imagined as above or below the material – it dwells, rather, precisely at its very surface.'[23] The surface is not shallow – transcendence at the surface opens the depth of the skin.

The BwO will be another station in the process of uncovering the surface of the skin to a timely dimension. But first, we can see how the surface of the skin can be the vehicle that crosses both categorical and essential boundaries.

The Topology of the Cross

The surface of the skin is teeming with potential; it possesses a virtual depth that can be manipulated. Here, at the level of the skin instead of the body, a diagrammatic transformation can be made. It will not be the vertical direction of a spirit descending into a body, but the multidimensional manipulation of the virtual folding into an actual state. This diagrammatic process has its basis in architecture (a simple definition of the diagram is a plan containing all the coordinates and measurements for the realization of a physical object), topology (an object drawn on this plan is folded and virtually manipulated into a completely different object), cartography (a plan provides a link to the imaginary, that is, it helps 'find one's bearings in thought'[24]) and finally, nineteenth-century biology (when the analogical process is still trained on the material and the physical). All of these elements work together yet independently towards one goal – they trawl the depths of the virtual for the material necessary to construct the actual.

Nineteenth-century biology seems out of place in the list of the previous paragraph but it is the theatre of Étienne Geoffroy Saint-Hilaire's nimble mind that skips over prefabricated, rigid categories of biological classification and shows how a cephalopod can be folded into a quadruped, if only virtually. When an animal does not seem to have a hyoid bone during dissection, it is assumed that it has one on a virtual level.[25] Geoffroy Saint-Hilaire navigates the virtual planes of the classificatory system with extraordinary ease. And a system does not simply consist of an organic ensemble of actual organs but also has virtual dimension: potential organs also belong to the system.[26] If the system holds actual and virtual dimensions, a biologist who relies on what he sees on the dissecting table runs the risk of missing that which is not there. Geffroy Saint-Hilaire's theory of the unified plan provides the opportunity to compare certain organs and bones of an animal with those that another animal possesses *in potentia*. The animal's virtual dimension is an anatomical plane that must be manipulated topologically.

Geoffroy Saint-Hilaire's analogical method revolves around a folding mechanism that provides a way for the bones and organs of a vertebrate to be reconfigured through torsion into a cephalopod. Whether or not these distortions can result in the twisted parts of Bacon's miasmic skeletons and ripped skin of the 1962 triptych, folds such as these occur before the stage of the actual. The functional plicature between heterogeneous elements occurs when the classificatory boundary is skipped over by thought. Analogy can pass over the physical limits and reconfigure a vertebrate into a cephalopod. In the passage between the virtual and the actual, even bones are rendered soft and malleable.

Anatomical analogy skips over the line drawn between species: a contraction of this sort can be witnessed in Mieke Bal's treatment of Jean-Baptiste-Siméon Chardin's painting of *The Ray* (1728). In this case, a fish is folded, contracted, into a crucified figure. This process illustrates the zones of indiscernibility, or the fuzzy border of becoming: 'Man becomes animal, but not without the animal becoming spirit at the same time, the spirit of man, the physical spirit of man presented in the mirror as Eumenides or Fate.'[27] Chardin's painting depicts a splayed ray hanging by a hook in a kitchen, surrounded by molluscs, fish, a cauldron and a cat. The ray holds the central position of the picture plane and has the shape of a diamond: 'This diamond is also like a crossroads: in it meet the different angles of vision located in the four corners of the painting, like the faces in the four corners of ancient maps.'[28] This ancient map, in the cartographic shape of the ray, can be abstracted in its four corners and provide the orientation the eyes of the viewer are to follow: the cat, the cauldron, the dead fish below, tracing, in effect, a cross. And in an extraordinary move, Bal uses this four point diagram to fold into the image of the ray, that of a crucified Christ. It is a topological manipulation: the geometrical shape of the cross turns into the diamond through 'continuous, elastic deformation'.[29] In this case, topological means: 'being or involving properties unaltered under a homeomorphism'.[30] Homeomorphism is the function through which a coffee cup can be reshaped into a donut: '[A] function that is a one-to-one mapping between sets such that both the function and its inverse are continuous and that in topology exists for geometric figures which can be transformed one into the other by an elastic deformation.'[31] It is not hard to imagine a diamond-shaped kite, the points of which are held up by a delicate wooden cross.

Bal does more than point out a simple analogy between the fish (incidentally, as she reminds us, a symbol of early Christianity) and Christ – she identifies the function that allows the comparison between both figures:

> The significance of this form is inevitable: the diamond shape, the representation of the body splayed open as if martyred, and the disposition

Skin, Aesthetics, Incarnation

of the corners all bring to mind the Crucifixion. But here the traditional form of the Crucifixion has been reversed in several different ways.[32]

First, the wounds on the surface of Christ's skin are compared to the single wound eviscerating the ray. Second, the extremities of the cross radiate out, whereas the ray's surface unifies these points, very much like the kite. Third, the volume of Christ's body is essential to the body's 'nature as incarnation'. The ray is flat, but the contrast is striking since 'the [ray] is also shown to be most definitely "hung", nailed like Christ on a hook that is clearly represented.'[33] In the Renaissance body, the three-dimensionality is demonstrated by the folds of the cloth hiding the body of Christ. In the case of the ray, the three-dimensionality is the tear in the mottled screen, the gap revealing a depth in the flat diamond, as the depth in the canvas slashed by Lucio Fontana. These three points need to be connected and followed for a homeomorphic translation to follow its course.

Leo Steinberg, on whose work Bal based her analysis of the crucifixion, describes the mental topography of the body of Christ – its diagram – necessary for artists to paint him in the full glory of pictorial realism. What is interesting in this virtual mapping of the body is that it was made in order to be covered up:

> For even if the body were partly draped, a decision had to be made how much to cover: whether to play the drapery down or send it fluttering like a banner; and whether the loincloth employed, opaque or diaphanous was to reveal or conceal. Only the painters and sculptors kept all of Christ's body in their mind's eye.[34]

This description of the process of painting a body covered with cloth can be considered an illustration of the virtual aspect of the diagrammatic structure. The body of the ray travelling on a continuous trajectory towards the shape of the crucified body of Christ dips momentarily into a tunnel, away from our view, only to emerge on the other side in another form. This process of transformation, this darkened indeterminate state, like a mysterious schema of art (to reshuffle Kant's characterization of his concept of imagination), is what is at stake in the virtual process of incarnation.

The virtual aspect of the diagram is the schema that is held up mentally between the ray and the figure of Christ on the cross. But this is the amorphous process that Bacon captures on the canvas. Tom Conley, in turn, describes the emblematic transposition of these anatomical acrobatics onto the plane of aesthetics and art, that is, Bacon's studies for figures at the base of the crucifixion. He explains the 'intensities' resulting from the figures' 'indeterminate state':

> they are amphibian, androgynous, polymorphous, simultaneously organic and inorganic – [they] offer the viewer an intense experience of painterly variation that runs through the bodies, in and along the spinal columns and nervous systems, of both the Figures that are grasped and the viewer who grasps them. In the dexter panel of *Three Studies for a Crucifixion* . . ., a splayed carcass reveals a dorsal column leading downward to a head with a gaping mouth whose teeth seem to be miniature vertebrae.[35]

It is precisely the materialist context of this incarnation and its falling away from the transcendental that Deleuze describes as coming into the form of meat. The furies' necks for the 1944 triptych are pointing downward at the fallen body. Perhaps this jumbled mass of organs, flesh, skin and bones could be emblematic of the dehierarchization crucial to Deleuze's philosophy?

Morose Time of Apprehension

Even though the torsions through which Bacon puts the bodies in his paintings remind Deleuze of BwO, I propose to go to *A Thousand Plateaus* to find the element of time necessary to give the vertical trait of the schema a vertical time line so that the schematic cross can be complete.

Skin, bones, organs, body, mouth, anus, nose and stomach: 'It has itself strung up to stop the organs from working; flayed, as if the organs clung to the skin.'[36] The organs are scrambled in their order, resembling the flayed and mixed up organs of Bacon's triptychs. But an organizing notion, however tenuous, is implied. After all, the chapter of Deleuze and Guattari's book is a 'how-to' guide called 'How Do You Make Yourself a Body without Organs?' This programme follows the morose time of a sadomasochistic schedule.

The mistress acts upon the subservient slave and sews all of his possible openings. The hierarchically determined body is then rendered into a single invariable surface as a programmatic:

> Mistress, 1) You may tie me down on the table, ropes drawn tight, for ten to fifteen minutes, time enough to prepare the instruments; 2) One hundred lashes at least, a pause of several minutes; 3) You begin sewing, you sew up the hole in the glans.[37]

Skin, Aesthetics, Incarnation

After the long quote is over and the narrator on the table has asked to be turned on his stomach, his buttocks sewn together, and whipped some more, Deleuze and Guattari add: this is not a fantasy, it is a programme.[38] It is a programme indeed. However, it is not a sadomasochistic relation, as Deleuze discovers in his book on Sacher-Masoch, where the slave is ordered by the mistress. The mistress is not doing anything. Nothing has been done. But a relationship has been established:

> It is nonstratified, unformed, intense matter, the matrix of intensity, intensity = 0; but there is nothing negative about that zero, there are no negative or opposite intensities. . . . That is why we treat the BwO as the full egg before the extension of the organism and the organization of the organs, before the formation of the strata; as the intense egg defined by axes and vectors, gradients and thresholds, by dynamic tendencies involving energy transformation and kinematic movements involving group displacement, by migrations: all independent of *accessory forms* because the organs appear and function here only as pure intensities.[39]

The programme of the BwO is praxis without being practiced. It is the virtual in the moment before the actual hatches. *Intensité zéro* is transformed into another object: *l'oeuf*, the shape of zero, or love in tennis (itself an English distortion of the French *tenez* exclaimed before the serve). At this stage, the BwO = zero in intensity. At this level of intensity, the egg represents the moment right before the formation and subsequent organization of organs. It is not the space, but the silent empty *vacuus*. Right before it breaks into the whole cinematics of style, right before the complete transformation of this space through speed, acceleration and deceleration, it is all waiting, expectation and trepidation. It is according to 'speeds and slownesses' that the virtual is incarnated into the actual:[40]

> The body without organs is *virtually* all the things we could be, but when we're in that state we're *actually* none of them. In order to actualize a virtuality, we need to conceptualize some step towards it as a possibility, and as a body without organs we have no concepts, so we are trapped in a catatonic state for a long as it lasts. The virtual is the realm of the prepossible, where there is no conception of what the alternative possibilities could be, so if anything happens, it happens without having those possibilities to guide or inform it.[41]

This particular time scale is filtered through masochism and defined as moroseness in terms of lateness: 'The masochist is morose: but his moroseness should be related to the experience of waiting and delay.'[42] For Deleuze, the morose mechanism remains incomprehensible if not given a form, a form that in turn makes the mechanism possible.[43] He stretches the definition of delay by complementing it with lateness:

> Formally speaking, masochism is a state of waiting; the masochist experiences waiting in its pure forms. Pure waiting divides naturally into two simultaneous currents, the first representing what is awaited, something essentially tardy, always late and always postponed, the second representing something that is expected and on which depends the speeding up of the awaited object.[44]

To this duality of what we are waiting for and what we expect to come, Deleuze adds another duality that inserts itself into the mechanism. It is the duality of pleasure and pain believed by Deleuze to be a necessary consequence. The mechanism of waiting constitutes the structure of masochism: it is the trepidation.

John Maybury's *Love is the Devil* (1998), the film representing the relationship between George Dyer (Daniel Craig) and Francis Bacon (Derek Jacobi), stages a scene of sadomasochistic sexual anticipation. After a meal in a stark apartment, Bacon and Dyer undress casually and fold their clothes neatly over chairs. Dyer then ropes a leather belt tightly around his fist, making it crack as it coils over his whitened knuckles. Bacon, for his part, kneels at the side of the bed: genuflexion away from the off camera sound of the belt tightening behind him, elbows over white sheets. After a cut that shifts to the post-coitus moment, Bacon's narrative monologue hovers above the lovers lying in bed. The artist matter-of-factly directs his attention to the food grumbling in his bowels: the flesh and what it infolds inside have been in some way uncoiled. The skin flayed from the leather belt, to the podgy flesh draped in white underwear to, finally, the meat in the belly.

Painting Skin

Let us turn our attention to the meat-stuffed diagram, so to speak. In *Francis Bacon: the Logic of Sensation*, the diagram is exactly made up of a duality that consists in the sensation and the frame.[45] Sensation is too fluid and the frame too abstract but together they form an equilibrium. We have already seen how the diagram is made up of another duality: tracing and mapping. The tracing is constraining and repeats what is already there like a photograph or an X-ray.[46] Mapping is expansive, it exposes pure potentiality. Together, they articulate a mechanism of constraint and expansion. There is, in Maybury's film, between Dyer and Bacon, a mapping of the flesh surveyed by the belt and the monologue that functions as an X-ray opening the belly to explain the meat moving through the bowels.

But this dual diagrammatic process can be witnessed in Eliot's *The Family Reunion*. His description of the loneliness and anonymity within a 'crowded desert' draws a directionless map where 'no direction / Leads anywhere but round and round in that vapour.'[47] If this verse serves as an illustration of the mapping of unexplored spaces, Eliot, in another passage, uncannily illustrates the process of colouration contained in Deleuze and Guattari's concept of tracing: 'While the slow stain sinks deeper through the skin / Tainting the flesh and discolouring the bone – / This is what matters, but it is unspeakable.'[48] Both the X-ray perspective of digested food and a stain reaching the bone are mediated by the skin.

The diagram is like a desert, or, to be more precise, the Sahara that erases the features of a painted face.[49] In Bacon's work, the diagram pushes the figure towards abstraction, creating zones of indiscernibility. Bacon would distract himself with photographs lying on his studio's floor while painting, so as to avoid clichés. Photographs would enter the painting, disturbing the configurations of traits. The result would be new dimensions full of potential.

The diagram, this controlled chance factor, this freedom from the expected within the act of painting, is 'like the emergence of a new world'.[50] And like Harry, the tormented character of Eliot's play shows, the unrepresentable erases the flesh into the world: 'I know it, I know it! / More potent than ever before, a vapour dissolving / All other worlds, and me into it.'[51] The vapour rubs out the contour of the figure and connects it to a world.

Incarnation is not simply the embodiment of the transcendental or the essential but the revelation of an ontological depth of the surface. It is not simply the spiritual in the skins of the actual but a descent that keeps going farther once the surface has been reached. 'One no longer paints "on" but "under".'[52] Or through, like Fontana's wounded canvases. This is shown not only in the representation of skin and flesh in Bacon's crucifixion triptychs but also in the structural diagram upholding these representations. There is the downward movement implied by Christ's incarnation and the underlying materiality shown in the mortification of the flesh. By taking the Deleuzean path traced by the virtual and the actual, our vision is trained on the surface of the skin and its potential for aesthetic manipulation of form. From cephalopod to quadruped, from the ray to the crucified Christ, the surface of the skin reveals its aesthetic elasticity. The shape of the cross is completed by a horizontal axis being added to the vertical line of descent. This horizontal axis is drawn by the moroseness of time functioning through virtual/actual stages of the trepidation experienced by the surface of the injured skin.

Conclusion

If we are to follow the concept of the diagram as the kernel inside Deleuze and Guattari's philosophical system, we do not see it coming on the scene from the very beginning, but elements of it would necessarily be present in the way that a system is organized according to the principle of constraint. The apparatus deployed in the preceding chapters served to locate zones in Deleuze and Guattari's writing that are at the cusp of a figure that remains incorporeal but not less real. The dimension between the text and image in Deleuze and Guattari's scholarship has not been actualized. This duality remains a particular problem.

Is a diagram a good tool with which to construct a system? Perhaps it is not ideal since it deals with instances of dissolution, with paradoxes and the unrepresentable. But it is an adequate map to guide our way through a system, to orient ourselves within the pages of a corpus made up of a multitude of discourses. After all, the diagram brings things together; it is philosophical and artistic, visual and textual. Its productive aspect appears where it is embodied. The problem has been to define an image, especially in view of the diagram. The diagram strategy was to capture an image of an unrepresentable, elusive site where images come into being. That is why Kant's schema has been an important part of the definition of the diagram. The schema, specifically as something that puts things together, has served as an apt analogy to the diagram's place within a system.

But can we speak of a system proper? The system as present in these pages has been elusive. When it was about to the captured, it dissolved into a multitude. The notion of the schema was at the edge of the contraction. It was observed at the site that appeared in the moment between its capture and release. Is a system a proper way through which to read Deleuze and Guattari's writings? Yes. The philosophers set up their theories according to an open system of multitudes but the system will change in relation to the map we design of their philosophy and the path we subsequently choose to follow on this map.

A joyful monotony must be followed to the various sites of what Deleuze calls a *Systématisation finale*. It comes from the images being used as devices within a philosophical argument. These focal points that emanate into the web of a system remain distorted and are put in relief through the chiaroscuro of the lines and drawings: the possibility of clarifying the concept of the diagram. Knowledge is dependent on illustrations and, since to some extent they carry knowledge, they can be steered towards a method that involves the intricate duality of text and image. This is done through the allagmatic that ontologizes the space within the analogizing, representational device of illustration and thought. But what kind of possibility does this compilation of knowledge hold for an ontology of thought? This is a complicated difficulty. Even though the diagram is based on a schematic model, this model is not without its spatial representations. If the diagram is spatial, then the spatial dimension can be extracted from Kant's transcendental philosophy. Heidegger underlines the schema within the dimension of time. But seen from a spatial perspective, we have isolated the principle of dynamism as function within the systematicity of knowledge and described the mechanics of the extraordinary contraction fuelled by an indiscernible style. This extraordinary contraction, the constrained, folded movement of thought, is based on geographical and anatomical constellations of images. It draws its base from images that are material and scientific and distorts them. It utilizes the mechanism that comes out of the duality of image and text in Deleuze and Guattari's system and delivers the impetus necessary for the further actualization of knowledge. The contraction is a delicate movement, like a breath or the anticipation of rhythm in the heart at rest. It is as elegant as the propulsion of a squid through the dark depths of the ocean. The idea is ontologized and made flesh: a paradoxical figure, to say the least. It is Deleuze's escape plan from the transcendental into the material: his inconspicuous notion of incarnation. Based on the concept of incarnation, which to fully function must base itself on a materiality already present in Deleuze so as to be a truly Deleuzean incarnation, images can be made into productive philosophical devices that are interwoven within a philosophical corpus as a carnal, material diagram. Concepts that are images and images that are concepts: this is the materiality of thought.

Of course, there have been blind spots in this analysis that have not been addressed. Peirce's philosophy was not given its proper place in the treatment of the diagram even though it has been very influential to the French philosophers. Within the Deleuze/Guattari duality, Guattari has not been given the proper weight especially since Deleuze considered him the diagram-persona. On the other hand, art and aesthetics have compensated for these shortcomings. Literature and painting served the purpose to open a dimension within the theory of the diagram beyond the scope of philosophy. The practical purpose of art was to articulate a concept that deals in illusive dimensions with an aspect of thought just beyond representation.

Notes

Introduction

[1] Gilles Deleuze, *Foucault*, trans. Seán Hand (Minneapolis: Minnesota UP, 1995), 31.
[2] Deleuze, *Foucault*, 31.
[3] Deleuze, *Foucault*, 32.
[4] Deleuze, *Foucault*, 32.
[5] Deleuze, *Foucault*, 32.
[6] Deleuze, *Foucault*, 33.
[7] Deleuze, *Foucault*, 33.
[8] Deleuze, *Foucault*, 34.
[9] Deleuze, *Foucault*, 34.
[10] Deleuze, *Foucault*, 34.
[11] Deleuze, *Foucault*, 34.
[12] Deleuze, *Foucault*, 34.
[13] Gilles Deleuze, 'Desire and Pleasure', in *Two Regimes of Madness: Text and Interviews 1975–1995*, ed. David Lapoujade, trans. Ames Hodges and Mike Taormina (New York: Semiotext(e), 2007), 125.
[14] Deleuze, *Foucault*, 85.
[15] Deleuze, *Foucault*, 101.
[16] Gilles Deleuze, 'Michel Foucault's Main Concepts', in *Two Regimes of Madness: Text and Interviews 1975–1995*, ed. David Lapoujade, trans. Ames Hodges and Mike Taormina (New York: Semiotext(e), 2007), 231.
[17] Deleuze, *Foucault*, 36.
[18] Michel Foucault, *Surveiller et punir* (Paris: Gallimard, 2004), 240.
[19] Deleuze, *Foucault*, 44.
[20] Deleuze, *Foucault*, 44.
[21] Peter Eisenman, *Written into the Void: Selected Writings 1990–2004*, intro. Jeffrey Kipnis (New Haven: Yale UP, 2007), 88.
[22] Eisenman, *Written into the Void*, 89.
[23] Eisenman, *Written into the Void*, 88.
[24] 'Reacting against an understanding of the diagram as what was thought to be an apparently essentialist tool, a new generation, fuelled by new computer techniques and a desire to escape its perceived Oedipal anxieties – the generation of their mentors – is today proposing a new theory of the diagram based partly on Gilles Deleuze's interpretation of Foucault's recasting of the diagram as "a series of machinic forces" and partly on their own cybernetic hallucinations. In their

polemic, the diagram has become a key word in the interpretation of the new. They challenge both the traditional geometric bases of the diagram and the sedimented history of architecture, and in so doing they question any relation of the diagram to architecture's anteriority or interiority.' Eisenman, *Written into the Void*, 89–90.
25. Eisenman, *Written into the Void*, 90.
26. Gilles Deleuze and Félix Guattari, *What Is Philosophy?*, trans. Hugh Tomlinson and Graham Burchell (New York: Columbia UP, 1994), 189.
27. Deleuze and Guattari, *What Is Philosophy?*, 187.
28. Deleuze and Guattari, *What Is Philosophy?*, 187.
29. Deleuze and Guattari, *What Is Philosophy?*, 180.
30. Gilles Deleuze, *Negotiations: 1972–1990*, trans. Martin Joughin (New York: Columbia UP, 1995), 33.
31. Gilles Deleuze, 'What Children Say', *Essays Critical and Clinical*, trans. Daniel W. Smith and Michael A. Greco (Minneapolis: U of Minnesota P, 1997), 62.
32. Gilles Deleuze and Félix Guattari, *A Thousand Plateaus: Capitalism and Schizophrenia*, trans. Brian Massumi (Minneapolis: U of Minnesota P, 2005), 13.
33. Deleuze, 'What Children Say', 63.
34. Deleuze and Guattari, *A Thousand Plateaus*, 12.
35. Merriam-Webster's Dictionary.
36. Deleuze and Guattari, *A Thousand Plateaus*, 12.
37. Deleuze and Guattari, *A Thousand Plateaus*, 13.
38. Deleuze and Guattari, *A Thousand Plateaus*, 91.
39. Noëlle Batt, 'L'expérience diagrammatique: un nouveau régime de pensée', in *Penser par le diagramme: de Gilles Deleuze à Gilles Châtelet*, ed. Noëlle Batt (Saint-Denis: Presses Universitaires de Vincennes, 2004), 15.
40. Robert Sasso and Arnaud Villani, eds, *Le Vocabulaire de Gilles Deleuze* (Paris: J. Vrin, 2003).
41. Gilles Deleuze, 'Écrivain non: un nouveau cartographe', *Critique*, 343 (1975): 1215 (my translation).
42. Deleuze, 'un nouveau cartographe', 1216.
43. Deleuze, 'un nouveau cartographe', 1216 (my translation).
44. Deleuze, 'un nouveau cartographe', 1216 (my translation).
45. Deleuze, 'un nouveau cartographe', 1217.
46. Deleuze, 'un nouveau cartographe', 1217 (my translation).
47. Charles S. Peirce, *Philosophical Writings of Peirce*, ed. Justus Buchler (New York: Dover Publications, 1955), 98.
48. Peirce, *Philosophical Writings*, 99.
49. Peirce, *Philosophical Writings*, 99.
50. Peirce, *Philosophical Writings*, 99.
51. Deleuze and Guattari, *A Thousand Plateaus*, 142.
52. Deleuze and Guattari, *A Thousand Plateaus*, 142.
53. Batt, 'L'expérience diagrammatique', 12.
54. Deleuze and Guattari, *A Thousand Plateaus*, 91.
55. Deleuze, 'Desire and Pleasure', 124–5.
56. Deleuze and Guattari, *A Thousand Plateaus*, 91.
57. Deleuze and Guattari, *A Thousand Plateaus*, 91.

58 Gilles Deleuze, *Francis Bacon: The Logic of Sensation*, trans. and intro. Daniel W. Smith, afterword Tom Conley (Minneapolis: U of Minnesota P, 2004).
59 Deleuze, in *Francis Bacon: The Logic of Sensation*, footnotes this exchange between Bacon and David Sylvester that he deemed very important:

> Bacon: Very often the involuntary marks are much more deeply suggestive than others, and those are the moments when you feel that anything can happen.
>
> Sylvester: You feel it while you're making those marks?
>
> Bacon: No, the marks are made, and you survey the thing like you would a sort of graph [*diagramme*]. And you see within this graph the possibilities of all types of fact being planted. This is a difficult thing; I'm expressing it badly. But you see, for instance, if you think of a portrait, you may be have to put the mouth somewhere , but you suddenly see through this graph that the mouth could go right across the face. And in a way you would love to be able in a portrait to make a Sahara of the appearance – to make it so like, yet seeming to have the distances of the Sahara. (*Interviews*, 56)

In another passage, Bacon explains that when he does a portrait, he often looks at photographs that have nothing to do with the model – for example, a photograph of a rhinoceros for the texture of the skin (*Interviews*, 32). Deleuze, *Francis Bacon*, 160 n. 3.
60 Deleuze, *Francis Bacon*, 81.
61 Deleuze, *Francis Bacon*, 82.
62 Deleuze, *Francis Bacon*, 82.
63 Deleuze, *Francis Bacon*, 83.
64 Deleuze, *Francis Bacon*, 83.
65 Deleuze, *Francis Bacon*, 128.
66 Deleuze, *Francis Bacon*, 126.
67 Deleuze, *Francis Bacon*, 126.
68 Deleuze, *Francis Bacon*, 126.
69 Deleuze, *Francis Bacon*, 126.
70 Deleuze, *Francis Bacon*, 126.
71 Deleuze, *Francis Bacon*, 126–7.
72 Deleuze, *Francis Bacon*, 127.
73 Batt, 'L'expérience diagrammatique', 14.
74 Batt, 'L'expérience diagrammatique', 14.
75 Batt, 'L'expérience diagrammatique', 17 (my translation).
76 Batt, 'L'expérience diagrammatique', 17.
77 Deleuze, *Foucault*, 39.
78 Deleuze, 'Foucault's Main Concepts', 253.
79 Deleuze, *Foucault*, 38.
80 Deleuze, 'un nouveau cartographe', 1216.
81 Deleuze, *Foucault*, 69.
82 Deleuze, *Foucault*, 68.
83 Immanuel Kant, *The Critique of Pure Reason*, trans. and ed. Paul Guyer and Allen W. Wood (Cambridge: Cambridge UP, 1998), A141/B180–1. A refers to the first edition of *The Critique of Pure Reason* published in 1781. B refers to the second edition published in 1787.

[84] Kant, *Critique of Pure Reason*, A138/B177.
[85] Deleuze, *Foucault*, 82.
[86] Deleuze, *Foucault*, 117.
[87] Deleuze, *Foucault*, 117.
[88] Deleuze, *Foucault*, 117.
[89] Deleuze, *Foucault*, 118.

Chapter 1

[1] Alain Badiou, *Deleuze: The Clamor of Being*, trans. Louise Burchill (Minneapolis: London, 2000).
[2] Gilles Deleuze and Claire Parnet, *Dialogues II*, trans. Hugh Tomlinson and Barbara Habberjam (New York: Columbia UP, 2002), 51.
[3] Gilles Deleuze and Claire Parnet, *Dialogues*, trans. Hugh Tomlinson and Barbara Habberjam (New York: Columbia UP, 1987), 70.
[4] Deleuze and Parnet, *Dialogues*, 69.
[5] Deleuze and Parnet, *Dialogues*, 69.
[6] Marcel Proust, *Sodom and Gomorrah*, trans. John Starrock (London: Allen Lane, Penguin Press, 2002), 5.
[7] 'Lacking the perspective of the geologist, I at least had that of the botanist, and gazed through the shutters on the stairs at the Duchesse's small shrub and the precious plant, exhibited in the courtyard.' Proust, *Sodom and Gomorrah*, 5.
[8] Proust, *Sodom and Gommorrah*, 11.
[9] See Henri Bergson, *L'évolution créatrice* (Paris: PUF, 2003), 171. Bergson discusses the stratagems orchids use to lure insects.
[10] Deleuze and Guattari, *A Thousand Plateaus*, 293.
[11] The philosophic study of knowledge: inquiry into the basis, nature, validity, and limits of knowledge. Merriam-Webster's Dictionary.
[12] Félix Guattari, *The Anti-Oedipus Papers*, ed. Stéphane Nadaud, trans. Kélina Gotman (New York: Semiotext(e), 2006), 415.
[13] Guattari, *Anti-Oedipus Papers*, 416.
[14] The Webster dictionary definition continues: '. . . from a supposed Greek *enkyklopaideia* (in MSS of the Roman rhetorician Quintilian), from Greek *enkyklios paedeia* general education, from *enkyklios* general – *paideia* educatio, rearing of a child, from *paid-*, *pais* child.'
[15] Gilles Deleuze, *Proust and Signs*, trans. Richard Howard (New York: George Braziller, 1972), 25.
[16] Deleuze, *Proust and Signs*, 4, 10.
[17] Ronald Bogue, *Deleuze on Music, Painting and the Arts* (London: Routledge, 2003), 31.
[18] Nicola Luckhurst, *Science and Structure in Proust's A la recherche du temps perdu* (Oxford: Clarendon Press, 2000), 199.
[19] Alberto Gualandi, *Deleuze* (Paris: Les Belles Lettres, 2003), 18 (my translation).
[20] Bogue, *Deleuze on Music*, 48.
[21] Gilles Deleuze, *Proust et les signes* (Paris: PUF, 1976), 139.
[22] Deleuze, *Proust et les signes*, 138.

23. David Bates, 'Cartographic Aberrations: Epistemology and Order in the Encyclopedic Map', in *Using the Encyclopédie: Ways of Knowing Ways of Reading*, ed. Daniel Brewer and Julie Candler Hayes (Oxford: Voltaire Foundation, 2002), 8.
24. Bates, 'Cartographic Aberrations', 9.
25. Bates, 'Cartographic Aberrations', 9. Bates is referring to Jean Ehard, 'L'arbre et le labyrinthe', in *L'Encyclopédie, Diderot, l'esthétique: mélange à Jacques Chouillet*, ed. Sylvain Auroux et al. (Paris: PUF, 1991).
26. Bates, 'Cartographic Aberrations', 9.
27. See Phillip Blom, *Encyclopédie: The Triumph of Reason in an Unreasonable Age* (London: Fourth Estate, 2004). It is an interesting account of the coming into being of the Encyclopedia.
28. David S. Ferris, 'Post-Modern Interdisciplinarity: Kant, Diderot and the Encyclopedic Project', *MLN*, 18.5 (2003): 1261.
29. Deleuze and Guattari, *A Thousand Plateaus*, 5.
30. Deleuze and Guattari, *A Thousand Plateaus*, 5.
31. Bates, 'Cartographic Aberrations', 9. Bates is referring to Ehard, 'L'arbre et le labyrinthe': 'Laissons donc se dessécher l'arbre, et engageons-nous dans le labyrinthe.'
32. Deleuze, *Foucault*, 125.
33. Julie Candler Hayes, *Reading the French Enlightenment: System and Subversion* (Cambridge: Cambridge UP, 1999), 3.
34. Candler Hayes, *French Enlightenment*, 5.
35. Candler Hayes, *French Enlightenment*, 191.
36. Deleuze and Guattari, *A Thousand Plateaus*, 6–7.
37. Deleuze and Guattari, *What Is Philosophy?*, 189.
38. Deleuze, *Foucault*, 82.
39. Gilbert Simondon, *Du mode d'existence des objets techniques* (Paris: Aubier-Montaigne, 1969), 97 (my translation).
40. Deleuze and Guattari, *A Thousand Plateaus*, 7.
41. Deleuze, *Negotiations*, 129.
42. Gilles Deleuze, *Pourparlers: 1972: 1990* (Paris: Les Éditions de Minuit, 2003), 177.
43. See Clément Rosset, *Le réel et son double: essai sur l'illusion* (Paris: Gallimard, 1976). Rosset uses *la bêtise*, stupidity as a strategy for illusion: 'Un réel qui n'est que le réel, et rien d'autre, est insignifiant, absurde, "idiot", comme le dit Macbeth. Macbeth a d'ailleurs raison, sur ce point du moins: la réalité est effectivement idiote. Car, avant de signifier imbécile, idiot signifie simple, particulier, unique de son espèce. Telle est bien la réalité, et l'ensemble des événements qui la composent: simple, particulière, unique – *idiotès* – "idiote".' Rosset, *Le réel et son double*, 50.
44. Clément Rosset, *Le réel: traité de l'idiotie* (Paris: Éditions de Minuit, 1977). 'Un mot exprime à lui seul ce double caractère, solitaire et inconnaissable, de toute chose au monde: le mot idioties. *Idôtès*, idiot, signifie simple, particulier, unique; puis, par une extension sémantique dont la signification philosophique est de grande portée, personne dénué d'intelligence, être dépourvu de raison. Toute chose, toute personne sont ainsi idiotes dès lors qu'elles n'existent qu'en elles, c'est-à-dire sont incapables d'apparaître dans le double du miroir.' Rosset, *Le réel*, 42.

Notes

45 Deleuze, *Negotiations*, 129.
46 Guattari, *Anti-Oedipus Papers*, 14.
47 Guattari, *Anti-Oedipus Papers*, 14.
48 Deleuze, *Negotiations*, 177.
49 Deleuze, *Negotiations*, 19–20.
50 Deleuze and Parnet, *Dialogues*, 30.
51 Alain Badiou, *Deleuze: The Clamor of Being*, trans. Louise Burchill (Minneapolis: U of Minnesota P, 2000), 5: 'Deleuze arrives at conceptual productions that I would unhesitatingly qualify as *monotonous*, composing a very particular regime of emphasis or almost infinite repetition of a limited repertoire of concepts, as well as a virtuosic variation of names, under which what is thought remains essentially identical.'
52 'Undoubtedly, between 1969 and 1975, he [Deleuze] was the mentor of that fraction of leftism for which all that mattered was desiring machines and nomadism, the sexual and the festive, free flux and the freedom of expression, the so-called free radio stations along with all the other spaces of freedom, the rainbow of minuscule differences, and the molecular protestation fascinated by the powerful moral configuration of Capital.' Badiou, *The Clamor of Being*, 95–6.
53 'They do not take literally enough the strictly "*machinic*" conception that Deleuze has, not only of desire (the famous "desiring-machines") but, even more so, of will or choice.' Badiou, *The Clamor of Being*, 11.
54 Badiou, *The Clamor of Being*, 17.
55 Badiou, *The Clamor of Being*, 15.
56 Badiou, *The Clamor of Being*, 16.
57 Deleuze and Guattari, *What Is Philosophy?*, 36.
58 Badiou, *The Clamor of Being*, 16.
59 Badiou, *The Clamor of Being*, 13.
60 Badiou, *The Clamor of Being*, 13.
61 Badiou, *The Clamor of Being*, 13.
62 Arnaud Villani, 'La métaphysique de Gilles Deleuze', *Multitude* (web), http://multitudes.samizdat.net/La-metaphysique-de-Deleuze.html
63 Villani, 'La métaphysique de Gilles Deleuze'.
64 Villani, 'La métaphysique de Gilles Deleuze'.
65 '. . . la philosophie de Deleuze nous apparaît hantée par un "démon de système" . . .' Gualandi, *Deleuze*, 15.
66 Gualandi, *Deleuze*, 16 (my translation).
67 Deleuze and Guattari, *A Thousand Plateaus*, 344.
68 Muriel Combes, *Simondon individu et collectivité: Pour une philosophie du transindividuel* (Paris: PUF, 1999), 12–13.
69 See Badiou, *The Clamor of Being*, 16–17.
70 Deleuze (and Guattari) mention Simondon several times in their corpus. In *Desert Island* Deleuze's review of Simondon is included. In *Difference and Repetition*, Simondon is discussed in relation to metastability, disparation and individuation as a way of understanding the virtual. In *Anti-Oedipus*, the philosophers invoque *Du mode d'existence des objets techniques*. In *A Thousand Plateau*, Deleuze and Guattari discuss transduction and hylemorphism. In *The Fold*, Deleuze writes about Simondon to explain modulation and in *Foucault* the topological

inversion of inside and outside, space and time is discussed through the notion of individuation.
71. Gilles Deleuze, 'Gilbert Simondon, *L'individu et sa genèse physico-biologique*', in *L'île déserte et autres textes: textes et entretiens 1953–1974*, ed. David Lapoujade (Paris: Les Éditions de Minuits, 2002), 120–4.
72. It is a biological term from which Simondon isolated a theory of systematic information sharing. A transduction is 'the transfer of genetic determinants from one microorganism to another or from one strain of microorganism to another by a viral agent.' Merriam-Webster's Dictionary.
73. Merriam-Webster's Dictionary.
74. Combes, *Simondon*, 14.
75. Gilbert Simondon, *L'individu et sa genèse physico-biologique* (Grenoble: Jérôme Millon, 1995), 196 (my translation).
76. Pascal Chabot, *La philosophie de Simondon* (Paris: J. Vrin, 2003), 81.
77. Chabot, *La philosophie de Simondon*, 81.
78. Chabot, *La philosophie de Simondon*, 81.
79. Chabot, *La philosophie de Simondon*, 81.
80. Chabot, *La philosophie de Simondon*, 81.
81. Chabot, *La philosophie de Simondon*, 81–2.
82. Chabot, *La philosophie de Simondon*, 82.
83. Chabot, *La philosophie de Simondon*, 82 (my translation).
84. Simondon, *L'individu*, quoted in Combes, *Simondon*, 22 (my translation).
85. Henri Atlan, *Entre le cristal et la fumée: essai sur l'organisation du vivant* (Paris: Éditions du Seuil, 1986), cited in Combes, *Simondon*, 22.
86. Combes, *Simondon*, 23 (my translation).
87. Combes, *Simondon*, 23–4. 'En effet, le pouvoir de découverte de l'analogie dans l'ordre de la pensée est lui-même conçu *par analogie* avec l'opération de cristallisation dans le domaine de l'individuation physique: "à partir d'un germe cristallin microscopique, on peut produire un monocristal de plusieurs décimètres cubes. L'activité de la pensée ne recèlerait-elle pas un processus comparable, *mutatis mutandis?*" (*IPC*, p. 62). Anne Fagot-Largeault, dans sa contribution au colloque consacré à Simondon en avril 1992, conclut de ce passage que la "fécondité de cette démarche analogique de la pensée est elle-même expliquée par une analogie physique".' *IPC* refers to *Individuation psychique et collective*. The conference consecrated to Simondon that took place in 1992 that Combes has in mind has been published. The text in question is: Anne Fagot-Largeault, 'L'individuation en biologie', *Gilbert Simondon, une pensée de l'individuation et de la technique. Actes du colloque organisé par le Collège International de Philosophie 31 mars–2 avril 1992* (Paris: Editions Albin Michel, 1994), 19–54.
88. Barbara Maria Stafford, *Visual Analogy: Consciousness as the Art of Connecting* (Cambridge: MIT Press, 1999), 106.
89. Alberto Toscano explaining the analogical short-circuit in relation to the notion of transduction: 'La disparation. Politique et sujet chez Simondon', *Multitudes* (web), http://multitudes.samizdat.net/spip.php?article1576
90. Gilbert Simondon, *L'individuation à la lumière des notions de forme et d'information* (Grenoble: Millon, 2005), 547–8.

[91] Anne Sauvagnargues, 'Deleuze. De l'animal à l'art', *La philosophie de Gilles Deleuze* (Paris: PUF, 2004), 133.
[92] See Martin Heidegger, 'The Origin of the Work of Art', *Poetry, Language, Thought*, trans. Albert Hofstadter (New York: Harper Collins, 2001). The rift in Heidegger's theory is constructive instead of a purely negative demarcation.
[93] Gilles Deleuze, *Difference and Repetition*, trans. Paul Patton (New York: Columbia UP, 1994), 235.
[94] Deleuze, *Difference and Repetition*, 236.
[95] Compare to the etymology of symbol: from late Latin *symbolum* baptismal creed, from late Greek *symbolon*, literally, token, sign, from Greek; in other senses, from Latin *symbolus*, *symbolum* token, sign, from Greek *symbolon* token of identity (verified by comparing its other half), sign, symbol, from *symballein* to throw together, compare, contribute, from syn- + ballein to throw.
[96] Valérie Carayol, *Communication organisationnelle: une perspective allagmatique* (L'Harmattan: Paris, 2004). The term is defined as *changement*.
[97] Jacques Roux, 'Penser le politique avec Simondon', *Multitudes* (web), http://multitudes.samizdat.net/article1573.html
[98] Simondon, *L'individuation*, 559–60 (my translation).
[99] Simondon, *L'individuation*, 559 (my translation).
[100] Simondon, *L'individuation*, 559 (my translation).
[101] Simondon, *L'individuaion*, 559–60 (my translation).
[102] Kant, *The Critique of Pure Reason*, A716–17/B744–5.
[103] Young Ahn Kang, *Schema and Symbol: A Study in Kant's Doctrine of Schematism* (Amsterdam: Free University Press, 1985), 48–9.
[104] Kant, *Critique of Pure Reason*, A717/B745.
[105] Kang, *Schema and Symbol*, 48–9.
[106] Kang, *Schema and Symbol*, 48–9.
[107] Kang, *Schema and Symbol*, 48–9.
[108] Kang, *Schema and Symbol*, 49.
[109] Kang, *Schema and Symbol*, 49.
[110] 'There is a simple general formula for the signifying regime of the sign (the signifying sign): every sign refers to another sign, and only to another sign, ad infinitum.' Out of this notion of exchange that leads to infinity, the road to transcendence, Deleuze and Guattari draw the following formula: 'It doesn't matter what it means, it's still signifying.' Deleuze and Guattari, *A Thousand Plateaus*, 112.
[111] *The Constructor (Self-Portrait)*, 1924, gelatin silver print, 19 × 21.2 cm. Los Angeles, Getty Research Institute.
[112] John E. Bowlt, 'Manipulating Metaphors: El Lissitzky and the Crafted Hand', in *Situating Lissitzky: Vitebsk, Berlin, Moscow*, ed. Nancy Perloff and Brian Reed (Los Angeles: Getty Research Institute, 2005), 136.
[113] Margarita Tupitsyn, 'After Vitebsk: El Lissitzky and Kazimir Maelvich, 1924–1929', in *Situating Lissitzky: Vitebsk, Berlin, Moscow*, ed. Nancy Perloff and Brian Reed (Los Angeles: Getty Research Institute, 2005), 179.
[114] Deleuze and Guattari, *A Thousand Plateaus*, 344.
[115] Deleuze, *Difference and Repetition*, 246.

116 Yves Citton, 'Sept résonances de Simondon', *Multitudes* (web), http://multitudes.samizdat.net/article1571.html: 'C'est la nature disparate de l'image perçue par mon œil gauche avec celle de mon œil droit qui me permet d'accéder à une perception de cette troisième dimension qu'est la profondeur; c'est la tension propre à de telles incompatibilités, à de telles *disparations*, qui nourrit l'émergence de significations nouvelles, et de formes supérieures d'individuation – et non leur conversion à la logique aplatissante de l'homogène.'

117 Clément Rosset, *Le réel: traité de l'idiotie* (Paris: Éditions de Minuit, 1977), 41 (my translation).

118 'Les ivrognes ont la réputation de voir double. L'homme possède deux yeux et par conséquent deux images du réel qui se superposent normalement l'une à l'autre; lorsqu'il est ivre la superposition se fait mal, d'où le fait que deux bouteilles au lieu d'une dansent devant les yeux de l'ivrogne. Mais cette duplication du réel est un phénomène purement somatique; elle n'engage pas en profondeur la perception ivrogne du réel. Tout au contraire: l'ivrogne perçoit simple, et c'est plutôt l'homme sobre qui, habituellement, perçoit double.' Rosset, *Le réel*, 41.

119 Deleuze, *Difference and Repetition*, 235. Where illusion is resolved by depth.

120 Simondon, *L'individuation*, 559.

121 Simondon, *L'individuation*, 559 (my translation).

122 Sauvagnargues, 'De l'animal à l'art', 138 (my translation).

123 Brian Massumi, 'The Diagram as Technique of Existence', *ANY*, 23 (1998): 44.

124 Massumi, 'The Diagram', 44.

125 Massumi, 'The Diagram', 45.

126 Massumi, 'The Diagram', 45.

127 Didier Debaise, 'Le langage de l'individuation (lexique Simondonien)', *Multitudes* (web), http://multitudes.samizdat.net/Le-langage-de-l-individuation.html?var_recherche=individuation

128 Debaise, 'Le langage' (my translation).

129 Debaise, 'Le langage' (my translation).

130 Debaise, 'Le langage' (my translation).

131 'Simondon l'appelle "disparation", en empruntant le terme au vocabulaire de la psychophysiologie de la perception, où il désigne la production de la profondeur dans la vision binoculaire (*ID*, 121). Chaque rétine est couverte d'une image bidimensionnelle, mais la différence de parallaxe empêche les deux images de coïncider: leur asymétrie produit par "disparation" la création d'une nouvelle dimension. Elle fait surgir la vision tridimensionnelle, comme résolution créatrice de la "disparité" entre les deux rétines. La différence n'est pas réduite: elle trouve sa résolution en inventant, en créant comme solution une nouvelle dimension: la tridimensionnalité. Le volume visuel se produit non par réduction, mais par "disparation" de la différence initiale.' Sauvagnargues, 'De l'animal à l'art', 13.

132 *Factum I* is at the Museum of Contemporary Art, Los Angeles and *Factum II* is at the MOMA in New York.

133 Debaise, 'Le langage' (my translation).

134 Branden W. Joseph, '"A Duplication Containing Duplications": Robert Rauschenberg's Split Screens', *October*, 95 (2001): 3–27.

[135] Deleuze, *Difference and Repetition*, 199.
[136] Guattari, *Anti-Oedipus Papers*, 420.
[137] Manuel DeLanda, 'Deleuze, Diagram, and the Genesis of Form', *ANY*, 23 (1998): 31.
[138] DeLanda, 'Deleuze, Diagram', 31.
[139] DeLanda, 'Deleuze, Diagram', 31.
[140] Sanford Kwinter, 'The Genealogy of Models: The Hammer and the Song', *ANY*, 23 (1998): 60.
[141] DeLanda, 'Deleuze, Diagram', 33.
[142] Kwinter, 'Genealogy of Models', 59.
[143] Kwinter, 'Genealogy of Models', 59.
[144] DeLanda, 'Deleuze, Diagram', 32.
[145] DeLanda, 'Deleuze, Diagram', 32.
[146] DeLanda, 'Deleuze, Diagram', 32.
[147] Compare to Gilles Thérien, *Sémiologies* (Montréal: Université de Québec à Montréal, 1985), 55. Thérien describes the notion of networks used as semiological levels of interpretation: the matrix of a network is constituted by several orders: economical, cultural, social, biological, ecological. They provide a lens through which to 'make appear sign-functions'.

Chapter 2

[1] Deleuze, *Foucault*, 38.
[2] Michel Foucault, *The Order of Things: An Archaeology of the Human Sciences* (London: Tavistock Publications, 1970), 144.
[3] Gilbert Simondon, *Du mode d'existence des objets techniques* (Paris: Aubier-Montaigne, 1969), 98. Making the same claims of written versus visual communication from the point of view of technology, Simondon, in *Du mode d'existence des objets techniques*, says that is the technological shift that demands a more precise manner of expression. Oral expression, he writes, uses already known concepts and, joining Foucault's argument here, it also carries emotions. It is not suited to transmit 'schemes of movements and precise material structures'.
[4] Foucault, *Order of Things*, 133.
[5] Simondon, *Du mode d'existence*, 97 (my translation).
[6] Simondon, *Du mode d'existence*, 97–8 (my translation).
[7] This is similar to Kant's view of this growth towards maturity as a symptom of human progress in the context of cosmopolitan politics in his 1784 essay 'What is Enlightenment?'
[8] Simondon, *Du mode d'existence*, 98 (my translation).
[9] Simondon, *Du mode d'existence*, 97 (my translation).
[10] Simondon, *Du mode d'existence*, 97 (my translation).
[11] Simondon, *Du mode d'existence*, 97 (my translation).
[12] Simondon, *Du mode d'existence*, 97.
[13] Roland Barthes, *New Critical Essays*, trans. Richard Howard (New York: Hill and Wang, 1980), 26.

[14] Barthes, *New Critical Essays*, 26–7.
[15] Roland Barthes, *Le degré zéro de l'écriture/Nouveaux essais critiques* (Paris: Éditions du Seuil, 1972), 92–3.
[16] Barthes, *Le degré zéro*, 93.
[17] Barthes, *New Critical Essays*, 29.
[18] Barthes, *New Critical Essays*, 29.
[19] Barthes, *New Critical Essays*, 31.
[20] Barthes, *New Critical Essays*, 33.
[21] Barthes, *New Critical Essays*, 33.
[22] Foucault, *Order of Things*, 135.
[23] Foucault, *Order of Things*, 133.
[24] Manuel DeLanda, *Intensive Science and Virtual Philosophy* (London: Continuum, 2002), 41.
[25] DeLanda, *Intensive Science*, 41–2.
[26] DeLanda, *Intensive Science*, 42.
[27] Sauvagnargues, 'De l'animal à l'art', 139 (my translation).
[28] Stephen Werner, *Blueprint: A Study of Diderot and the Encyclopédie Plates* (Birmingham: Summa Publications, 1993).
[29] Deleuze and Guattari, *A Thousand Plateaus*, 344. Deleuze and Guattari are here writing about Klee's programme to render the Cosmos visible.
[30] Deleuze and Guattari, *A Thousand Plateaus*, 344.
[31] Werner, *Blueprint*, 110.
[32] Deleuze and Guattari, *A Thousand Plateaus*, 344.
[33] Werner, *Blueprint*, 110.
[34] Werner, *Blueprint*, 110.
[35] Deleuze and Guattari, *A Thousand Plateaus*, 505.
[36] Deleuze and Guattari, *A Thousand Plateaus*, 505 (bold is mine).
[37] Deleuze and Guattari, *A Thousand Plateaus*, 505–6.
[38] *Discours, figure* was Lyotard's doctoral dissertation and Deleuze was on his defence committee.
[39] Lyotard Jean-François, *Discours, figure* (Paris: Klincksieck, 2002), 9. All quotes from *Discours, figure* have been translated from French to English by myself since there is no English translation of this book that was first published in 1971.
[40] Lyotard, *Discours, figure*, 9.
[41] Lyotard, *Discours, figure*, 9.
[42] Lyotard, *Discours, figure*, 9.
[43] David Carroll, *Paraesthetics: Foucault, Lyotard, Derrida* (London: Routledge, 1987).
[44] David S. Ferris, 'Post-Modern Interdisciplinarity: Kant, Diderot and the Encyclopedic Project', *MLN*, 18.5 (2003): 1262. To contrast with what Ferris sees as the insensible objectivity of the encyclopedists: 'Now, both the possibility of a "figured system" or "encyclopedic tree" and the response to the arbitrariness produced by that possibility are articulated according to a thematics of sight. It is, in fact, this sense that gives access to the "insensible nuances" that provide a basis for the rationalization of knowledge. But, in order to avoid the annihilating consequences of this arbitrariness, such a sense must now fail to see even as it exercises its power to see; it is the sense of insensibility.'

45 Lyotard, *Discours, figure*, 17.
46 Deleuze, *Difference and Repetition*, 28–9.
47 'The ground [*fond*] as it appears in a homogeneous extensity is notably a projection of something "deeper" [*profond*]: only the latter may be called *Ungrund* or groundless. The law of the figure and ground would never hold for objects distinguished from a neutral background or a background of other objects unless the object itself entertained a relation to its own depth. The relation between figure and ground is only an extrinsic place relation which presupposes an internal, voluminous relation between surfaces and the depth which they envelop. This synthesis of depth which endows the object with its shadow, but makes it emerge from that shadow, bears witness to the furthest past and to the coexistence of the past with the present. We should not be surprised that the pure spatial syntheses here repeat the temporal synthesis previously specified: the explication of extensity rests upon the first synthesis, that of habit or the present; but the implication of depth rests upon the second synthesis, that of Memory and the past. Furthermore, in depth the proximity and simmering of the third synthesis make themselves felt, announcing the universal "ungrounding".' Deleuze, *Difference and Repetition*, 229–30.
48 'En fait, telle révélation partielle apparaît dans tel domaine de signes, mais s'accompagne parfois de régressions dans d'autres domaines, se noie dans une déception plus générale, quitte à réapparaître ailleurs, toujours fragile, tant que la révélation de l'art n'a pas systématisé l'ensemble.' Deleuze, *Proust et les signes*, 36.
49 'Apprendre à discerner non pas donc le vrai du faux, tous deux définis en termes de consistance interne d'un système ou d'opérativité sur un objet de référence; mais apprendre à discerner entre deux expressions celle qui est là pour déjouer le regard (pour le capturer) et celle qui est là pour le démesurer, pour lui donner l'invisible à voir.' Lyotard, *Dicours, figure*, 17.
50 Gilles Deleuze and Félix Guattari, *Anti-Oedipus: Capitalism and Schizophrenia*, trans. Robert Hurley, Mark Seem and Helen R. Lane (New York: Penguin Books, 2009), 243.
51 Deleuze and Guattari, *Anti-Oedipus*, 243.
52 Cf. *Discours, figure*, 15.
53 Deleuze and Guattari, *Anti-Oedipus*, 244.
54 Deleuze, *Difference and Repetition*, 202.
55 Deleuze, *Difference and Repetition*, 202.
56 Deleuze, *Difference and Repetition*, 202.
57 Carl Linnaeus, *Species Plantarum: A Facsimile of the First Edition, 1753, Vol. 1*, intro. William Thomas Stearn (London: Ray Society, 1957), 1. Stearn, in the introduction to Linnaeus' *Species Plantarum*, explains how Linnaeus' taxonomy, published for the first time in 1753, was widely accepted as the origin of modern of nomenclature of botany: 'Botanical published before 1753 thus have no standing in modern nomenclature.'
58 Foucault, *Order of Things*, 135. Erasmus Darwin's text on botany and nature is written in verse that describes fabulously natural processes that are illustrated on the page. Perhaps, it is close to the idea Foucault finds interesting in Linnaeus. See Erasmus Darwin, *The Botanic Garden, 1791* (Menston: Scolar Press, 1973).

[59] Michel Foucault, *This Is Not a Pipe*, trans. James Harkness (Berkeley: U of California P, 1983), 22.
[60] Foucault, *This Is Not a Pipe*, 22.
[61] Foucault, *This Is Not a Pipe*, 15.
[62] Foucault, *This Is Not a Pipe*, 23.
[63] Foucault, *This Is Not a Pipe*, 22.
[64] Foucault, *This Is Not a Pipe*, 33.
[65] Foucault, *This Is Not a Pipe*, 33.
[66] Christine Buci-Glucksman, 'Of the Diagram in Art', trans. Josh Wise, *ANY* 23 (1998): 34.
[67] Gilles Deleuze, *The Fold: Leibniz and the Baroque*, trans. Tom Conley (Minneapolis: U of Minnesota P, 2004), 14–15.
[68] Mireille Buydens, *Sahara: l'esthétique de Gilles Deleuze* (Paris: J. Vrin, 1990), 25 (my translation).
[69] Buydens, *Sahara*, 25–6.
[70] Deleuze, *The Fold*, 15.
[71] DeLanda, *Intensive Science*, 31–2.
[72] Gilles Deleuze, Michel Foucault and Adrian Rifkin, *Photogenic Painting: Gérard Fromanger* (London: Black Dog Publishing, 2001).
[73] Deleuze and Guattari, *A Thousand Plateaus*, 344.
[74] Deleuze and Guattari, *What Is Philosophy?*, 197.
[75] Deleuze, *The Fold*, 15.
[76] Lyotard, *Discours, figure*, 231.
[77] Deleuze, *Negotiations*, 69–70. In 'Letter to Serge Daney: Optimism, Pessimism, and Travel', Deleuze considers the question of false depth in the context of cinema: '*Montage* became secondary, giving way not only to the famous "sequence shot", but to new forms of composition and combination. Depth was condemned as "deceptive", and the image took on the flatness of a "surface without depth", or a *slight depth* rather like the oceanographer's shallows.'
[78] Klee quoted in Lyotard, *Discours, figure*, 231. '[R]eprésenter la lumière par la clarté n'est que neige d'antan (. . .). J'essaie maintenant de rendre la lumière simplement comme déploiement d'énergie. Du moment que sur un blanc présupposé je traite l'énergie en noir, il faut que cela aussi mène au but. Je rappellerai ici le noir absolument rationnel de la lumière sur les négatif photographiques.'
[79] Sauvagnargues, 'De l'animal à l'Art', 140, 144.
[80] Brian Massumi, *A User's Guide to Capitalism and Schizophrenia: Deviations from Deleuze and Guattari* (Cambridge: MIT Press, 1992).
[81] Massumi, *A User's Guide*, 16.
[82] Deleuze, *Proust and Signs*, 76.
[83] Deleuze, *Proust and Signs*, 165.
[84] Deleuze and Guattari, *What Is Philosophy?*, 194.
[85] DeLanda, *Intensive Science*, 32.
[86] Lyotard, *Discours, figure*, 211.
[87] Lyotard, *Discours, figure*, 231.
[88] Lyotard, *Discours, figure*, 237–8.
[89] Lyotard, *Discours, figure*, 237–8.

Notes

[90] Martin Heidegger, *Kant and the Problem of Metaphysics*, trans. Richard Taft (Bloomington: Indiana UP, 1990), 65–6.
[91] Heidegger, *Kant and the Problem of Metaphysics*, 65–6.
[92] Heidegger, *Kant and the Problem of Metaphysics*, 65–6.
[93] Heidegger, *Kant and the Problem of Metaphysics*, 66.
[94] Heidegger, *Kant and the Problem of Metaphysics*, 66.
[95] Heidegger, *Kant and the Problem of Metaphysics*, 66.
[96] Heidegger, *Kant and the Problem of Metaphysics*, 66.
[97] Heidegger, *Kant and the Problem of Metaphysics*, 66.
[98] Heidegger, *Kant and the Problem of Metaphysics*, 66.
[99] 'Only on your face and at the bottom of your black hole and upon your white wall will you be able to set faciality traits free like birds, not in order to return to a primitive head, but to invent the combinations by which those traits connect with landscapity trait that have themselves been freed from the landscape and with traits of picturality and musicality that have also been freed from their respective codes.' In the notion of faciality, the black holes/white walls system, black holes are the depth and the white wall the surface. Deleuze and Guattari, *A Thousand Plateaus*, 189.
[100] Deleuze and Guattari, *A Thousand Plateaus*, 167.
[101] Deleuze and Guattari, *A Thousand Plateaus*, 168.
[102] Deleuze and Guattari, *A Thousand Plateaus*, 173.
[103] Deleuze and Guattari, *A Thousand Plateaus*, 190.
[104] Deleuze and Guattari, *A Thousand Plateaus*, 189.
[105] Deleuze and Guattari, *What Is Philosophy?*, 41.
[106] Deleuze and Guattari, *What Is Philosophy?*, 39–40.
[107] Deleuze and Guattari, *What Is Philosophy?*, 40.
[108] Gilles Deleuze and Félix Guattari, *Qu'est-ce que la philosophie?* (Paris: Les Éditions de Minuit, 2005), 43.
[109] Deleuze, *Francis Bacon*, 82.
[110] Deleuze and Guattari, *What Is Philosophy?*, 53.
[111] Deleuze and Guattari, *What Is Philosophy?*, 55.
[112] Deleuze and Guattari, *A Thousand Plateaus*, 190.
[113] Gilles Deleuze, *Cinema 2: The Time-Image*, trans. Hugh Tomlinson and Robert Galeta (Minneapolis: U of Minnesota P, 1989), 122.
[114] Deleuze, *Cinema 2*, 123.
[115] Simplicius of Cilicia, *On Aristotle's 'Categories 1–4'*, trans. Michael Chase (Ithaca: Cornell UP, 2003), 184. Simplicius offers commentaries on Aristotle's categories, the enumerations of the division of things.
[116] Simplicius, *On Aristotle*, 184.
[117] Deleuze, *Cinema 2*, 123.
[118] Massumi, *A User's Guide*, 6.
[119] Massumi, *A User's Guide*, 4.
[120] Massumi, *A User's Guide*, 5.
[121] Massumi, *A User's Guide*, 5.
[122] Massumi, *A User's Guide*, 16.
[123] Ben Van Berkel and Caroline Bos, 'Diagrams – Interactive Instruments in Operation', *ANY*, 23 (1998): 21.

210 Notes

124 Massumi, *A User's Guide*, 16.
125 Massumi, *A User's Guide*, 16.
126 'Truth is defined neither by conformity or common form, nor by a correspondence between the two forms. There is a disjunction between speaking and seeing, between the visible and the articulable: "what we see never lies in what we say", and vice versa. The conjunction is impossible for two reasons: the statement has its own correlative object and is not a proposition designating a state of things or a visible object, as logic would have it; but neither is the visible a mute meaning, a signified of power to be realized in language, as phenomenology would have it.' Deleuze, *Foucault*, 64. This is part of the diagram described as a machine that is almost blind, almost dumb but that allows to see, allows to speak. The diagram names the dimension that is aformal.
127 Badiou, *The Clamor of Being*, 22.
128 Félix Guattari, *Molecular Revolution: Psychiatry and Politics*, trans. Rosemary Sheed (Harmondsworth: Penguin Books, 1984), 95.
129 Massumi, 'The Diagram as Technique of Existence', 43.
130 Deleuze, *Difference and Repetition*, 28.
131 Deleuze, *Difference and Repetition*, 28.
132 Deleuze, *Difference and Repetition*, 28–9.
133 Kant, *Critique of Pure Reason*, A141–2/B180–1.
134 'Now what we call a science – the schema of which must contain the outline of the whole (*monogramma*) and the division of the whole into members in conformity with the idea, that is, contain them *a priori*, and must distinguish it from all other wholes securely and according to principles – cannot be produced technically, that is, not due to the similarity of its manifold parts or the contingent use of knowledge *in concreto* for this or that external end, but only architectonically, on the basis of the affinity of its parts and their derivation from a single supreme and inner end through which alone the whole becomes first of all possible.' Kant, *Critique of Pure Reason*, A833–4/B861–2.

Chapter 3

1 Deleuze and Guattari, *A Thousand Plateaus*, 13.
2 Deleuze and Guattari, *A Thousand Plateaus*, 551.
3 'The very fact of this allusion to the systematic place of the Schematism chapter within the ordering of the stages of the ground-laying betrays the fact that these eleven pages of the *Critique of Pure Reason* must constitute the central core for the whole voluminous work.' Martin Heidegger, *Kant and the Problem of Metaphysics*, trans. Richard Taft (Bloomington: Indiana UP, 1990), 60.
4 Gary, Banham, *Kant's Transcendental Imagination* (New York: Palgrave Macmillan, 2006), 159.
5 See Deleuze, *Francis Bacon*, 160 n. 3.
6 Van Berkel and Bos, 'Diagrams', 22.
7 Van Berkel and Bos, 'Diagrams', 22.
8 Van Berkel and Bos, 'Diagrams', 22.
9 Van Berkel and Bos, 'Diagrams', 22.

[10] Marcel Proust, *À la recherche du temps perdu* (Paris: Gallimard, 1999), 173 (my translation).
[11] 'Un écrivain non: un nouveau cartographe' was published in *Critique* in 1975 and reprised in the chapter titled 'A New Cartographer', in *Foucault*.
[12] Deleuze, *Foucault*, 68–9.
[13] Deleuze, *Foucault*, 38. Deleuze conflates the non-place with the informal diagram.
[14] 'On one occasion Foucault gives it its most precise name: it is a "diagram".' Deleuze, *Foucault*, 34.
[15] Michel Foucault, *Discipline and Punish: The Birth of the Prison*, trans. Alan Sheridan (New York: Vintage Books, 1995), 205.
[16] Deleuze, *Foucault*, 200.
[17] Deleuze, *Foucault*, 205.
[18] Deleuze, *Foucault*, 205.
[19] Deleuze, *Foucault*, 171.
[20] Deleuze, *Foucault*, 34.
[21] Deleuze, *Foucault*, 68.
[22] Deleuze, *Foucault*, 68.
[23] Deleuze, *Foucault*, 68.
[24] Deleuze, *Foucault*, 82.
[25] Sanford Kwinter, 'The Genealogy of Models. The Hammer and the Song', *ANY* 23 (1998): 57.
[26] Kwinter, *Genealogy of Models*, 57.
[27] Kwinter, *Genealogy of Models*, 57.
[28] Kwinter, *Genealogy of Models*, 57.
[29] Kwinter, *Genealogy of Models*, 58.
[30] Kant quoted in Heidegger, *Kant and the Problem of Metaphysics*, 80.
[31] Hugh Tomlinson and Barbara Habberjam, Introduction to Gilles Deleuze, *Kant's Critical Philosophy: The Doctrine of the Faculties* (Minneapolis: U of Minnesota P, 1999), xvi. They are possibly referring to the following lecture by Deleuze: Gilles Deleuze, *Les cours de Gilles Deleuze: Deleuze/Kant. Cours Vincennes 04/04/1978*, www.webdeleuze.com/php/texte.php?cle=66&groupe=Kant&langue=2. Deleuze states in a lecture on Kant: 'It's an excessive atmosphere, but if one holds up, and the important thing above all is not to understand, the important thing is to take on the rhythm of a given man, a given writer, a given philosopher, if one holds up, all this northern fog which lands on top of us starts to dissipate, and underneath there is an amazing architecture. When I said to you that a great philosopher is nevertheless someone who invents concepts, in Kant's case, in this fog, there functions a sort of thinking machine, a sort of creation of concepts that is absolutely frightening.'
[32] Gilles Deleuze, 'On Four Poetic Formulas Which Might Summarize the Kantian Philosophy', in *Kant's Critical Philosophy: The Doctrine of the Faculties*, trans. Hugh Tomlinson and Barbara Habberjam (Minneapolis: U of Minnesota P, 1999). The four formulas include Shakespeare's Hamlet's pronouncement: 'The time is out of joint'; Rimbaud's 'I is another'; Kafka's 'The Good is what the Law says'; and Rimbaud again with 'A disordering (*dérèglement*) of all the senses.'

[33] 'It is not always easy to be Heideggerian. . . . It had to be a philosopher, as if shame had to enter into philosophy itself. He wanted to rejoin the Greeks through the Germans, at the worst moment in their history.' (Deleuze and Guattari, *What Is Philosophy?*, 108).

[34] Deleuze and Guattari, *What Is Philosophy?*, 56.

[35] Deleuze and Guattari, *What Is Philosophy?*, 85.

[36] Deleuze and Guattari, *What is Philsophy?*, 85.

[37] Deleuze, *Kant's Critical Philosophy*, 22.

[38] Deleuze and Guattari, *What Is Philosophy?*, 85.

[39] Deleuze and Guattari, *What Is Philosophy?*, 85.

[40] Deleuze and Guattari, *What Is Philosophy?*, 85.

[41] Deleuze and Guattari, *What Is Philosophy?*, 23. The concept has surfaces and contours, it is spatial, it has junctions, detours, bridged. Deleuze and Guattari, *What Is Philosophy?*, 21: Even though, the concept 'does not have spatiotemporal coordinates', it does not mean that it is not represented spatially. Deleuze and Guattari, *What Is Philosophy?*, 37: Furthermore, concepts populate the plane of immanence: 'The plane is like a desert that concepts populate without dividing up. The only regions of the plane are concepts themselves, but the plane is all that holds them together. The plane has no other regions than the tribes populating and moving around on it. It is the plane that secures conceptual linkages with ever increasing connections, and it is concepts that secure the populating of the plane on an always renewed and variable curve. The plane of immanence . . . [is] the image of thought, the image thought gives itself of what it means to think, to make use of thought, to find one's bearings in thought.'

[42] Deleuze, *Difference and Repetition*, 218.

[43] Deleuze, 1978 Lecture on Kant.

[44] Deleuze, 1978 Lecture on Kant.

[45] Deleuze, 1978 Lecture on Kant.

[46] Deleuze, 1978 Lecture on Kant.

[47] Deleuze, 1978 Lecture on Kant.

[48] I am referring to chapter 11 of *A Thousand Plateaus*, '1837: Of the Refrain', 310–50.

[49] Deleuze, 1978 Lecture on Kant.

[50] Deleuze, 1978 Lecture on Kant.

[51] Deleuze, 1978 Lecture on Kant.

[52] Deleuze, 1978 Lecture on Kant.

[53] Deleuze, 1978 Lecture on Kant.

[54] Deleuze, 1978 Lecture on Kant.

[55] Stephen R. Palmquist, *Kant's System of Perspectives: An Architectonic Interpretation of the Critical Philosophy* (Lanham: UP of America, 1993).

[56] Max Black, *Models and Metaphors* (Ithaca: Cornell UP, 1962), 236.

[57] Black, *Models and Metaphors*, 237 quoted in Palmquist *Kant's System*, 11.

[58] Black, *Models and Metaphors*, 41.

[59] Although it has to be made clear that the mapping Palmquist has in mind comes from a different philosophical tradition than what Deleuze has in mind, at least on the surface: 'Philosophical devices such as "conceptual mapping", popularized by various analytic philosophers in this century, can be regarded as at least

Notes

213

indirectly related to the use of models described in this section.' Palmquist, *Kant's System*, 15 n. 9.
[60] Black, *Models and Metaphors*, 44–5 quoted in Palmquist, *Kant's System*, 11.
[61] Black, *Models and Metaphors*, 231.
[62] Mark A. Cheetham, *Kant, Art and Art History: Moments of Discipline* (Cambridge: Cambridge UP, 2001). Cheetham considers Deleuze and Guattari's caricature of Kant included in the pages of *What Is Philosophy?*
[63] Andrea Alciati, *A Book of Emblems: the Emblematum liber in Latin and English*, trans. and ed. John F. Moffitt (Jefferson, NC; London: McFarland & Co., 2004).
[64] Tom Conley, 'From Multiplicities to Folds: On Style and Form in Deleuze', *South Atlantic Quarterly*, 96.3 (1997): 632.
[65] Palmquist, *Kant's System*, 13.
[66] Deleuze and Guattari, *What Is Philosophy?*, 187.
[67] Deleuze and Guattari, *What Is Philosophy?*, 187.
[68] Deleuze and Guattari, *What Is Philosophy?*, 187.
[69] Deleuze and Guattari, *What Is Philosophy?*, 187.
[70] See Deleuze and Guattari, *What Is Philosophy?*, 85.
[71] Diane Morgan, *Kant Trouble: The Obscurities of the Enlightenment* (London: Routledge, 2000), 6–7. Morgan explores the architectural implication in Kant's philosophy: About Kant's use of architectural metaphors she writes the following: 'it is the practical and economic preoccupations of building that are used to express the need, even for speculative philosophy, for measured progress and a gradual building up from firm foundations, which here are rooted in the "ground of experience". Although the edifice rises away from empirical conditions, it cannot be constructed in a haphazard fashion, without design. Indeed, the need for a securely constructed framework arises exactly when one has left the ground of experience – it is then that architectonic is crucial. Philosophy is required to emulate architecture for the exact reasons that often lead to the latter's disparagement: it is an art that nevertheless has its feet firmly on the ground.' Morgan, *Kant Trouble*, 6–7.
[72] '. . . – building as cultivating. Latin *colere, cultura*, and building as the raising up of edifices, *aedificare* – are comprised within genuine building, that is, dwelling. Building as dwelling, that is, as being on the earth.' Martin Heidegger, 'Building, Dwelling, Thinking', in *Poetry, Language, Thought*, trans. Albert Hofstadter (New York: Harper Collins, 2001), 145.
[73] Kant, *Critique of Pure Reason*, A707/B735.
[74] Kant, *Critique of Pure Reason*, A707/B735.
[75] Kant, *Critique of Pure Reason*, A141/B180–1.
[76] Kant, *Critique of Pure Reason*, A141/B180–1.
[77] Hannah Arendt, *Lectures on Kant's Political Philosophy*, ed. Ronald Beiner (Chicago: Chicago UP, 1982).
[78] Arendt, *Lectures on Kant*, 81.
[79] Arendt, *Lectures on Kant*, 81.
[80] Arendt, *Lectures on Kant*, 81.
[81] Jean-Jacques Wunenburger, *Philosophie des images* (Paris: PUF, 2001), 3. The definition of the image here is broad. Wunenburger offers an initial definition of image which tries to be as expansive as possible: 'On peut convenir d'appeler

image une représentation concrète, sensible (au titre de reproduction ou de copie) d'un objet (modèle référent) matériel (une chaise) ou idéel (un nombre abstrait), présent ou absent du point de vue perceptif, et qui entretient un lieu tel avec son référant qu'elle peut être tenue pour son représentant et permet donc de reconnaître ou de penser le premier. En ce sens, l'image se distingue aussi bien des choses réelles en elles-mêmes, considérées en dehors de leur représentation sensible, que de leur représentation sous forme de concept, qui n'entretien, à première vue, pas de relation de ressemblance ou de participation avec la chose, puisque séparée de toute intuition sensible de son contenue.' The schema is not a representational image. After explaining the signification of the root of image as the Greek *eikon* (icon), Wunenburger shows that the schema, as a form of image, signifies the way that a thing is held together, in effect, underlining the synthetic aspect of the schema in Kant at the crux of the system: 'Ainsi *eidolon*, au sens d'image, non dérivé de *eidos*, qui signifie "aspect, forme", de la racine *weid* – "voir", bien attestée dans les langues indo-européennes. *Eidolon* a partie liée avec l'irréalité, en tant que reflet, et on trouve associé au mensonge, "vision, songe ou fantôme", issue d'une racine qui signifie "faire briller" et donc rendre visible (voir le verbe *phaino*). Le terme d'eikon voisine, de manière générale avec ceux d' *eidos et d'eidolon*, dont on peut rapprocher *idea*, aspect qu'une réalité offre à un moment de son apparition. Ces représentations renvoient à des formes immanentes, mentales ou matérielles, la *morphé* (stature, ordre apparent), *le skhèma* (manière dont une chose se tient), le *typos* (marque ou cachet laissé par un coup). Dans cette perspective, l'image apparaît bien comme une forme visible, qui se rapporte à une expérience passée, présente ou à venir.' Wunenburger, *Philosophie des images*, 4–5.

[82] Arendt, *Lectures on Kant*, 82.
[83] Heidegger, *Kant and the Problem of Metaphysics*, 60.
[84] Kant, *Critique of Pure Reason*, A141/B180–1.
[85] John Onians, 'Architecture, Metaphor and the Mind', *Architectural History* 35 (1992): 194. Onians provides the etymology of 'plan': 'Although related to the Latin *planus*, "flat", and referring essentially to a flat diagram, it also goes back through the Italian *pianta* to the Latin *planta* or "sole of the foot", the Latin being in turn related to the Greek *ichnos*, "footprint" or "track" – *ichnographia* being the word for round-plan used by Vitruvius.' Onians, 'Architecture', 194.
[86] Heidegger, *Kant and the Problem of Metaphysics*, 64.
[87] Heidegger, *Kant and the Problem of Metaphysics*, 64–5.
[88] Heidegger, *Kant and the Problem of Metaphysics*, 65.
[89] Heidegger, *Kant and the Problem of Metaphysics*, 66.
[90] 'But admittedly, Kant wrote in his last years (1797): "In general, the Schematism is one of the most difficult points. Even Herr Beck cannot find his way therein. – I hold this chapter to be the most important."' Heidegger, *Kant and the Problem of Metaphysics*, 77.
[91] Gilles Deleuze, *Bergsonism*, trans. Hugh Tomlinson and Barbara Habberjam (New York: Zone Books, 1991), 24–5. We have in mind the Bergsonian concept building technique through perception by the subtraction of elements described by Deleuze in *Bergsonism*: 'So that perception is not the object *plus* something, but the object *minus* something, minus everything that does not interest us.' Deleuze, *Bergsonism*, 24–5.

[92] Heidegger, *Kant and the Problem of Metaphysics*, 61.
[93] Deleuze, 1978 Lecture on Kant.
[94] Martin Heidegger, *Introduction to Metaphysics*, trans. Gregory Fried and Richard Polt (New Haven: Yale UP, 2000), 195.
[95] Martin Heidegger, *Being and Time*, trans. Joan Stambaugh (Albany: SUNY Press, 1996), 336.
[96] Heidegger, *Introduction to Metaphysics*, 195.
[97] Heidegger, *Introduction to Metaphysics*, 195.
[98] Heidegger, *Introduction to Metaphysics*, 195 n. 91.
[99] Heidegger, 'Building, Dwelling, Thinking', 154.
[100] Heidegger, *Being and Time*, 338.
[101] Heidegger, *Being and Time*, 338.
[102] Heidegger, *Introduction to Metaphysics*, 61.
[103] Deleuze and Guattari, *What Is Philosophy?*, 41.
[104] 'The rift is fixed in place by a *Grund-riss* as well as an *Auf-riss*, that is, by a plan and an elevation, whereby the twofold nature of spatiality again becomes apparent.' Christian Norberg-Schulz, 'Heidegger's Thinking on Architecture', *Perspecta*, 20 (1993): 66.
[105] Heidegger, *Introduction to Metaphysics*, 61.
[106] Kant, *Critique of Pure Reason*, A23/B37.
[107] Kant, *Critique of Pure Reason*, A141–2/B181–2 (bold is mine).
[108] Kant, *Critique of Pure Reason*, A142/B181.
[109] Heidegger, *Kant and the Problem of Metaphysics*, 61.
[110] Immanuel Kant, *Géographie (Physische Geographie)*, trans. Michèle Cohen-Halimi, Max Marcuzzi and Valérie Seroussi (Paris: Aubier, 1999), 11.
[111] See Bruno Schilhaas and Ingird Hönsch, 'History of German Geography: Worldwide Reputation and Strategies of Nationalisation and Institutionalisation', in *Geography: Discipline, Profession and Subject since 1870*, ed. Gary S. Dunbar (Dordrecht: Kluver Academic Publishers, 2001), 9–44. Schilhaas and Hönsch describe how the discipline of geography in Germany was becoming a discreet science starting in the eighteenth century. Also, Philippe Despoix, *Le monde mesuré: dispositifs de l'exploration à l'âge des Lumières* (Genève: Droz, 2005). Despoix speculates about how Kant figured out his categories of space and time to be a priori only after the limits of the world had been measured through world exploration. Kant taught geography for 30 years in Konigsburg. This resulted in the publication of his *Physische Geographie* in 1802. Cf. the introduction to the French translation of Kant's *Géographie*. Trans. Michèle Cohen-Halimi, Max Marcuzzi and Valérie Seroussi (Paris: Aubier, 1999) for a description and contextualization of Kant and his relationship with the discipline of geography. J. A. May, *Kant's Concept of Geography and Its Relation to Recent Geographical Thought* (Toronto: U of Toronto P, 1970). May's book is often mentioned in the introduction to the French translation of Kant's *Geographie* because it is an excellent source of everything that is both Kantian and geographical. Richard Hartshorne, 'The Nature of Geography: A Critical Survey of Current Thought in the Light of the Past', *Annals of the Association of American Geographers*, 29.3 (1939): 173–412, and Richard Hartshorne, 'The Concept of Geography as a Science of Space, from Kant and Humbolt to Hettner', *Annals of the Association of American Geographers*, 48.2 (1958): 97–108, fit Kant within a general history of

[112] Kant, *Critique of Pure Reason*, A235–6/B294–5 (bold is mine).
[113] Deleuze and Guattari, *What Is Philosophy?*, 20.
[114] Hartshorne, 'Nature of Geography', 221.
[115] Hartshorne, 'Nature of Geography', 221.
[116] Immanuel Kant, *Political Writings*, ed. Hans Reiss, trans. H. B. Nisbet (Cambridge: Cambridge UP, 1991), 52.
[117] Kant, *Political Writings*, 52.
[118] Kant, *Géographie*, 67.
[119] Paul De Man, *Aesthetic Ideology*, ed. Andrzej Warminski (Minneapolis: U of Minnesota P, 1996).
[120] De Man, *Aesthetic Ideology*, 80. Quoting from *The Critique of Judgement*, 196.
[121] De Man, *Aesthetic Ideology*, 126.
[122] De Man, *Aesthetic Ideoloy*, 46.
[123] 'Exhibition or *hypotyposis* – the vivid sketching or illustration of an idea – involves providing an intuition that matches up with a concept and confirms its objective reference.' Kirk Pillow, 'Jupiter's Eagle and the Despot's Hand Mill: Two Views on Metaphor in Kant', *The Journal of Aesthetics and Art Criticism*, 59.2 (2001): 194.
[124] De Man, *Aesthetic Ideology*, 46.
[125] De Man, *Aesthetic Ideology*, 46.
[126] De Man, *Aesthetic Ideology*, 48.
[127] De Man, *Aesthetic Ideology*, 127.
[128] Hartshorne, 'Nature of Geography', 214.
[129] Kant, *Géographie*, 66 (my translation).
[130] Jack Goody, *The Domestication of the Savage Mind* (Cambridge: Cambridge UP, 1977). Goody explains the instrumentality of graphics in the development of knowledge.
[131] Deleuze and Guattari, *What Is Philosophy?*, 58.
[132] Deleuze and Guattari, *What Is Philosophy?*, 52.
[133] Deleuze and Guattari, *What Is Philosophy?*, 53.

Chapter 4

[1] Sauvagnargues, 'De l'animal à l'art', 143.
[2] François Dagognet, *Le catalogue de la vie: Étude méthodologique sur la taxonomie* (Paris: PUF, 1970), 97.
[3] Deleuze and Guattari, *What Is Philosophy?*, 96.
[4] 'Through having reached the percept as "the sacred source", through having seen Life in the living or the Living in the lived, the novelist or painter returns breathless and with bloodshot eyes. They are athletes – not athletes who train their bodies and cultivate the lived . . . but bizarre athletes of the "fasting-artist" type, or "great Swimmer" who does not know how to swim.' Deleuze and Guattari, *What Is Philosophy?*, 172.

[5] '... car les maîtres baigneurs sont prudents, sachant rarement nager ...' Marcel Proust, À la recherche du temps perdu (Paris: Gallimard, 1999), 543.
[6] 'August 2. Germany has declared war on Russia. – Swimming in the afternoon.' Franz Kafka, The Diaries of Franz Kafka: 1914–1923, ed. Max Brod (New York: Schocken Books, 1971), 75.
[7] Kafka in Anne Carson, Plainwater: Essays and Poetry (New York: Vintage Books, 2000), 12.
[8] Henri Bergson, L'évolution créatrice (Paris: PUF, 2003), 193–5.
[9] Bergson, L'évolution créatrice, 193–4.
[10] Gilles Deleuze, 'Causes et Raisons des Îles Désertes', in L'île déserte et autres textes: textes et entretiens 1953–1974, ed. David Lapoujade (Paris: Les Éditions de Minuit, 2002), 11–17.
[11] 'For no one has thus far determined the power of the body, that is, no one has yet been taught by experience what the body can do merely by the laws of nature, in so far as nature is considered merely as corporeal and what it cannot do, save when determined by the mind. For no one has yet had a sufficiently accurate knowledge of the construction of the human body as to be able to explain all its functions: in addition to which there are many things which are observed in brutes which far surpass human sagacity, and many things which sleep-walkers do which they would not dare, were they awake: all of which sufficiently shows that the body can do many things by the laws of its nature alone at which the mind is amazed.' Benedictus de Spinoza, Ethics, trans. G. H. R. Parkinson (Oxford: Oxford UP, 2000), Prop. 49 part II.
[12] Edward Casey, Getting Back into Place: Toward a Renewed Understanding of the Place-World (Bloomington: Indiana UP, 1993), 27–8.
[13] Casey, Getting Back, 24–5.
[14] Casey, Getting Back, 24. Casey cites Jean-François Lyotard, 'Scapeland', The Lyotard Reader, ed. Andrew Benjamin (Oxford: Blackwell, 1989).
[15] Jean-François Lyotard, The Differend: Phrases in Dispute, trans. Georges Van Den Abbeele (Minneapolis: U of Minnesota P, 1987), 130–1.
[16] Lyotard, Differend, 130.
[17] Deleuze, Difference and Repetition, 208–9.
[18] Immanuel Kant, Critique of judgement, trans. J. H. Bernard (New York: Hafner Press, 1951), 197–8.
[19] Lyotard, Differend, 131.
[20] As mentioned in the previous chapter, the fog analogy comes from Deleuze's seminar on Kant: 'In 1978 Deleuze gave a number of seminars on Kant ... In those seminars Deleuze still kept his distance from Kant, speaking of the "fog of the north" and the "suffocating atmosphere" of his work (Seminar of 14 March 1978) ...' Tomlinson and Habberjam in Gilles Deleuze, Kant's Critical Philosophy, trans. Hugh Tomlinson and Barbara Habberjam (Minneapolis: U of Minnesota P, 1999), xvi.
[21] Massumi, A User's Guide, 16.
[22] Deleuze, Cinema 2, 46–7.
[23] Deleuze, Cinema 2, 46–7.
[24] Deleuze, Negotiations, 68–9.
[25] Deleuze, Negotiations, 69.

218   Notes

26. Deleuze, *Negotiations*, 70.
27. Deleuze, *Difference and Repetition*, 283. In the original French: 'Soit l'Idée d'île: la dramatisation géographique la différencie, on en divise le concept d'après deux types, le type océanique originel qui marque une éruption, un soulèvement hors de l'eau, le type continental dérivé qui renvoie à une désarticulation, à une fracture.' Gilles Deleuze, *Différence et répétition* (Paris: PUF, 1997), 219.
28. Gilles Deleuze, 'Desert Islands', in *Desert Islands and Other Texts. 1953–1974*, ed. David Lapoujade, trans. Michael Taormina (Los Angeles: Semiotext(e), 2004), 9.
29. Deleuze, 'Desert Islands', 9.
30. Deleuze, 'Desert Islands', 9.
31. Deleuze, *Difference and Repetition*, 219–20. In the original French:'Mais le rêveur de l'île retrouve ce double dynamisme, puisqu'il rêve qu'il se sépare infiniment, à l'issue d'une longue dérive, et aussi qu'il recommence absolument, dans une fondation radicale.' Deleuze, *Différence et répétition*, 283.
32. Robert Smithson, 'A Sedimentation of the Mind: Earth Projects (1968)', in *Robert Smithson: The Collected Writings*, ed. Jack Flam (Berkeley: U of California P, 1996), 100.
33. Smithson, 'Sedimentation', 100.
34. Deleuze and Guattari, *What Is Philosophy?*, 96.
35. Deleuze and Parnet, *Dialogues*, 102.
36. Sauvagnargues, 'De l'animal à l'art', 139 (my translation).
37. Muriel Combes, *Simondon individu et collectivité: pour une philosophie du transindividuel* (Paris: PUF, 1999), 25 (my translation).
38. Deleuze and Guattari, *What Is Philosophy?*, 96.
39. Deleuze and Guattari, *What Is Philosophy?*, 37.
40. Deleuze and Guattari, *What Is Philosophy?*, 35.
41. Deleuze and Guattari, *What Is Philosophy?*, 39.
42. Deleuze and Guattari, *What Is Philosophy?*, 37.
43. Deleuze and Guattari, *What Is Philosophy?*, 41.
44. Deleuze and Guattari, *What Is Philosophy?*, 20.
45. Adrian Parr, ed., *The Deleuze Dictionary* (New York: Columbia UP, 2005).
46. Deleuze and Guattari, *What Is Philosophy?*, 20.
47. Deleuze and Guattari, *What Is Philosophy?*, 41.
48. Gilles Deleuze, *Essays Critical and Clinical*, trans. Daniel W. Smith and Michael A. Greco (Minneapolis: Minnesota UP, 1997), 110–11.
49. Guattari, *Anti-Oedipus Papers*, 420.
50. 'Consequently, we react to it like a shocked Soviet bureaucrat in the Rabinovitch joke: we are startled, it is absurd and nonsensical; the proposition 'the Spirit is a bone' provokes in us a sentiment of radical, unbearable contradiction; it offers an image of grotesque discord, of an extremely negative relationship.' Slavoj Žižek, *The Sublime Object of Ideology* (London: Verso, 1998), 207.
51. Deleuze and Guattari, *What Is Philosophy?*, 36 (bold is mine).
52. Deleuze, *Difference and Repetition*, 281.
53. Deleuze, *Difference and Repetition*, 281.
54. Deleuze, *Difference and Repetition*, 282.
55. 'The highest class of Mollusca containing the squids, cuttlefishes, octopuses, nautiluses, ammonites, and related forms all having around the front of the head

a group of elongated muscular arms usually furnished with prehensile suckers or hooks, a highly developed head with large well-organized eyes showing remarkable resemblance to the vertebrate eye, usually a cartilaginous brain case, a pair of powerful horny jaws shaped like a parrot's beak, and in most existing forms a bag of inklike fluid which they can eject from the siphon, the higher forms (as the cuttlefishes and squids) being able to swim rapidly by ejecting a jet of water from the tubular siphon beneath the head.' Merriam-Webster's Dictionary.

[56] Sauvagnargues, 'De l'animal à l'art', 144 (my translation and bold).
[57] Michel Foucault, *The Order of Things: An Archaeology of the Human Sciences* (London: Tavistock Publications, 1970), 133.
[58] Deleuze, *Essays Critical and Clinical*, 77.
[59] Deleuze, *Essays Critical and Clinical*, 78.
[60] Toby A. Appel, *The Cuvier-Geoffroy Debate: French Biology in the Decades Before Darwin* (New York: Oxford UP, 1987), 204.
[61] 'Vertebrates, molluscs, articulates (insects and crustaceans), radiates.' Merriam-Webster's Dictionary.
[62] Appel, *Cuvier-Geoffroy*, 145.
[63] Hervé Le Guyader, *Étienne Geoffroy Saint-Hilaire, 1772–1844: le naturaliste visionnaire* (Paris: Belin, 1998), 116.
[64] Le Guyader, *Étienne Geoffroy Saint-Hilaire*, 116–18.
[65] Appel, *Cuvier-Geoffroy*, 146.
[66] Appel, *Cuvier-Geoffroy*, 148.
[67] Appel, *Cuvier-Geoffroy*, 147–8.
[68] Appel, *Cuvier-Geoffroy*, 9.
[69] Appel, *Cuvier-Geoffroy*, 9.
[70] Appel, *Cuvier-Geoffroy*, 7.
[71] Appel, *Cuvier-Geoffroy*, 38.
[72] Appel, *Cuvier-Geoffroy*, 38.
[73] Appel, *Cuvier-Geoffroy*, 181.
[74] Appel, *Cuvier-Geoffroy*, 181.
[75] Appel, *Cuvier-Geoffroy*, 41.
[76] Appel, *Cuvier-Geoffroy*, 41.
[77] Appel, *Cuvier-Geoffroy*, 70.
[78] Appel, *Cuvier-Geoffroy*, 85.
[79] Appel, *Cuvier-Geoffroy*, 85.
[80] Appel, *Cuvier-Geoffroy*, 85.
[81] Appel, *Cuvier-Geoffroy*, 83.
[82] Appel, *Cuvier-Geoffroy*, 83.
[83] Appel, *Cuvier-Geoffroy*, 83.
[84] Appel, *Cuvier-Geoffroy*, 98–9.
[85] Le Guyader, *Étienne Geoffroy Saint-Hilaire*, 116.
[86] Foucault, *Order of Things*, 139.
[87] Foucault, *Order of Things*, 139.
[88] Foucault, *Order of Things*, 263.
[89] Mireille Buydens, *Sahara: l'esthétique de Gilles Deleuze* (Paris: Vrin, 1990), 17. There she explains the organization of systems in Deleuze through Simondon's metastability, the notion of intensity and multiplicity.

90. Foucault, *Order of Things*, 264–5.
91. Foucault, *Order of Things*, 263–4.
92. Le Guyader, *Étienne Geoffroy Saint-Hilaire*, 122 (my translation).
93. Le Guyader, *Étienne Geoffroy Saint-Hilaire*, 123 (my translation).
94. Tom Conley, 'A Politics of Fact and Figure', in *Francis Bacon: The Logic of Sensation*, trans. Daniel W. Smith (Minneapolis: U of Minnesota Press, 2004), 140.
95. Tom Conley, 'From Multiplicities to Folds: On Style and Form in Deleuze', *South Atlantic Quarterly*, 96.3 (1997): 637.
96. Deleuze and Guattari, *A Thousand Plateaus*, 6.
97. Kathryn Hume, 'William S. Burroughs's Phantasmic Geography', *Contemporary Literature*, 40.1 (1999): 111–12.
98. Hume, 'William S. Burroughs', 132.
99. David Porush, 'Review of *The Soft Machine. Cybernetic Fiction.* New York and London: Methuen, 1985', *Poetics Today*, 6.3 (1985): 565.
100. Deleuze, *The Fold*, 9–10.
101. '. . . quand l'animal déjoue la prévision, regardons le foetus (sorte de diagramme de cristallisation ou encore l'organisme davantage dispersé, avant le moment des superpositions.' Dagognet, *Le catalogue*, 99. The link between the diagram and the foetus is clearly made here so that the foetus could be a physical manifestation of the diagram.
102. 'Species do not resemble the differential relations which are actualised in them; organic parts do not resemble the distinctive points which correspond to these relations. Species and parts do not resemble the intensities which determine them. As Dalcq says, when a caudal appendix is induced by its intensive environment, that appendix corresponds to a certain level of morphogenetic potential and depends upon a system in which "nothing is *a priori* caudal". The egg destroys the model of similitude.' Deleuze, *Difference and Repetition*, 251.
103. Albert Dalcq, *L'œuf et son dynamisme organisateur* (Paris: Albin Michel, 1941). A good primer on the subject of embryology is by Herman Denis, *De l'œuf à l'embryon: Introduction à la biologie du développement* (Paris: Le Pommier – Fayard, 2000).
104. Deleuze and Guattari, *A Thousand Plateaus*, 40.
105. Deleuze, *Difference and Repetition*, 216.
106. Deleuze, *Difference and Repetition*, 215–16.
107. Deleuze, *Difference and Repetition*, 216.
108. Deleuze, *Difference and Repetition*, 216.
109. Manuel DeLanda, *Intensive Science and Virtual Philosophy* (London: Continuum, 2002), 51–2.
110. Deleuze, *Difference and Repetition*, 277.
111. '. . . two different embryological processes, one behind the *spatial structuration* of organisms through cellular migration, folding and invagination, and the other behind the *qualitative differentiation* of neutral cells into fully specialized muscle, bone, blood, nerve and other cell types. Metaphorically, an egg may be compared to a topological space which undergoes a progressive spatial and qualitative differentiation to become the metric space represented by a fully formed organism. But in what sense can eggs and organisms be said to form spaces? As I said in the previous chapter, the distinction between metric and

nonmetric spaces boils down to the way in which neighbourhoods (or the linkages between the points that form a space) are defined, either through exact lengths or through non-exact topological relations of proximity. In this sense, the fertilized egg, defined mostly by chemical gradients and polarities, as well as the early embryo defined by neighbourhoods with fuzzy borders and ill defined qualities, may indeed be viewed as a topological space which acquires a rigidly metric *anatomical structure* as tissues, organs and organ systems become progressively better defined and relatively fixed in form.' DeLanda, *Intensive Science*, 51–2.

112 DeLanda, *Intensive Science*, 54.
113 DeLanda, *Intensive Science*, 54.
114 DeLanda, *Intensive Science*, 54.
115 Deleuze, *Difference and Repetition*, 214.
116 DeLanda, *Intensive Science*, 46.
117 Deleuze, *Difference and Repetition*, 215.
118 Gilles Deleuze, *The Logic of Sense*, trans. Mark Lester, ed. Constantin V. Boundas (New York: Columbia UP, 1990), 88. Deleuze extracts the concept from Artaud in *The Logic of Sense*: 'To these values the glorious body corresponds, being a new dimension of the schizophrenic body, an organism without parts which operates entirely by insufflation, respiration, evaporation, and fluid transmission (the superior body or body without organs of Antonin Artaud).' Deleuze notes on 342 n. 8: 'See in *84*, 1948: "No mouth No tongue No teeth No larynx No esophagus No stomach No intestine No anus I shall reconstruct the man that I am." (The body without organs is fashioned of bone and blood alone.)'
119 Deleuze and Guattari, *A Thousand Plateaus*, 47.
120 Sauvagnargues, 'De l'animal à l'art', 141 (my translation).
121 Sauvagnargues, 'De l'animal à l'art', 145 (my translation).
122 Sauvagnargues, 'De l'animal à l'art', 140 (my translation).
123 Deleuze, *Difference and Repetition*, 183.
124 Deleuze, *Difference and Repetition*, 184–5.
125 Deleuze, *Difference and Repetition*, 184–6.
126 Deleuze, *Difference and Repetition*, 173–4.
127 Deleuze, *Difference and Repetition*, 183.
128 Sauvagnargues, 'De l'animal à l'art', 144 (my translation).

Chapter 5

1 T. S. Eliot, *The Complete Poems and Plays* (London: Faber and Faber, 2004), 308.
2 Deleuze, *Francis Bacon*, 49.
3 Barbara Maria Stafford, *Visual Analogy: Consciousness as the Art of Connecting* (Cambridge: MIT Press, 1999), 106.
4 Peter Fenves, 'The Genesis of Judgment: Spatiality, Analogy, and Metaphor in Benjamin's "On Language as Such and on Human Language"', in *Walter Benjamin: Theoretical Questions*, ed. David S. Ferris (Stanford: Stanford UP, 1996), 226 n. 10.

5. Deleuze and Guattari, *What Is Philosophy?*, 21.
6. Deleuze and Guattari, *What Is Philosophy?*, 178.
7. Michael Hardt, 'Exposure: Pasolini and the Flesh', in *A Shock to Thought: Expression after Deleuze and Guattari*, ed. Brian Massumi (London: Routledge, 2002), 78.
8. Hardt, 'Exposure', 78.
9. Hardt, 'Exposure', 78.
10. Deleuze, *Difference and Repetition*, 76.
11. Deleuze, *Difference and Repetition*, 212.
12. Deleuze, *Difference and Repetition*, 208.
13. Deleuze, *Proust et les Signes*, 76 (my translation). Richard Howard's translation reads as follows: '"Real without being present, ideal without being abstract." This ideal reality, this virtuality, is essence, [Howard continues the sentence that Deleuze finished] which is realized or incarnated in involuntary memory.' Deleuze, *Proust and Signs*, 60. I wanted to make sure that the terms 'present' was understood as 'actual' and also thought that 'ideal reality' did not have the precise meaning of 'ideal real', terms important to Deleuze's whole corpus. The original French reads: '"Réels sans être actuels, idéaux sans être abstraits." Ce réel idéal, ce virtuel, c'est l'essence. L'essence se réalise ou s'incarne dans le souvenir involontaire. Ici comme dans l'art, l'enveloppement, l'enroulement, reste l'état supérieur de l'essence. Et le souvenir involontaire en retient les deux pouvoirs: la différence dans l'ancien moment, la répétition dans l'actuel. Mais l'essence se réalise dans le souvenir involontaire à un degré plus bas que dans l'art, elle s'incarne dans une matière plus opaque.' Deleuze, *Proust et les signes*, 76–7.
14. Deleuze, *Proust et les signes*, 76–7 (my translation).
15. Deleuze, *Proust and Signs*, 43.
16. Deleuze, *Difference and Repetition*, 212.
17. Deleuze, *Proust and Signs*, 43.
18. Deleuze, *Proust et les signes*, 122 (my translation).
19. Deleuze, *Proust et les signes*, 122 (my translation).
20. Deleuze, *Difference and Repetition*, 210.
21. Hardt, 'Exposure', 78–9.
22. Hardt, 'Exposure', 78–9.
23. Hardt, 'Exposure', 78–9.
24. Deleuze and Guattari, *What Is Philosophy?*, 37.
25. Le Guyader, *Étienne Geoffroy Saint-Hilaire*, 123.
26. Le Guyader, *Étienne Geoffroy Saint-Hilaire*, 123 (my translation).
27. Deleuze, *Francis Bacon*, 20.
28. Mieke Bal, *The Mottled Screen: Reading Proust Visually*, trans. Anna-Louise Milne (Stanford: Stanford UP, 1997), 32.
29. Merriam-Webster's Dictionary.
30. Merriam-Webster's Dictionary.
31. Merriam-Webster's Dictionary.
32. Bal, *Mottled Screen*, 32–3.
33. Bal, *Mottled Screen*, 33.
34. Leo Steinberg, *The Sexuality of Christ in Renaissance Art and in Modern Oblivion* (Chicago: U of Chicago P, 1996), 17.

[35] Conley in Deleuze, *Francis Bacon*, 140.
[36] Deleuze and Guattari, *A Thousand Plateaus*, 150.
[37] Deleuze and Guattari, *A Thousand Plateaus*, 151.
[38] Deleuze and Guattari, *A Thousand Plateaus*, 151.
[39] Deleuze and Guattari, *A Thousand Plateaus*, 153.
[40] Deleuze, *Difference and Repetition*, 185.
[41] Andrew Ballantyne, *Deleuze and Guattari for Architects* (London: Routledge, 2007), 35.
[42] Gilles Deleuze, *Masochism* (New York: Zone Books, 1989), 71.
[43] Deleuze, *Masochism*, 71.
[44] Deleuze, *Masochism*, 71.
[45] Deleuze, *Francis Bacon*, 91.
[46] Deleuze and Guattari, *A Thousand Plateaus*, 13.
[47] Eliot, *Complete Poems*, 294.
[48] Eliot, *Complete Poems*, 294.
[49] Deleuze, *Francis Bacon*, 82.
[50] Deleuze, *Francis Bacon*, 82.
[51] Eliot, *Complete Poems*, 311.
[52] Deleuze and Guattari, *What Is Philosophy?*, 194.

Bibliography

Alciati, Andrea. *A Book of Emblems: The Emblematum Liber in Latin and English*. Translated and edited by John F. Moffitt. Jefferson, NC; London: McFarland & Co., 2004.
Appel, Toby A. *The Cuvier-Geoffroy Debate: French Biology in the Decades before Darwin*. New York: Oxford UP, 1987.
Arendt, Hannah. *Lectures on Kant's Political Philosophy*. Edited by Ronald Beiner. Chicago: Chicago UP, 1982.
Atlan, Henri. *Entre le cristal et la fumée: essai sur l'organisation du vivant*. Paris: Éditions du Seuil, 1986.
Badiou, Alain. *Deleuze: The Clamor of Being*. Translated by Louise Burchill. Minneapolis: London, 2000.
Bal, Mieke. *The Mottled Screen: Reading Proust Visually*. Translated by Anna-Louise Milne. Stanford: Stanford UP, 1997.
Ballantyne, Andrew. *Deleuze and Guattari for Architects*. London: Routledge, 2007.
Banham, Gary. *Kant's Transcendental Imagination*. New York: Palgrave Macmillan, 2006.
Barthes, Roland. *Le degré zéro de l'écriture/Nouveaux essais critiques*. Paris: Éditions du Seuil, 1972.
—. *New Critical Essays*. Translated by Richard Howard. New York: Hill and Wang, 1980.
Bates, David. 'Cartographic Aberrations: Epistemology and Order in the Encyclopedic Map'. In *Using the Encyclopédie: Ways of Knowing Ways of Reading*, edited by Daniel Brewer and Julie Candler Hayes, 1–20. Oxford: Voltaire Foundation, 2002.
Batt, Noëlle. 'L'expérience diagrammatique: un nouveau régime de pensée'. In *Penser par le diagramme: de Gilles Deleuze à Gilles Châtelet*, edited by Noëlle Batt, 9–28. Saint-Denis: Presses Universitaires de Vincennes, 2004.
Bergson, Henri. *L'évolution créatrice*. Paris: PUF, 2003.
Black, Max. *Models and Metaphors*. Ithaca: Cornell UP, 1962.
Blom, Phillip. *Encyclopédie: The Triumph of Reason in an Unreasonable Age*. London: Fourth Estate, 2004.
Bogue, Ronald. *Deleuze on Music, Painting and the Arts*. London: Routledge, 2003.
Bowlt, John E. 'Manipulating Metaphors: El Lissitzky and the Crafted Hand'. In *Situating Lissitzky: Vitebsk, Berlin, Moscow*, edited by Nancy Perloff and Brian Reed, 129–53. Los Angeles: Getty Research Institute, 2005.
Buci-Glucksman, Christine. 'Of the Diagram in Art'. Translated by Josh Wise. *ANY* 23 (1998): 34–6.
Buydens, Mireille. *Sahara: l'esthétique de Gilles Deleuze*. Paris: J. Vrin, 1990.

Candler Hayes, Julie. *Reading the French Enlightenment: System and Subversion*. Cambridge: Cambridge UP, 1999.
Carayol, Valérie. *Communication organisationnelle: une perspective allagmatique*. Paris: L'Harmattan, 2004.
Carroll, David. *Paraesthetics: Foucault, Lyotard*, Derrida. London: Routledge, 1987.
Carson, Anne. *Plainwater: Essays and Poetry*. New York: Vintage Books, 2000.
Casey, Edward. *Getting Back into Place: Toward a Renewed Understanding of the Place-World*. Bloomington: Indiana UP, 1993.
Chabot, Pascal. *La philosophie de Simondon*. Paris: J. Vrin, 2003.
Cheetham, Mark A. *Kant, Art and Art History: Moments of Discipline*. Cambridge: Cambridge UP, 2001.
Citton, Yves. 'Sept résonances de Simondon'. *Multitudes* (web), http://multitudes.samizdat.net/article1571.html
Combes, Muriel. *Simondon individu et collectivité: Pour une philosophie du transindividuel*. Paris: PUF, 1999.
Conley, Tom. 'A Politics of Fact and Figure'. In *Francis Bacon: The Logic of Sensation*, translated by Daniel W. Smith, 130–49. Minneapolis: U of Minnesota Press, 2004.
—. 'From Multiplicities to Folds: On Style and Form in Deleuze'. *South Atlantic Quarterly* 96.3 (1997): 629–46.
Dagognet, François. *Le catalogue de la vie: Étude méthodologique sur la taxonomie*. Paris: PUF, 1970.
Dalcq, Albert. *L'œuf et son dynamisme organisateur*. Paris: Albin Michel, 1941.
Darwin, Erasmus. *The Botanic Garden, 1791*. Menston: Scolar Press, 1973.
De Man, Paul. *Aesthetic Ideology*. Edited by Andrzej Warminski. Minneapolis: U of Minnesota P, 1996.
Debaise, Didier. 'Le langage de l'individuation (lexique Simondonien)'. *Multitudes* (web), http://multitudes.samizdat.net/Le-langage-de-l-individuation.html?var_recherche=individuation
DeLanda, Manuel. 'Deleuze, Diagram, and the Genesis of Form'. *ANY* 23 (1998): 30–4.
—. *Intensive Science and Virtual Philosophy*. London: Continuum, 2002.
Deleuze, Gilles. *Bergsonism*. Translated by Hugh Tomlinson and Barbara Habberjam. New York: Zone Books, 1991.
—. 'Causes et Raisons des Îles Désertes'. In *L'île déserte et autres textes: textes et entretiens 1953–1974*, edited by David Lapoujade, 11–17. Paris: Les Éditions de Minuit, 2002.
—. *Cinema 2: The Time-Image*. Translated by Hugh Tomlinson and Robert Galeta. Minneapolis: U of Minnesota, 1989.
—. 'Desert Islands'. In *Desert Islands and Other Texts. 1953–1974*, edited by David Lapoujade and translated by Michael Taormina, 9–14. Los Angeles: Semiotext(e), 2004.
—. 'Desire and Pleasure'. In *Two Regimes of Madness: Text and Interviews 1975–1995*, edited by David Lapoujade and translated by Ames Hodges and Mike Taormina, 112–34. New York: Semiotext(e), 2007.
—. *Difference and Repetition*. Translated by Paul Patton. New York: Columbia UP, 1994.

—. *Différence et répétition*. Paris: PUF, 1997.
—. 'Écrivain non: un nouveau cartographe'. *Critique* 343 (1975): 1207–27.
—. *Essays Critical and Clinical*. Translated by Daniel W. Smith and Michael A. Greco. Minneapolis: Minnesota UP, 1997.
—. *The Fold: Leibniz and the Baroque*. Translated by Tom Conley. Minneapolis: U of Minnesota P, 2004.
—. *Foucault*. Translated by Seán Hand. Minneapolis: Minnesota UP, 1995.
—. *Francis Bacon: The Logic of Sensation*. Translated and with an introduction by Daniel W. Smith. Afterword by Tom Conley. Minneapolis: U of Minnesota P, 2004.
—. 'Gilbert Simondon, *L'individu et sa genèse physico-biologique*'. In *L'île déserte et autres textes: textes et entretiens 1953–1974*, edited by David Lapoujade, 120–4. Paris: Les Éditions de Minuits, 2002.
—. *Kant's Critical Philosophy: The Doctrine of the Faculties*. Translated by Hugh Tomlinson and Barbara Habberjam. Minneapolis: U of Minnesota P, 1999.
—. *Les cours de Gilles Deleuze: Deleuze/Kant. Cours Vincennes 04/04/1978*, www.webdeleuze.com/php/texte.php?cle=66&groupe=Kant&langue=2
—. *The Logic of Sense*. Translated by Mark Lester and edited by Constantin V. Boundas. New York: Columbia UP, 1990.
—. *Masochism*. New York: Zone Books, 1989.
—. 'Michel Foucault's Main Concepts'. In *Two Regimes of Madness: Text and Interviews 1975–1995*, edited by David Lapoujade and translated by Ames Hodges and Mike Taormina, 246–65. New York: Semiotext(e), 2007.
—. *Negotiations: 1972–1990*. Translated by Martin Joughin. New York: Columbia UP, 1995.
—. *Pourparlers: 1972: 1990*. Paris: Les Éditions de Minuit, 2003.
—. *Proust and Signs*. Translated by Richard Howard. New York: George Braziller, 1972.
—. *Proust et les Signes*. Paris, PUF, 1976.
—. 'What Children Say'. In *Essays Critical and Clinical*, translated by Daniel W. Smith and Michael A. Greco, 61–7. Minneapolis: U of Minnesota P, 1997.
Deleuze, Gilles and Claire Parnet. *Dialogues*. Translated by Hugh Tomlinson and Barbara Habberjam. New York: Columbia UP, 1987.
—. *Dialogues II*. Translated by Hugh Tomlinson and Barbara Habberjam. New York: Columbia UP, 2002.
Deleuze, Gilles and Félix Guattari. *Anti-Oedipus: Capitalism and Schizophrenia*. Translated by Robert Hurley, Mark Seem and Helen R. Lane. New York: Penguin Books, 2009.
—. *Qu'est-ce que la philosophie?* Paris: Les Éditions de Minuit, 2005.
—. *A Thousand Plateaus: Capitalism and Schizophrenia*. Translated by Brian Massumi. Minneapolis: U of Minnesota P, 2005.
—. *What Is Philosophy?* Translated by Hugh Tomlinson and Graham Burchell. New York: Columbia UP, 1994.
Deleuze, Gilles, Michel Foucault and Adrian Rifkin. *Photogenic Painting: Gérard Fromanger*. London: Black Dog Publishing, 2001.
Denis, Herman. *De l'œuf à l'embryon: Introduction à la biologie du développement*. Paris: Le Pommier – Fayard, 2000.
Despoix, Philippe. *Le monde mesuré: dispositifs de l'exploration à l'âge des Lumières*. Genève: Droz, 2005.

Eisenman, Peter. *Written into the Void: Selected Writings 1990–2004*. New Haven: Yale UP, 2007.
Eliot, T. S. *The Complete Poems and Plays*. London: Faber and Faber, 2004.
Fagot-Largeault, Anne. 'L'individuation en biologie'. In *Gilbert Simondon, une pensée de l'individuation et de la technique. Actes du colloque organisé par le Collège International de Philosophie 31 mars–2 avril 1992*, 19–54. Paris: Editions Albin Michel, 1994.
Fenves, Peter. 'The Genesis of Judgment: Spatiality, Analogy, and Metaphor in Benjamin's "On Language as Such and on Human Language"'. In *Walter Benjamin: Theoretical Questions*, edited by David S. Ferris, 75–93. Stanford: Stanford UP, 1996.
Ferris, David S. 'Post-Modern Interdisciplinarity: Kant, Diderot and the Encyclopedic Project'. *MLN* 18.5 (2003): 1251–77.
Foucault, Michel. *Discipline and Punish: The Birth of the Prison*. Translated by Alan Sheridan. New York: Vintage Books, 1995.
—. *The Order of Things: An Archaeology of the Human Sciences*. London: Tavistock Publications, 1970.
—. *Surveiller et punir*. Paris: Gallimard, 2004.
—. *This Is Not a Pipe*. Translated by James Harkness. Berkeley: U of California P, 1983.
Goody, Jack. *The Domestication of the Savage Mind*. Cambridge: Cambridge UP, 1977.
Gualandi, Alberto. *Deleuze*. Paris: Les Belles Lettres, 2003.
Guattari, Félix. *The Anti-Oedipus Papers*. Edited by Stéphane Nadaud and translated Kélina Gotman. New York: Semiotext(e), 2006.
—. *Molecular Revolution: Psychiatry and Politics*. Translated by Rosemary Sheed. Harmondsworth: Penguin Books, 1984.
Hardt, Michael. 'Exposure: Pasolini and the Flesh'. In *A Shock to Thought: Expression after Deleuze and Guattari*, edited by Brian Massumi. London: Routledge, 2002.
Hartshorne, Richard. 'The Concept of Geography as a Science of Space, from Kant and Humbolt to Hettner'. *Annals of the Association of American Geographers* 48.2 (1958): 97–108.
—. 'The Nature of Geography: A Critical Survey of Current Thought in the Light of the Past'. *Annals of the Association of American Geographers* 29.3 (1939): 173–412.
Heidegger, Martin. *Being and Time*. Translated by Joan Stambaugh. Albany: SUNY Press, 1996.
—. 'Building, Dwelling, Thinking'. In *Poetry, Language, Thought*, translated by Albert Hofstadter, 141–59. New York: Harper Collins, 2001.
—. *Introduction to Metaphysics*. Translated by Gregory Fried and Richard Polt. New Haven: Yale UP, 2000.
—. *Kant and the Problem of Metaphysics*. Translated by Richard Taft. Bloomington: Indiana UP, 1990.
—. 'The Origin of the Work of Art'. In *Poetry, Language, Thought*, translated by Albert Hofstadter, 15–86. New York: Harper Collins, 2001.
Hume, Kathryn. 'William S. Burroughs's Phantasmic Geography'. *Contemporary Literature* 40.1 (1999): 111–35.
Joseph, Branden W. '"A Duplication Containing Duplications": Robert Rauschenberg's Split Screens'. *October* 95 (2001): 3–27.

Kafka, Franz. *The Diaries of Franz Kafka: 1914-1923*. Edited by Max Brod. New York: Schocken Books, 1971.

Kang, Young Ahn. *Schema and Symbol: A Study in Kant's Doctrine of Schematism*. Amsterdam: Free University Press, 1985.

Kant, Immanuel. *Critique of Judgement*. Translated by J. H. Bernard. New York: Hafner Press, 1951.

—. *The Critique of Pure Reason*. Translated and edited by Paul Guyer and Allen W. Wood. Cambridge: Cambridge UP, 1998.

—. *Géographie (Physische Geographie)*. Translated by Michèle Cohen-Halimi, Max Marcuzzi and Valérie Seroussi. Paris: Aubier, 1999.

—. *Political Writings*. Edited by Hans Reiss. Translated by H. B. Nisbet. Cambridge: Cambridge UP, 1991.

Kwinter, Sanford. 'The Genealogy of Models: The Hammer and the Song'. *ANY* 23 (1998): 57-62.

Le Guyader, Hervé. *Étienne Geoffroy Saint-Hilaire, 1772-1844: le naturaliste visionnaire*. Paris: Belin, 1998.

Linnaeus, Carl. *Species Plantarum: A Facsimile of the First Edition, 1753*. Vol. 1. Introduction by William Thomas Stearn. London: Ray Society, 1957.

Littell, Jonathan. *Les bienveillantes*. Paris: Gallimard, 2006.

Luckhurst, Nicola. *Science and Structure in Proust's A la recherche du temps perdu*. Oxford: Clarendon Press, 2000.

Lyotard, Jean-François. *The Differend: Phrases in Dispute*. Translated by Georges Van Den Abbeele. Minneapolis: U of Minnesota P, 1987.

—. *Discours, figure*. Paris: Klincksieck, 2002.

—. 'Scapeland'. In *The Lyotard Reader*, edited by Andrew Benjamin, 212-19. Oxford: Blackwell, 1989.

Massumi, Brian. 'The Diagram as Technique of Existence'. *ANY* 23 (1998): 42-7.

—. *A User's Guide to Capitalism and Schizophrenia: Deviations from Deleuze and Guattari*. Cambridge: MIT Press, 1992.

May, J. A. *Kant's Concept of Geography and Its Relation to Recent Geographical Thought*. Toronto: U of Toronto P, 1970.

Morgan, Diane. *Kant Trouble: The Obscurities of the Enlightenment*. London: Routledge, 2000.

Norberg-Schulz, Christian. 'Heidegger's Thinking on Architecture'. *Perspecta* 20 (1993): 61-8.

Onians, John. 'Architecture, Metaphor and the Mind'. *Architectural History* 35 (1992): 192-207.

Palmquist, Stephen R. *Kant's System of Perspectives: An Architectonic Interpretation of the Critical Philosophy*. Lanham: UP of America, 1993.

Parr, Adrian, ed. *The Deleuze Dictionary*. New York: Columbia UP, 2005.

Peirce, Charles S. *Philosophical Writings of Peirce*. Edited by Justus Buchler. New York: Dover Publications, 1955.

Pillow, Kirk. 'Jupiter's Eagle and the Despot's Hand Mill: Two Views on Metaphor in Kant'. *Journal of Aesthetics and Art Criticism* 59.2 (2001): 193-209.

Porush, David. 'Review of *The Soft Machine. Cybernetic Fiction*. New York and London: Methuen, 1985'. *Poetics Today* 6.3 (1985): 565.

Proust, Marcel. *À la recherche du temps perdu*. Paris: Gallimard, 1999.

—. *Sodom and Gomorrah*. Translated by John Starrock. London: Allen Lane, Penguin Press, 2002.

Rosset, Clément. *Le réel et son double: essai sur l'illusion*. Paris: Gallimard, 1976.

—. *Le réel: traité de l'idiotie*. Paris: Éditions de Minuit, 1977.

Roux, Jacques. 'Penser le politique avec Simondon'. *Multitudes* (web), http://multitudes.samizdat.net/article1573.html

Sasso, Robert and Arnaud Villani, eds. *Le Vocabulaire de Gilles Deleuze*. Paris: J. Vrin, 2003.

Sauvagnargues, Anne. 'Deleuze. De l'animal à l'art'. *La philosophie de Gilles Deleuze*. Paris: PUF, 2004.

Schilhaas, Bruno and Ingird Hönsch. 'History of German Geography: Worldwide Reputation and Strategies of Nationalisation and Institutionalisation'. In *Geography: Discipline, Profession and Subject since 1870*, edited by Gary S. Dunbar, 9–44. Dordrecht: Kluver Academic Publishers, 2001.

Simondon, Gilbert. *Du mode d'existence des objets techniques*. Paris: Aubier-Montaigne, 1969.

—. *L'individuation à la lumière des notions de forme et d'information*. Grenoble: Million, 2005.

—. *L'individu et sa genèse physico-biologique*. Grenoble: Jérôme Million, 1995.

Simplicius of Cilicia. *On Aristotle's 'Categories 1–4'*. Translated by Michael Chase. Ithaca: Cornell UP, 2003.

Smithson, Robert. 'A Sedimentation of the Mind: Earth Projects (1968)'. In *Robert Smithson: The Collected Writings*, edited by Jack Flam, 100–13. Berkeley: U of California P, 1996.

Spinoza, Benedictus de. *Ethics*. Translated by G. H. R. Parkinson. Oxford: Oxford UP, 2000.

Stafford, Barbara Maria. *Visual Analogy: Consciousness as the Art of Connecting*. Cambridge: MIT Press, 1999.

Steinberg, Leo. *The Sexuality of Christ in Renaissance Art and in Modern Oblivion*. Chicago: U of Chicago P, 1996.

Thérien, Gilles. *Sémiologies*. Montréal: Université de Québec à Montréal, 1985.

Toscano, Alberto. 'La disparation. Politique et sujet chez Simondon'. *Multitudes* (web), http://multitudes.samizdat.net/spip.php?article1576

Tupistsyn, Margarita Tupitsyn. 'After Vitebsk: El Lissitzky and Kazimir Maelvich, 1924–1929'. In *Situating Lissitzky: Vitebsk, Berlin, Moscow*, edited by Nancy Perloff and Brian Reed, 177–96. Los Angeles: Getty Research Institute, 2005.

Van Berkel, Ben and Caroline Bos. 'Diagrams – Interactive Instruments in Operation'. *ANY* 23 (1998): 19–23.

Villani, Arnaud. 'La métaphysique de Gilles Deleuze'. *Multitudes* (web), http://multitudes.samizdat.net/La-metaphysique-de-Deleuze.html

Werner, Stephen. *Blueprint: A Study of Diderot and the Encyclopédie Plates*. Birmingham: Summa Publications, 1993.

Wunenburger, Jean-Jacques. *Philosophie des images*. Paris: PUF, 2001.

Žižek, Slavoj. *The Sublime Object of Ideology*. London: Verso, 1998.

Index

Abrioux, Yves 14
abstract geology 151
abstract machines 16, 20, 21, 35, 96, 97, 109, 113
  and language 17
  reality functioning through 63
  stratification of 62
abstraction 10, 35, 42, 73, 75, 113–14, 120, 142
  dissolution into 9
action, and geometer 50–1
aesthetics 22, 26, 43, 59, 66, 69, 73, 77, 81, 86, 88, 90, 91, 120, 121, 137, 140, 143, 144, 149, 153, 174, 177, 179, 182, 183, 187, 192, 195
Alciati, Andrea 213n. 63
allagmatic 25, 43, 49, 50, 51, 52, 54–6, 58–61, 64, 65, 80, 101, 165, 194
Allen, Woody,
  The Purple Rose of Cairo 101
analogy 7, 19, 21, 24, 25, 26–7, 32, 43–4, 46, 51–2, 54–5, 56, 61–2, 65, 72, 106, 114, 171, 175, 185–6, 193, 194, 217n. 20
  as extraordinary contraction 141
  incarnation and 182
  metaphors and 55
  and ontology 47–8, 57–60, 101, 194
anonymity– individuation duality 15
anticliché 111, 121
apparition 128–9
appearance and apparition, distinction between 128–9
appearing, concept of 129
Appel, Toby 163, 164, 219nn. 60, 62, 65–84
  The Cuvier-Geoffroy Debate: French Biology in the Decades Before Darwin 160

archipelago 57, 116, 134, 139, 142, 144–7, 149, 153–8, 166, 176
architectonic 21, 108, 110, 115, 123–4, 126, 133–4, 136, 137, 146, 147, 210n. 134, 213n. 71
architecture 2, 5, 6, 7–13, 14, 21, 23, 31, 33, 34, 48, 73, 89, 104, 109, 110, 112–14, 120, 122–5, 129, 140, 167, 172–3, 185, 197n. 24, 211n. 31, 213n. 71
Arendt, Hannah 125, 213nn. 77–80, 214n. 82
art 2, 11, 18, 29, 30, 32, 55, 60, 74, 75, 80, 82, 84, 88–9, 91, 99, 107, 111, 118, 122, 123, 124, 126, 129–30, 166–7, 178, 182, 187, 195
assemblage 16–17, 24–5, 41, 60, 61, 65, 74, 176
  comparison with block 28
  in system 25–35
Atlan, Henri 202n. 85
auto-didacticism 68

Bacon, Francis 18–20, 98, 110, 111, 121, 126, 166, 167, 177, 178, 179, 181, 183, 187, 191, 198n. 59
  Painting 19, 20
  Second Version of Triptych 1944 180
  Three Studies for a Crucifixion 178, 180, 188
  Three Studies for Figures at the Base of a Crucifixion 178, 179, 180
  Triptych – Inspired by T. S. Eliot's Poem 'Sweeney Agonistes' 180
Badiou, Alain 36, 40, 41–2, 43, 44, 46, 62, 65, 105, 199n. 1, 201nn. 51–6, 58–61, 69, 210n. 127
  Deleuze: The Clamor of Being 25, 39

Bal, Mieke 186, 222nn. 28, 32–3
Balzac, Honoré de 163
Banham, Gary 210n. 4
Barthes, Roland 66, 69–70, 74, 102, 205n. 13, 206nn. 14–21
Bates, David 30, 200nn. 23–6, 31
Batt, Noëlle 20, 197n. 39, 198nn. 73–6
   L'expérience diagrammatique:un nouveau régime de pensée' (*Penser par le diagramme: de Gilles Deleuze à Gilles Châtelet*) 14
Bentham, Jeremy 5, 7, 113
Bergson, Henri 84, 143, 199n. 9, 217nn. 8–9
   L'évolution créatrice 144
Berkel, Ben Van 104, 110, 120, 123, 209n. 123, 210nn. 6–9
Black, Max 121, 212nn. 56–8, 213nn. 60–1
   Models and Metaphors 120
blind spot 57–8, 60, 97, 100, 101, 194
block 100
   comparison with assemblage 28
Blom, Phillip 200n. 27
blueprint 73–5
   virtual side of 75
Body without Organs (BwO) 44, 142, 155, 158, 159, 169, 171, 174, 185, 188, 189
Bogue, Ronald 30, 199n. 17
Bos, Caroline 104, 110, 120, 123, 209n. 123, 210nn. 6–9
break-flow 80
Buci-Glucksman, Christine 84, 208n. 66
Buffon, Georges-Louis Leclerc Comte de 68
   Histoire naturelle 47, 68
Burroughs, William S. 111, 168, 169, 177
   The Ticket That Exploded 169
burrow model 34
Buydens, Mireille 86, 208nn. 68–9, 219n. 89

Cache, Bernard,
   Earth Moves 122
calligram 82–3
Calvino, Italo 29

Carayol, Valérie 203n. 96
Carroll, David 206n. 43
Carson, Anne 217n. 7
cartography 10–13, 84, 100, 113
   see also map
Casey, Edward 144, 217nn. 12–14
   Getting Back into Place 145
Chabot, Pascal 47, 202nn. 76–83
Chardin, Jean-Baptiste-Siméon, *The Ray* 186
Cheetham, Mark A. 213n. 62
chiaroscuro effect 80, 81, 91, 99, 106
Citton, Yves 204n. 116
   Sept résonances de Simondon 56
Claudel, Paul 77
collectivity 26, 35
Combes, Muriel 46, 152, 201n. 68, 202nn. 74, 84–7, 218n. 37
comparative anatomy 164
concepts 156–7, 212n. 41
   and space-time, correspondence between 118 *see also* image
concrete concept and concept of concrete, nuances between 40
concrete machines 20
Conley, Tom 121, 166, 167, 187, 213n. 64, 220nn. 94–5, 223n. 35
connectivity 2, 7, 10–11, 12, 21, 22–3, 25, 26, 28, 33, 35, 65
constraint 25, 65, 66, 71–2, 118
   etymological 182
   and monotony, in system 36–43
   and typology 72
continuity–contiguity duality 15
contraction 20, 24, 62, 67, 104, 108, 115, 131, 132, 141–77, 186, 193, 194
cosmopolitanism 135
cross, topology of 185–8
crystallization 45, 47, 48–9
Cuvier, Georges 73, 141, 158, 159, 161, 162, 163–4, 166

d'Alembert, Jean 25, 30, 31, 35
Dagognet, François 216n. 2, 220n. 101
   Le catalogue de la vie: études méthodologiques sur la taxonomie 141

Index 233

Dalcq, Albert 220nn. 102–3
  L'oeuf et son dynamisme organisateur 170
Daney, Serge 149
Darwin, Erasmus 207n. 58
Da-sein 129, 130
Daubenton, Louis-Jean-Marie 68
  Instruction pour les bergers et pour les propriétaires de troupeaux 68
  L'histoire naturelle 68
de Man, Paul 136, 137–8, 216nn. 119–22, 124–7
Debaise, Didier 58, 204nn. 127–30, 133
deframing 123
DeLanda, Manuel 13, 14, 25, 43, 61–3, 66, 71–2, 87, 93, 165, 171, 172–3, 205nn. 137–9, 141, 144–6, 206nn. 24–6, 208nn. 71, 85, 220n. 109, 221nn. 111–14, 116
  Deleuze, Diagrams, and the Genesis of Form 61
  Intensive Science and Virtual Philosophy 71
Deleuze, Gilles,
  Anti-Oedipus 80
  Cinema 2: The Time-Image 101, 147
  Désir et plaisir 13
  Desire and Pleasure 17
  Deux régimes de fous 13
  Dialogues 155
  Difference and Repetition 13, 14, 61, 81, 105, 106, 116, 117, 150, 157, 158, 160, 163, 170, 171, 175, 176
  Écrivain non: un nouveau cartographe 2, 21
  Essays Critical and Clinical 13
  The Fold: Leibniz and the Baroque 6, 13, 85, 89, 122, 170, 174
  Foucault 2–13, 20–3, 34, 109, 112, 114
  Francis Bacon: The Logic of Sensation 2, 18–20, 190
  Kafka: Towards a Minor Literature 34
  Kant's Critical Philosophy 116
  on Kant's schema 114–23
  Le pli 167
  Logic of Sense 174
  Mille plateaux 13, 167
  Negotiations 11
  On Several Regimes of Signs 55
  Pourparlers 36
  Proust and Signs 30, 183
  Sur les principaux concepts de Michel Foucault 13
  A Thousand Plateaus 2, 11, 15–18, 20, 32, 33, 35, 41, 44, 62, 89, 92, 99, 109, 121, 158, 160, 162, 167, 171, 174, 188
  What Children Say? 11
  What Is Philosophy? 9, 13, 34, 89, 93, 97, 116, 122, 142, 143, 144, 156, 182 see also *individual entries*
depth metaphor 83–4
dérive principle 155
deterritorialization 12, 15, 16, 17, 28, 44, 73, 100, 117, 160
diagram,
  anti-programmatic nature of, and tonality 111
  architectural 8–10
  conceptual 1, 9
  Deleuzoguattarian 9
  desire and 16
  feudal 6
  Greek 6
  house and 10
  and map, comparison between 6, 7, 10–12
  Napoleonic 6, 15
  as new informal dimension 2–5
  pastoral 6
  phase 61
  proto 25, 43
  sources of 13–14
    Bacon and sensation diagram and 18–20
    Foucault as cartographer and 14–15
    Foucault, diagram and thought and 20–3
    A Thousand Plateaus and linguistic diagram and 15–18
  of surveillance 5–7, 24
diagrammaticism 15, 22, 114
Diderot, Denis 25, 30, 31, 70
dimension 20, 21, 23, 30, 56–9, 66, 71, 73, 75, 76, 80, 84–91, 96, 99,

101, 107, 108, 114, 126, 129, 139, 146, 148, 152, 154, 155, 166, 167–8, 174, 179, 185, 187, 194, 210n. 126, 221n. 118
  diagram as new informal 2–5
  graphic 50
  imaginary textual 31
  informal 66, 109, 112
  materialistic 79
  ontological 41, 48, 54, 55, 60, 79
  of real language 70
  semiotic 67 *see also* space; time
discursive formation 3
disparation 56, 57, 58, 60
dispositif 13, 20, 113
dissipative process 60
Dulaure, Antoine 36

egg 37, 142, 167–76, 189, 220nn. 102, 111
Eisenman, Peter 8, 9, 196nn. 21–3, 197nn. 24–5
Eisenstein, Sergei 149
Eliot, T. S. 221n. 1, 223nn. 47–8, 51
  The Family Reunion 180, 191
embodiment 5, 8–9, 18, 20, 23, 178, 193
encyclopedia 29–30, 40, 65, 67, 71, 149–50, 206n. 44
  and heterogeneous assemblage 31
  human quality of image of 69, 70
  as multidisciplinary map 34–5
  ontology and 68
  as tool for philosophers 31–2
Encyclopédie 25, 30, 31, 66, 68, 69, 73–5, 76, 90
Enlightenment 31, 33, 47, 68
essences and incarnation 184
evolutionary strata model 64
expression and silence 36–7
extraordinary contraction 141–2, 194
  egg cinematics and 167–76
  geography and anatomy and 142–58
  of Saint-Hilaire 158–67

faciality 81, 88, 96, 97, 98, 99, 209n. 99
far-from-equilibrium 85
Fenves, Peter 221n. 4

Ferris, David S. 31, 32, 200n. 28, 206n. 44
feudal assemblage 26
figural space 80, 81, 93
figurative space 93
film 92, 93, 96, 100–2, 147–9, 190, 191
flexibility 1, 33, 86, 101, 142, 157, 165, 172, 176
flux-schiz 80
fold 23, 73, 85–6, 89, 115, 159, 171, 173, 184, 185
Fontana, Lucio 187
force 6, 9, 20, 22, 44, 45, 63, 73, 86, 93, 114, 145, 152, 157, 182, 184
  abstract 7, 24, 106
  analogical 171
  machinic 196n. 24
  ontological 45, 52
  repressive 38
Foucault 2
  architecture and cartography in 7–13
  diagram as new informal dimension in 2–5
  diagrams as display of relations as pure functions in 5–7
Foucault, Michel 2, 4, 66, 69, 70, 73, 77, 78, 81–4, 104–5, 106, 110, 113, 159, 166, 196n. 18, 205nn. 2–4, 206nn. 22–3, 207n. 58, 208nn. 59–65, 72, 211nn. 14–15, 219nn. 57, 86–8, 220nn. 90–1
  as cartographer 14–15
  Ceci n'est pas une pipe 81, 82–3
  Discipline and Punish 3, 5, 13, 112, 113
  The Order of Things 66, 67, 71, 81, 101, 165, 174
frames 94–6, 122, 123, 127
Freud, Sigmund,
  The Interpretation of Dreams 79
function 51–2, 60, 61
  process of 63
furies, studies of 179–81

gaps 37
Geoffroy Saint-Hilaire, Étienne 73, 106, 141, 142, 152, 169, 171, 172, 173, 174, 175, 176, 185
  extraordinary contraction of 158–67

geographical system 134–5
geography 10–11, 13, 36, 38, 59, 64, 99, 100, 109, 115–17, 119–20, 123, 133–6, 138–9, 142–6, 148, 150–8, 166, 168–70, 177, 194
geological strata model 63–4
geology, genetics and society, functional arc between 62
geometer 50–1, 52–3, 55
geophilosophy 116, 117
Goody, Jack 216n. 130
graphics 126
  illustrations and 66–76
  and schema 126
ground 207n. 47
  autonomous 105
Gualandi, Alberto 29, 43, 199n. 19, 201nn. 65–6
Guattari, Félix 10, 12, 24, 26, 27, 28, 35, 38, 40, 57, 60, 73, 74, 75, 99, 102, 105, 106, 110, 117, 123, 125, 131, 134, 139, 144, 151, 153, 154, 156, 166
  Anti-Oedipus 80
  Kafka: Towards a Minor Literature 34
  On Several Regimes of Signs 55
  A Thousand Plateaus 2, 11, 15–18, 20, 32, 33, 35, 41, 44, 62, 89, 99, 109, 121, 158, 160, 162, 167, 171, 174, 188
  What Is Philosophy? 9, 13, 34, 89, 93, 97, 116, 122, 142, 143, 144, 156, 182 see also *individual notes*

Habberjam, Barbara 211nn. 31–2, 214n. 91, 217n. 20
hachure 98
Hardt, Michael 184, 222nn. 7–9, 21–3
  'Exposure: Pasolini and the Flesh' 183
harmony 117–18
Hartshorne, Richard 134, 215n. 111, 216nn. 114–15, 128
Hayes, Julie Candler 33, 200nn. 33–5
Heidegger, Martin 95–6, 116, 123–31, 194, 203n. 92, 209nn. 90–8, 210n. 3, 211n. 30, 213n. 72, 214nn. 83, 86–90, 215nn. 92, 94–102, 105, 109

Being and Time 129, 130
Kant and the Problem of Metaphysics 94
The Origin of the Work of Art 129
heterogeneity 3–4, 5, 7, 9, 11, 17, 19, 20, 21, 24, 25, 26, 29, 30, 31, 65, 92, 118, 142, 186
  and assemblage 27–8, 41
  and connection duality 35
  discursive 33
homeomorphism 186
homosexual coupling, and assemblage 26–7
Hume, Kathryn 168, 169, 220nn. 97–8
hypotyposis 136–7, 216n. 123

idiom 38, 39
illustrations 66, 81–7
  decoy in system and 76–81
  diagrammatic traits and 97–106
  graphics of classifying and 66–76
  line and traits and 88–97
image 2, 10, 11, 22, 24–5, 26, 43, 50, 57, 58, 59, 60, 88, 96, 127–9, 147–52, 156, 158, 160, 167, 168, 169–70, 208n. 77, 213n. 81, 218n. 50
  anatomical 142, 194
  connected 65
  disparate 177
  duality of 121
  encyclopedic 69, 70
  fluid 94
  geographic 36, 120, 123, 134, 136, 142, 145, 146, 194
  of geometer 51, 55
  mental 46, 47
  and metaphors 121
  of pairing 27
  photographic 94–5
  rhizomatic 30, 31
  and schema 107, 124, 125–6, 132–3, 138
  superimposition of 55–6
  text and 66–9, 71, 75, 76, 78, 80–3, 86, 103, 105, 107, 121, 177, 193, 194
  thought and 1, 42, 57, 99, 117, 139, 155, 157, 212n. 41

tree 32
unrepresentational 100, 129, 130, 193
vegetational 29–30 *see also* concepts; photographs
imagination 1, 15–16, 28, 31, 124, 131, 139, 155, 163, 180, 187
    in concept creation 125
    geographical and spatial 134
    productive 107, 118, 132
    reproductive 118
    schema and 21, 114, 125, 128, 133
immanence 13, 20, 42, 61, 69, 97, 98, 99, 116, 131, 134, 142, 149, 153, 154–5, 212n. 41
incarnation 13, 14, 37, 61, 122, 147, 157, 169, 171, 175, 176, 178–9, 187, 191, 194
    as downward movement 181–5
incongruence *see* incongruity
incongruity 3–5, 22–3, 34, 49, 56, 57–8, 114, 121, 130, 132, 141–2
indiscernibility 12, 13, 17, 18, 19, 28, 155, 160, 186, 191
individuation 44, 45, 46, 47, 49, 56, 57, 72, 173
    and anonymity 15
inflection 87
intelligibility 37
interpretant, of first sign 16
interworld 87
intuition 21, 53, 95, 96, 99, 114, 118, 125, 132, 145, 216n. 123
    empirical 21, 110, 124, 126, 146
    pure 110, 117, 128

Joseph, Branden W. 204n. 134
Jouffroy, Alain, *L'Aube à l'antipode* 82
judgement, notion of 53, 145–6, 147

Kafka, Franz 143, 217nn. 6–7
Kang, Young Ahn 53, 54, 203nn. 105–9
    Schema and Symbol: A Study in Kant's Doctrine of Schematism 52
Kant, Immanuel 21, 53, 55, 107–8, 109, 110, 123–9, 133–9, 176, 198n. 83, 199n. 84, 203nn. 102, 104, 205n. 7, 210n. 133, 211n. 30, 213nn. 71, 73–6, 214nn. 84, 90, 215nn. 106–8, 110–11, 216nn. 112, 116–18, 129, 217nn. 18, 20
    The Critique of Judgement 136, 146
    The Critique of Pure Reason 21, 52, 54, 108, 124, 126, 133
    First Critique 52, 123, 125
    Geography 138, 139
    Physische Geographie 138
    schema, Deleuze on 114–23
    Third Critique 136, 145, 146, 147
    Transcendental Aesthetic 132
Klee, Paul 80, 81, 83, 84–5, 86, 88–94, 98, 112, 114, 208n. 78
    Arrow in the Garden (painting) 89
    Italian City (painting) 89
    Southern Gardens (painting) 85
    Twittering Machine (painting) 89, 90
    Unstable Equilibrium (painting) 85
    Villa R. (painting) 89
    Wandbild aus dem Tempel du Sehnsucht Dorthin (painting) 85
Kwinter, Sanford 62, 63, 114, 159, 205nn. 142–3, 211nn. 25–9

L'Autre Journal 36
labyrinth, significance of 31–3
language 1, 3, 13, 15–18, 33, 35, 37, 67, 68, 71, 76, 83–4, 114, 138, 155, 167, 210n. 126
    models 35, 70
    philosophical 136
    real 70
    as spatial 130
    spoken 69, 70
    uncertainty of 137
    visual 66, 69
Le Guyader, Hervé 161, 164, 219nn. 63–4, 85, 220nn. 92–3, 222n. 25–6
Lhote, André 80, 86, 88, 90, 91, 94, 98
line 75–6, 86–7, 106–7
    and traits, and illustrations 88–97
linguistic models *see* language
Linnaeus, Carl 207n. 57
Lissitzky, El 55

Index

Littell, Jonathan 179
Lowry, Malcolm,
   Under the Volcano 56
Luckhurst, Nicola 29, 199nn. 18, 20
Lyotard, Jean-François 78–9, 81, 83,
   90–1, 93, 94, 145–7, 206nn.
   38–42, 207nn. 45, 49, 208nn. 76,
   78, 86–9, 217nn. 15–16, 19
   Discours, figure 76, 77–8, 86, 90

Magritte 83
   Treachery of the Image 82
map,
   and diagram, comparison between 6,
      7, 10–12
   superimposition of 100
   and tracing 12, 17, 34, 41, 71, 89,
      109, 118, 191
Marker, Chris,
   La Jetée (film) 101–2
Massumi, Brian 58, 92, 102, 103–4,
   147, 204nn. 123–6, 209nn.
   118–22, 210nn. 124–5, 129,
   217n. 21
   The Diagram as Technique of
      Existence 57
materiality 84, 89, 94, 113, 173, 183,
   184, 191
May, J. A. 215n. 111
Maybury, John,
   Love is the Devil 190
Melville, Herman 155–6, 159
mental landscapes 11, 139, 151–3
meshwork model 62, 64
metaphors 10, 29, 36, 43, 77, 124, 133,
   152, 220n. 111
   analogy and 55
   art as 129–30
   depth 83–4
   and images, integration of 121
   as models 120, 122
   photographic 94
   vegetal 30, 39
   visual 32
   within philosophical system 120
metaphysics 53–4
metastability 45, 46

mind and earth, interconnection
   between 151
monogram 22, 107, 108
Morgan, Diane 213n. 71
morose time 179
   of apprehension 188–90
multidisciplinarity 28, 31, 36
   encyclopedia and 34–5
multiplicity 14–15, 20, 22, 25, 26, 28,
   30, 36, 46, 51, 65, 75, 76, 80, 93,
   104, 105, 110, 167, 175

natural history, function of 67
negative space 57, 81
non-discursive formation 3
non-place 20, 114

oceanic islands 150
One 25, 39–40, 44, 49
Onians, John 214n. 85
ontology 25, 41, 43–5, 54–7, 61, 64, 67,
   79, 101, 105, 122, 123, 142, 159,
   165–6, 172, 182, 191
   and analogy 47–8, 57–60, 101, 194
   encyclopedias and 68
   and geography 143
   and operation and structure 50, 52
   and sketch 99
   visual and textual and 76
operation 45, 55, 56–7, 59, 111
   and structure 50–2

painting 2, 18–20, 59, 77, 80, 82–5,
   88–91, 93–4, 96–7, 99–100, 102,
   111, 121, 126, 133, 166, 167, 177,
   178, 180, 181, 186–8, 190–2
Palmquist, Stephen R. 120–1, 212nn.
   55, 59, 213n. 65
panopticon 5, 7, 21, 104, 112–13, 119
Parnet, Claire 36, 152, 199nn. 2–5,
   218n. 35
   Dialogues 155
parody 59
Parr, Adrian 218n. 45
passage, notion of 146–7, 173
Peirce, Charles Sanders 15–16, 105,
   106, 194, 197nn. 47–50

penal law and formation type 3
photogram 55
photographs 11, 12, 55, 75, 91–2, 94–6, 101–2, 109, 127, 191, 198n. 59
    see also image
Pillow, Kirk 216n. 123
plicature 13, 142, 159, 160, 164–6, 177
    forced 158
    functional 186
portée 98, 99
potentiality 10, 31, 46, 56, 57, 80, 107, 110, 123, 142, 165, 166, 168, 170, 179, 185, 192, 220n. 102
    pure 12, 17, 191
power relations 6
pragmatics 16
Prigogine, Ilya 60
prison system and formation type 3, 5
process, notion of 60
Proust, Marcel 28, 110, 111, 143, 146, 199nn. 6–8, 211n. 10, 217n. 5
    À la recherche du temps perdu 24, 26, 29, 30
    Recherche 29, 30
    Sodom and Gomorrah 27
puissance 20

Rauschenberg, Robert,
    Factum I 59
    Factum II 59
real, reading of 77–9
real language, dimensions of 70
Real-Abstract 16
reality 11, 15, 16, 26, 40, 50, 52, 58, 65, 70, 77, 91, 97, 115
    empirical 41, 48
    ideal 222n. 13
    objective 137
    spheres of 64
    three-dimensional 56
    through abstract machines 63
relationality 35, 51, 58, 65, 71
Renaissance 91
repression and expression, link between 38
Resnais, Alain 101
    My American Uncle 100

rhizome model 11, 12, 17, 25, 30, 31, 33, 34, 35, 39, 40–1, 62, 75, 86, 94, 99
rift, as sketch and fissure 130–1
root-book model 32–4
Rossellini, Roberto,
    Stromboli 147–8
Rosset, Clément 56, 200nn. 43–4, 204nn. 117–18
Roux, Jacques 203n. 97

Sasso, Robert 197n. 40
    Le Vocabulaire de Gilles Deleuze 14
Sauvagnargues, Anne 92, 158, 174, 176, 203n. 91, 204nn. 122, 131, 206n. 27, 216n. 1, 218n. 36, 219n. 56, 221nn. 120–2, 128
    'Deleuze. De l'animal à l'art' 49, 72–3
schema 21–2, 47, 52, 68, 108, 110, 146, 157, 187, 193, 210n. 134, 214n. 81
    as art 126
    as dynamic device 125
    and image 107, 124, 125–6, 132–3, 138
    of Kant, Deleuze on 114–23
    sketch and 126–30, 138
    and symbol 137
    time and space constituting 132–3, 139
sedimentary model 62, 63–4
seeing-without-being-seen function 4, 7
self-emptying 183
self-reflexivity 29, 30, 33, 52, 84, 97, 101, 133
semiotic theory 15, 43, 67, 69, 76, 80, 88, 91 *see also* symbol
signifier 34, 77, 80–1, 91, 93
Simondon, Gilbert 25, 43, 45–51, 54, 55, 56, 66, 69, 70, 71, 77, 165, 175, 176, 200n. 39, 201n. 70, 202nn. 72, 75, 84, 90, 203nn. 98–101, 204nn. 120–1, 205nn. 3, 5–6, 8–12, 219n. 89
    Du mode d'existence des objects techniques 68
    L'individu et sa genèse physico-biologique 44
    L'individuation psychique et collective 44

singularities 61, 87
sketch 8, 18, 73, 91, 98, 99, 108, 116, 123, 133, 139, 154, 162, 170–1, 184
　rift as 130–1
　and schema 126–30, 138
　temporal 130
skin 178–9
　painting 190–2
Smithson, Robert 218nn. 32–3
　Spiral Jetty 151
sobriety 44, 56, 73, 74, 86, 90
social field 4, 5, 7, 14, 16, 20, 35, 113
social strata model 64
space 61, 83–4, 93–4, 115, 119
　appearing as concept and 129
　body and landscape and 145
　concentration on 73
　and constraint, and vacuoles 37–8, 43
　Dasein and 130
　figural 80, 81, 93
　floating 103
　graphic 71
　negative 57, 81
　and rift 131
　and schema 132
　static 129
　textual 93
space-time and concepts, correspondence between 118
Spinoza, Benedictus de 217n. 11
squid 141, 142, 155, 156, 158, 159, 160, 167, 176, 194, 218n. 55
Stafford, Barbara Maria 202n. 88, 221n. 3
Steinberg, Leo 187, 222n. 34
Stengers, Isabelle 60
strata 64–5
　models 63–4
structure 165, 175
　and operation 50–2, 71
　and visibility 82
sublime 136, 138
superimposition 8, 27, 59, 100
　of images 55–6
　of maps 7, 12

Sylvester, David 18, 198n. 59
symbol 53, 55, 68, 84, 85, 88, 106, 136–7, 145–7, 149, 186, 203n. 95
synallagmatic 50
system 24, 43, 165, 166
　analogy, allagmatic, and proto-diagrams and 43–65
　assemblage in 25–35
　constraint and monotony and 36–43
　decoy in, and illustrations 76–81
　geographical 134
　mapping of 121
　reliance, on graphics 67

Thérien, Gilles 205n. 147
time 3, 8, 20, 72, 73, 101–2, 115, 117–19, 128–30, 135, 139, 148, 149, 157, 171–2, 176, 202n. 70, 215n. 111
　morose 179, 188–90
　non-chronological 100
　schema and 132, 133, 194
　skin and 178–9
Tomlinson, Hugh 211nn. 31–2, 214n. 91, 217n. 20
topological spaces 61
Toscano, Alberto 202n. 89
tracing 50, 51, 161
　and mapping 12, 17, 34, 41, 71, 89, 109, 118, 191
　static 11
transcendence 42, 54, 58, 117, 132, 143, 182–4
　and authority 137
　false 91
Transcendental Deduction 128
Transcendental Doctrine of Elements 123
transduction 44, 45, 46, 173, 201n. 70, 202nn. 72, 89
tree-as-phylum duality 32
tree model 12, 32–3, 62, 64, 75, 168
Tupitsyn, Margarita 203n. 113
typological thinking 72

unconsciousness 12, 93, 152
univocity 54, 174

vacuoles, and space and constraint 37–8, 43
Villani, Arnaud 42, 197n. 40, 201nn. 62–4
Le Vocabulaire de Gilles Deleuze 14
virtuality 5, 7, 8, 12, 42, 43, 46, 57, 62–4, 72–5, 84–7, 89, 92–3, 97, 107, 110, 113, 122, 146–7, 165–6, 170–9, 183–7, 189, 192, 201n. 70, 222n. 13
visibility 3, 9, 12, 20–1, 23, 66, 67, 71, 113–15, 119, 139, 166, 182, 210n. 126
structure and 82

vision, and disparation 58

wasp–orchid duality 100
and assemblage 26, 27–8
Werner, Stephen 66, 73–4, 206nn. 28, 31, 33–4
Blueprint: A Study of Diderot and the Encyclopédie Plates 73
white wall/black hole system 96, 97, 209n. 99
Wunenburger, Jean-Jacques 213n. 81, 214n. 81

Žižek, Slavoj 218n. 50

Lightning Source UK Ltd.
Milton Keynes UK
UKOW05f1812220514

232146UK00003B/36/P

9 781472 526199